Drummer's Guide
Preface

In the past few years, rock has ceased to be the illegitimate... able forms of music. It has become an authentic hybrid of Blues, Jazz, and more recently, Gospel and Country music. It has emerged unscathed from the Shoo-bop, Shoo-bop era a separate and legitimate music form, still in its infancy granted, but nevertheless, an honest form with a new direction.

Rhythmically, Rock has advanced by leaps and bounds. As a result, much emphasis has been placed on the drummer. This is one in a series of books and it deals with one of the most important aspects of rock drumming: **RHYTHMIC IMPROVISATION.**

The object of this text is to **encourage and develop the drummer's ability to create and develop his own ideas from a basic format.** Rock music is, or should be, a form of personal expression. There can be no right or wrong ways to play. Everything must be reduced to the individual level. There should be very few general rules. If something works for an individual, then for that particular drummer it is right. **If something works for you, do it!**

John Pickering

AUDIO CONTENTS

1	Ex. 1 & 2	page 14	14	Ex. 28 & 29	page 16
2	Ex. 3 & 4	page 14	15	Ex. 30 & 31	page 16
3	Ex. 5 & 6	page 14	16	Ex. 32 & 33	page 16
4	Ex. 7 & 8	page 14	17	Ex. 34 & 35	page 16
5	Ex. 9 & 10	page 14	18	Ex. 36 & 37	page 16
6	Ex. 11 - 13	page 14	19	Ex. 38 - 40	page 16
7	Ex. 14 & 15	page 15	20	Ex. 55 - 60	page 18
8	Ex. 16 & 17	page 15	21	Ex. 68 - 73	page 19
9	Ex. 18 & 19	page 15	22	Ex. 82 - 87	page 20
10	Ex. 20 & 21	page 15	23	Ex. 95 - 100	page 21
11	Ex. 22 & 23	page 15	24	Ex. 109 & 110	page 22
12	Ex. 24 & 25	page 15	25	Ex. 1 & 2	page 39
13	Ex. 26 & 27	page 15			

Select examples are presented on the audio recording as an aid to learning.

Recording by Frank Briggs

Online Audio www.melbay.com/93301EB

1 2 3 4 5 6 7 8 9 0

© 1972 BY MEL BAY PUBLICATIONS, INC., PACIFIC, MO 63069.
ALL RIGHTS RESERVED. INTERNATIONAL COPYRIGHT SECURED. B.M.I. MADE AND PRINTED IN U.S.A.
No part of this publication may be reproduced in whole or in part, or transmitted in any form or by any means, electronic, mechanical, photocopy, recording, or otherwise, without written permission of the publisher.

Visit us on the Web at www.melbay.com — E-mail us at email@melbay.com

TABLE OF CONTENTS

THE ROCK FEELING: An explanation of some of the different "feels" used in rock. A few exercises showing three basic high hat patterns, and their relationship to the overall feeling of a rhythm.

THE VARIATIONS AND DEVELOPMENT OF A BASIC FIGURE: A method of obtaining variations from a basic figure by 1) Changing the tonal structure of a figure 2) Changing the rhythmic structure of a figure.

RHYTHMIC IMPROVISATION: A study into the concept of improvising rhythmically. Improvising off of a basic rhythmic structure much in the manner of melodic improvisation.

CHAPTER ONE: Variations of a basic beat.

A series of eight 8 Bar solos built from the exercises in Chapter One.

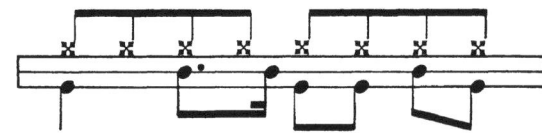

CHAPTER TWO: Variations of a basic beat.

A series of eight 8 Bar solos built from the exercises in Chapter Two.

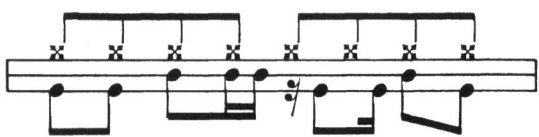

CYMBAL VARIATIONS WITH THE RIGHT HAND: A few exercises demonstrating the technique of varying the rhythm of the right hand and integrating it into the overall rhythm.

THE ROCK FEELING

Before going any further, an attempt must be made at explaining how to feel a rock rhythm. Every drummer has his own way of feeling a figure, but in general they all must give a rock sound.

Technical execution is not nearly as important as the feeling generated by the drummer. The most prevalent feeling in the newer tunes is borrowed from the Black Music of today. It is a combination of three or four feels combining together to give an overall effect.

Tempo is of utmost importance when discussing feeling. The figures in this book were designed to be played no faster than between ♩ = 112 to 120. As a general rule, it would be advisable to play every figure at many different tempos ranging between ♩ = 60 and 112. ANY TIME SPENT TRYING TO PLAY THESE FIGURES AT RIDICULOUS TEMPOS IS WASTED!!

(A) Except for the obvious differences such as shuffles and 6/8 figures there is always an "8 to the bar" feeling. Usually it is played with the right hand, either on the ride cymbal or on a closed high hat. On occasion it is not so necessary to play this figure as it is to IMPLY it. As in all types of music, what the band is doing will govern what you, the drummer, will play behind them. Whether or not you choose to actually play the "8 to the bar", that feeling must always be there. Sometimes straight quarter notes suit the arrangement much better but they are still felt in eight. Don't think of just straight eighth notes in 4/4 but of an 8/8 time signature. Try counting 1 2 3 4 5 6 7 8, instead of 1 & 2 & 3 & 4 &.

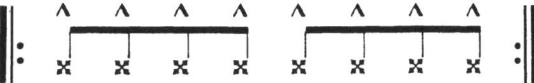

Note: Play each eighth note with an upstroke rather than a downstroke feeling. This gives the rhythm a lift and emphasizes the 8/8 feel.

© Copyright 1972 by Mel Bay Publications, Inc.   -:-   International Copyright Secured   -:-   Printed in U.S.A.   -:-   All Rights Reserved

THE ROCK FEELING (Cont.)

(B) Superimposed on top of (A) is a cut time or upbeat feeling. When played, it is most often done by the high hat, or on occasion, on the bass drum. Usually though it is merely insinuated.

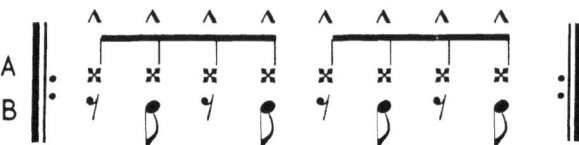

(C) Next is the everpresent "4 to the bar" feeling. It is most effective when played by the high hat with the left foot, leaving the right foot and both hands free to play the rest of the figure. Once again, it isn't so necessary to play it as it is to IMPLY it.

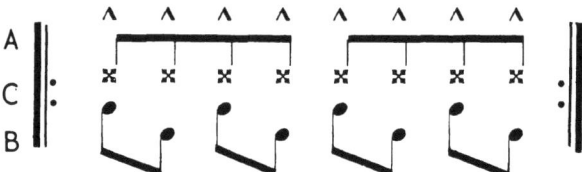

(D) Last but not least, is the steady sixteenth note figure that rides on top of everything else. It isn't necessarily used in every arrangement. Some things sound better with an eighth note ride and not the sixteenth figure. It can be played by the tambourine or when the tempo and the arrangement will allow, it can be played by the right hand. It is most effective when played on a closed high hat.

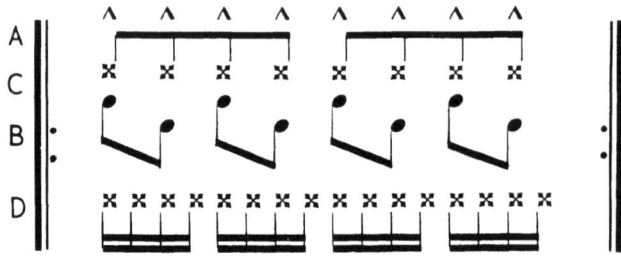

THE ROCK FEELING (Cont.)

Note: When practicing the right hand cymbal rhythm alone, counting in 8/8, (1 2 3 4 5 6 7 8) can be of great help in finding the intended upstroke feeling. However, to be realistic, most rock tunes are written in 4/4 but played with the upstroke feeling. They are not as a rule written in an 8/8 time signature. Therefore to avoid confusion, from this point on, all figures should be counted in 4/4 (1 & 2 & 3 & 4 &).

The following simple exercises should help clarify what is meant by an "upbeat" feeling.

Play a steady eighth note pattern on the ride cymbal with the right hand. Then along with that play the high hat (with a nice tight "chick" sound) on the offbeat eighth notes. (1 & 2 & 3 & 4 &) Note that the high hat pattern gives almost a cut time effect.

Using these two cymbal patterns as a basis,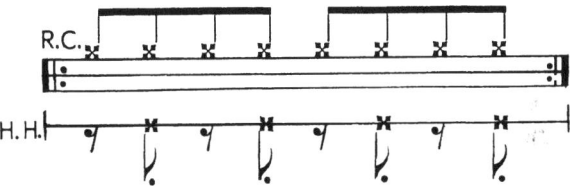

Try playing some simple 4/4 snare and bass drum figures against them.

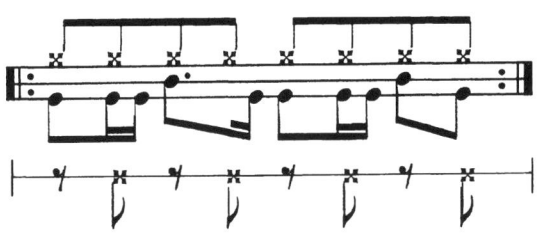

Repeat the above examples, using the same snare, bass, and high hat patterns, only this time change the ride cymbal figure from eighth notes to steady sixteenth notes. This gives the examples an entirely new sound and feeling. It cannot be stressed enough that every exercise and figure in this text be played against both a steady eighth note and sixteenth note ride rhythm.

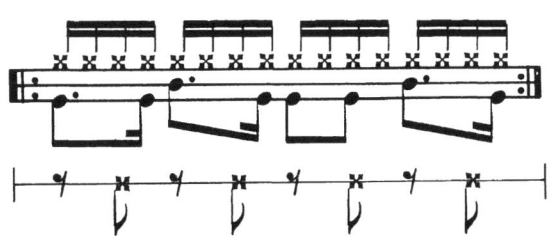
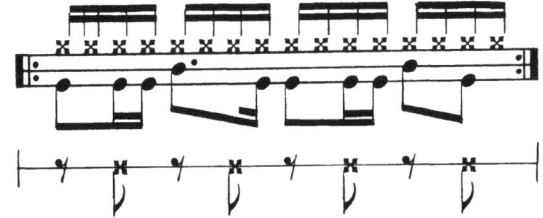

THE ROCK FEELING (Cont.)

The pattern played by the H.Hat, whether it be "2 and 4, 1 2 3 4, or 1 & 2 & 3 & 4 &, is essential to the overall feeling of the rhythm. A change in the H. Hat pattern can cause a marked difference in the pulse of the figure being played on the drums.

Example #1 has an upbeat feeling.   Example #2 has a more straight ahead "4 to the bar" feel.

   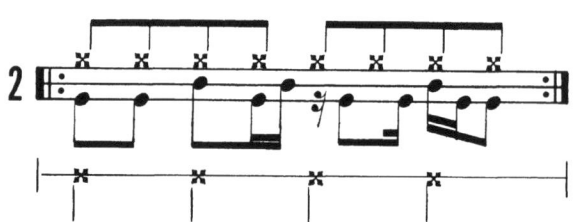

There are three basic patterns that can be played on the H.Hat. They are:

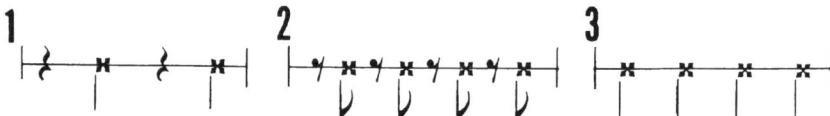

Each of these provides a different feeling to the rhythm. The feels generated by these different H. Hat patterns can be used separately or they can be combined. For example, try playing the H.Hat on 2 and 4, but playing the ride cymbal with the upbeat feeling implied by the 1 & 2 & 3 & 4 & H.Hat pattern.

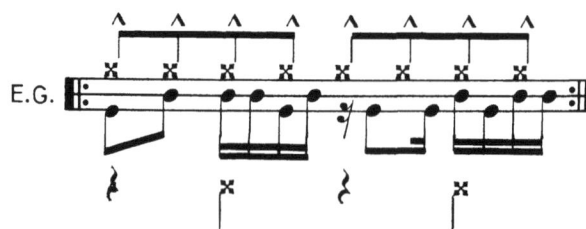

Note: IT IS IMPERATIVE THAT EACH ONE OF THE ABOVE THREE HIGH HAT PATTERNS BE PLAYED IN CONJUNCTION WITH EVERY EXERCISE CONTAINED IN CHAPTERS ONE AND TWO.

THE VARIATIONS AND DEVELOPMENT OF A BASIC FIGURE

The developing of variations from a simple basic beat is the first and most important step to improvising rhythmically.

Before starting to change the figure at all, first try experimenting with the tonality of the original pattern. That simply means trying all the different possible hand and foot combinations without changing the original figure. Note that by changing the hand and foot combinations of the same riff, the sound is changed, thus in effect, creating a "new beat".

FOR EXAMPLE:

Figure #1 is the basic beat.

Figure #2 is rhythmically the same as figure #1 but with a different tonal structure, thereby making it a slightly different beat.

After experimenting with the tonality, the next step would be to vary the rhythmic structure slightly. Always take care to make sure that the figure, after any changes made, will still maintain the same pulse and general rhythm as the original beat. THE VARIATION MUST COMPLIMENT THE ORIGINAL!!

FOR EXAMPLE:

Figure #1 is the basic beat.

Figure #3 has a slightly different rhythmic structure, but still maintains the same pulse as figure #1. It compliments instead of duplicating the original.

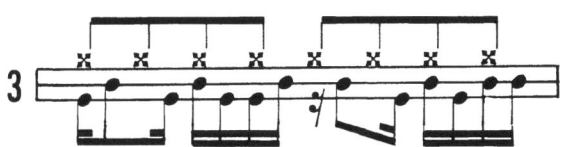

VARIATIONS AND DEVELOPMENT (Cont.)

It must be noted that the principle of changing the tonal structure of the basic beat can also be applied to the variation. Thus making the number of variations off of any given figure very nearly infinite.

FOR EXAMPLE:

Figure #3 is the variation obtained on the previous page by varying the rhythmic structure of figure #1.

Figure #4 is rhythmically the same as figure #3, but the tonality has been changed, and thus another new variation has been obtained.

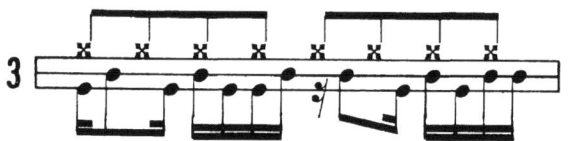

TONALITY

The principle of changing the tonal structure is basically a very simple one. However, a brief explanation is in order.

As was previously stated, the tonality, as referred to in this text, is limited to the different hand and foot combinations obtainable by the drummer. To be more specific, the combinations possible between the snare and bass drums. The high hat, cymbals, and tom-toms can also be utilized, but at present tonality will be confined to the snare and bass drums.

EXAMPLE: Below is a one bar figure, separated into sections, with some of the hand and foot combinations demonstrated.

TONALITY (Cont.)

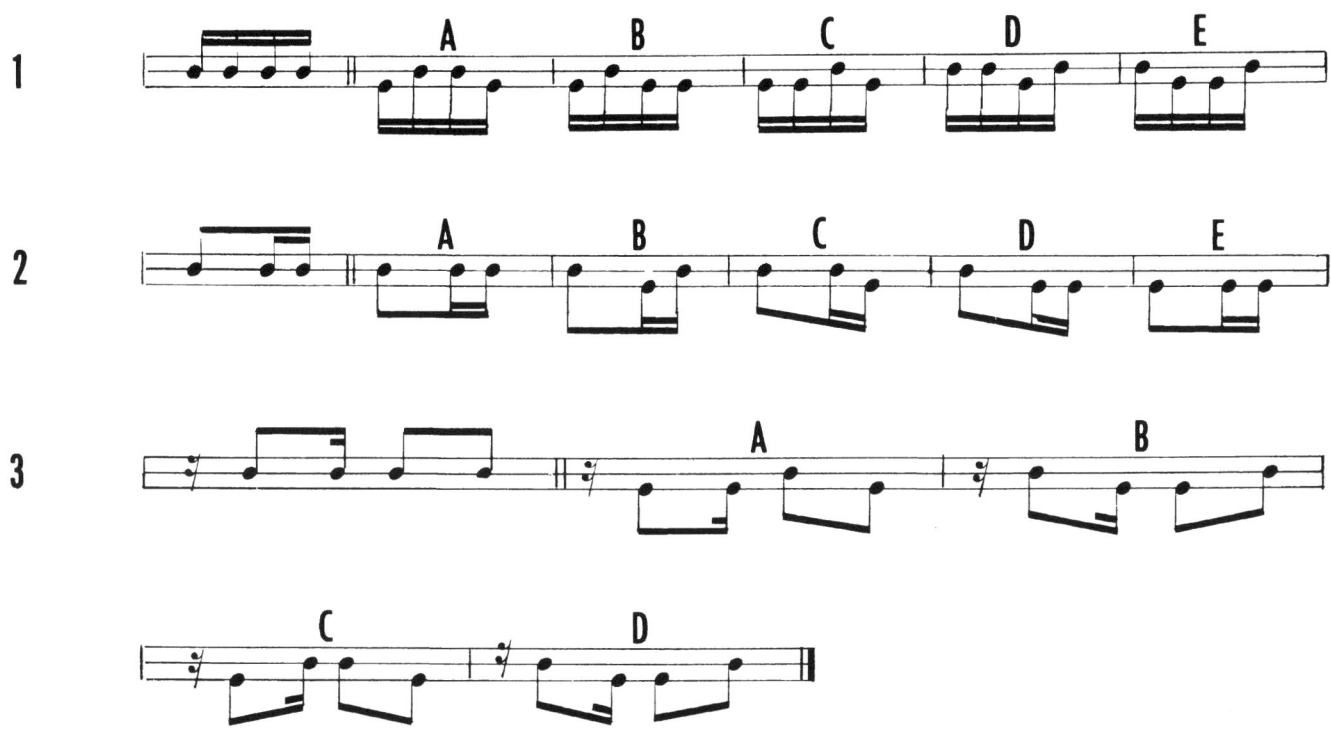

By combining a variation from each section, a new one bar figure is formed. For example: Try combining (1)a with (2)b and (3)c. Now combine (1)b with (2)b and (3)c, then (1)a with (2)a and (3)c and so on. It's easy to see that there are many possible combinations. The following are just a few examples.

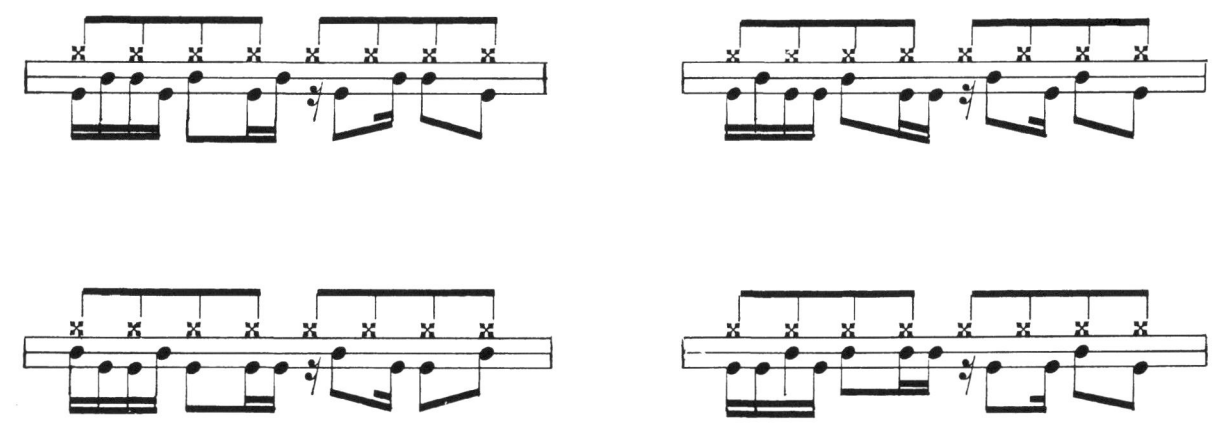

It must be noted however, that not every combination of tonal and rhythmic variations are applicable in every instance. Each musical situation is different and must be dealt with accordingly.

Note: See the first section of Chapter Two for more examples of changing the tonal structure of a riff.

RHYTHMIC IMPROVISATION

The majority of rock and jazz rock tunes are based on some kind of vamp or riff. A vamp being a constantly repeated figure played throughout the tune. It can be played by the bass player alone, or by the entire rhythm section, and on occasion by the brass and/or reed section as well. It would logically follow then that the best way of playing within the rock idiom would be to learn to think and play creatively off of and around a given vamp or riff.

That, in essence, is the concept of rhythmic improvisation. It simply means improvising around a basic rhythm pattern in the same manner as the more melodic instruments might improvise around a melody. It gives the drummer the chance to play longer more linear phrases, instead of being trapped in the rigidity of a one or two bar pattern.

In order to maintain some semblance of musical coherence when improvising, the player must play within the chord structure of the tune and also keep the melody in mind. The same principle applies to the drummer when improvising rhythmically. He should keep in mind, the rhythmic structure of the arrangement and his playing should maintain the same pulse, feeling, and overall effect as generated by the basic original pattern.

The following is an example of one basic figure and two variations, one more applicable than the other:

VARIATION #1

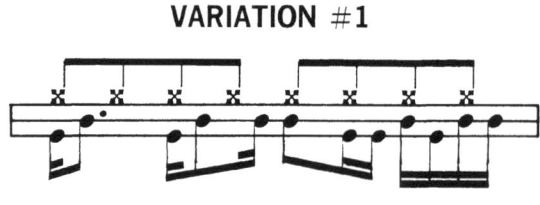

EXAMPLE

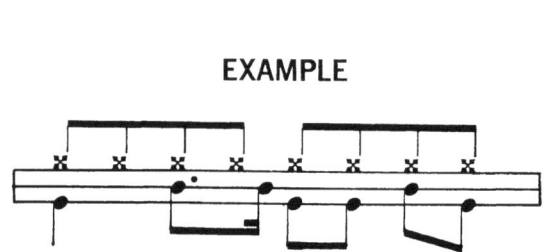

VARIATION #2

If played alongside the example, variation #1 would sound forced and feel very uncomfortable, whereas variation #2 has a tendency to roll with and compliment the original pattern.

RHYTHMIC IMPROVISATION (Cont.)

A close examination of the newer rock tunes would reveal that the basic rhythm patterns used in most of them could be traced back to a handful of simple figures. The following pages are an extensive study into the variations and development of two of the most widely used figures. Most of the beats being played by today's drummers are variations of these patterns.

Each of these figures can be used separately as a basic beat, or they can be connected together to form longer more flowing rhythmic lines. If the basic one or two bar figure is constantly repeated without any variation, the effect would be a very rigid, "boxed in" feeling. By varying the basic beat slightly during a phrase, the rhythm has much more room to come alive and really "cook". An excellent idea would be to follow the bass player, and to use the variations to play off of his ideas. The professional doesn't need to be told, but a good general rule for the student would be to "ALWAYS LISTEN TO THE BASS PLAYER".

The following is an example of how to connect some of the variations together to form a longer more flowing phrase, giving a more linear effect while all the while maintaining the same rhythmic pulse as generated by the original beat.

Note: Once the concept itself is thoroughly understood, the individual drummer will find it very easy to develop his own variations and to mold them to his own particular style. That being the primary objective.

CHAPTERS ONE AND TWO
MUST BE STUDIED SIMULTANEOUSLY!!

In order to obtain maximum benefit from this text, chapters one and two must be studied simultaneously. Practicing one or two pages at a time from each chapter would achieve by far, the best results. This text is not a technical exercise and it is not necessary to finish chapter one before starting chapter two. No constructive purpose would be served by studying them separately.

IT IS IMPERATIVE THAT EVERY VARIATION IS PLAYED TWICE! ONCE WITH A STEADY EIGHTH NOTE PATTERN ON THE RIGHT HAND, THEN AGAIN WITH A STEADY SIXTEENTH NOTE PATTERN ON THE RIGHT HAND.

FOR EXAMPLE:

1ST X

2ND X

CHAPTER I

BASIC FIGURE: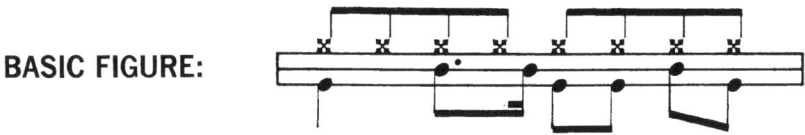

As was previously stated, the primary objective of this text is to show the development and some of the variations of two of the most used figures in rock drumming. Chapter One is a study into what could possibly be the oldest "fat-back" beat in rock.

When rock finally broke away from the original drum beat of 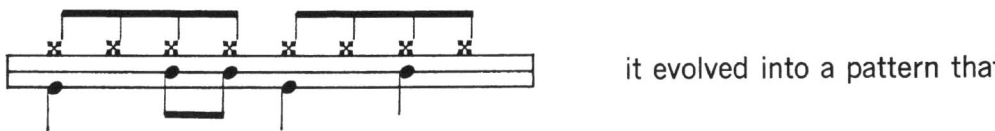 it evolved into a pattern that could be described as the basis for the majority of drum beats being played by the rock drummers of today.

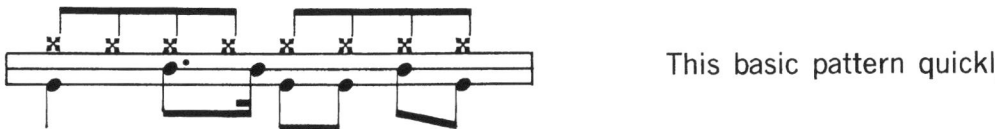 This basic pattern quickly progressed onto the more sophisticated variations described in this text. In the newer arrangements this figure is seldom used in its basic form. However, its variations are among the most played beats in rock.

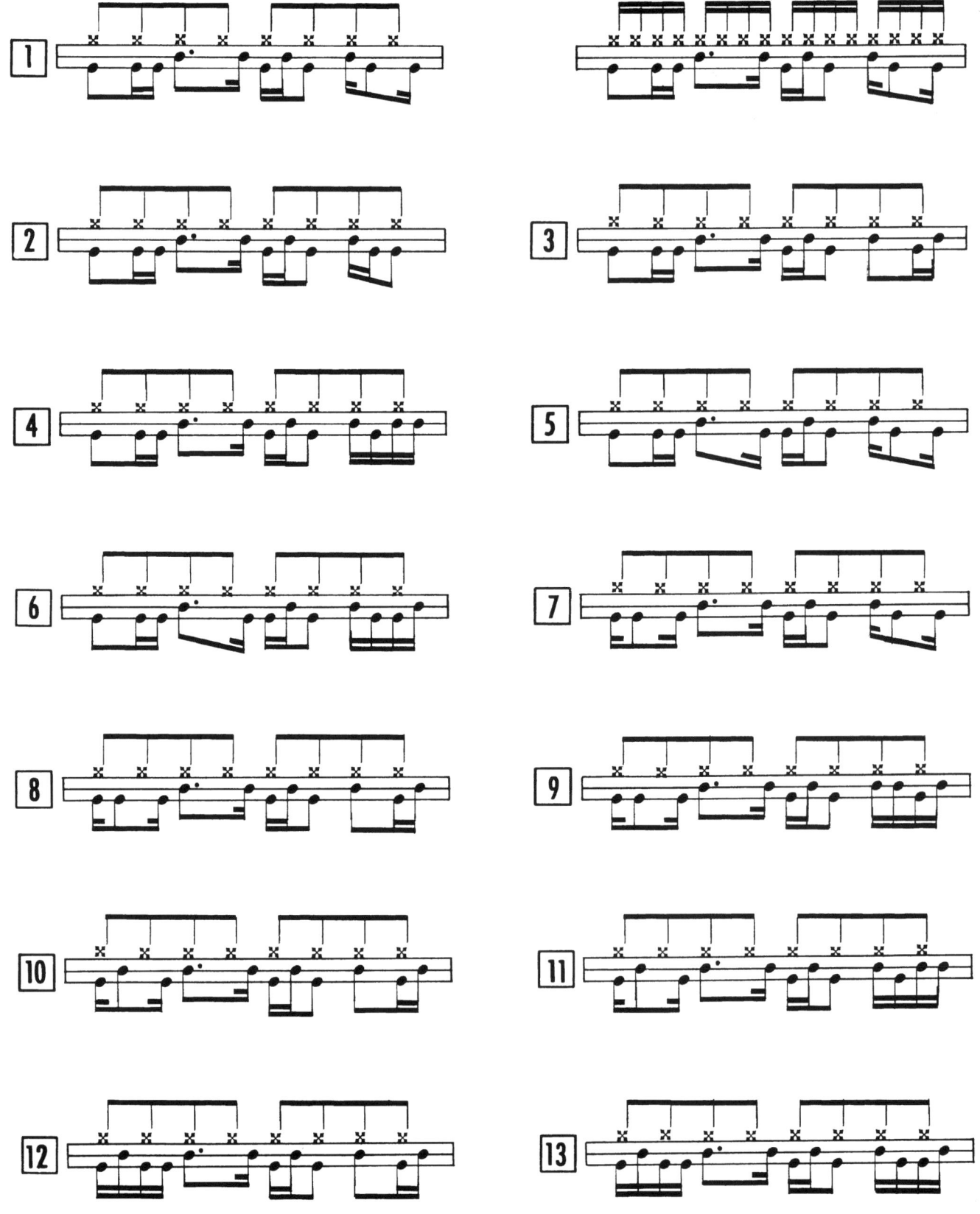

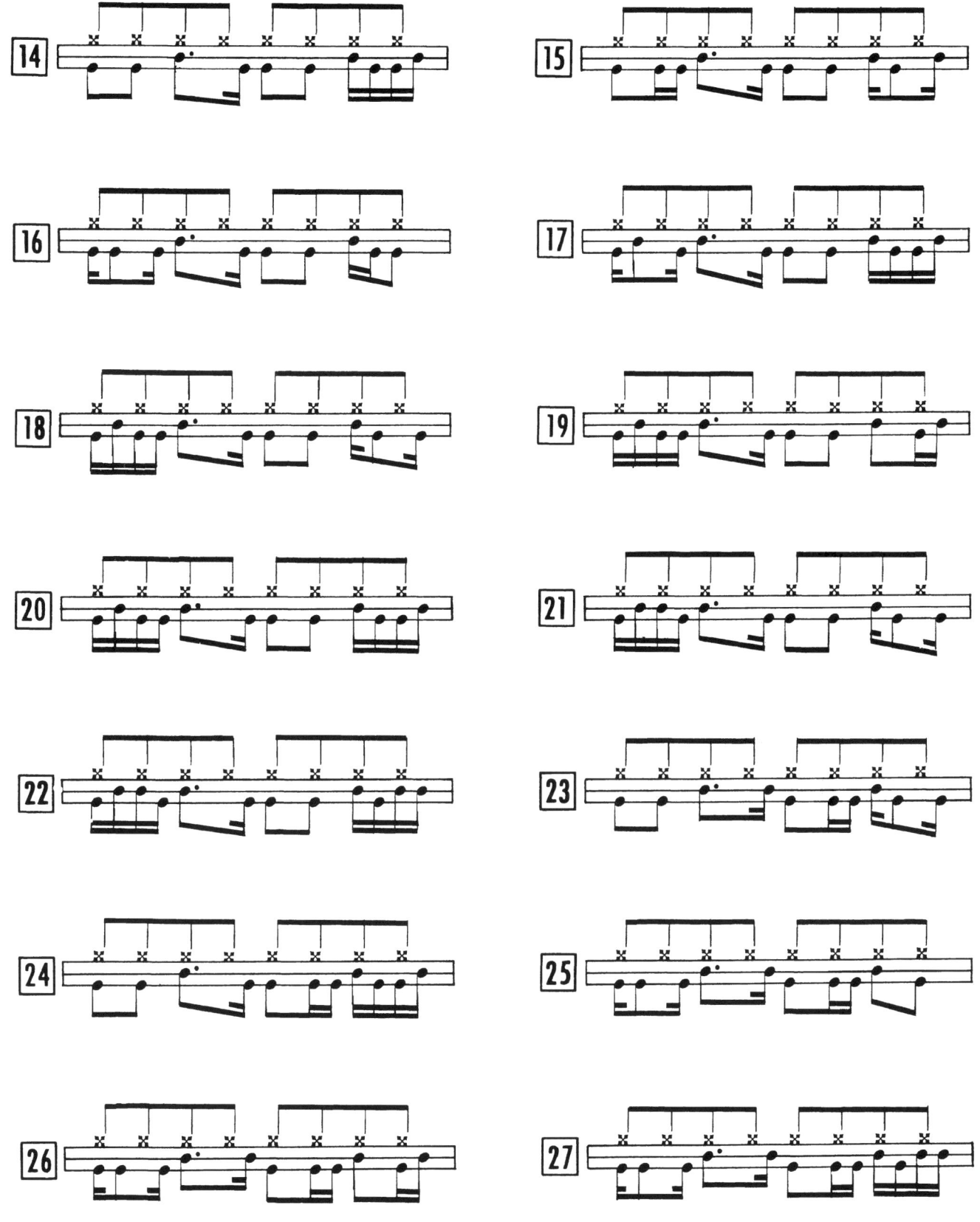

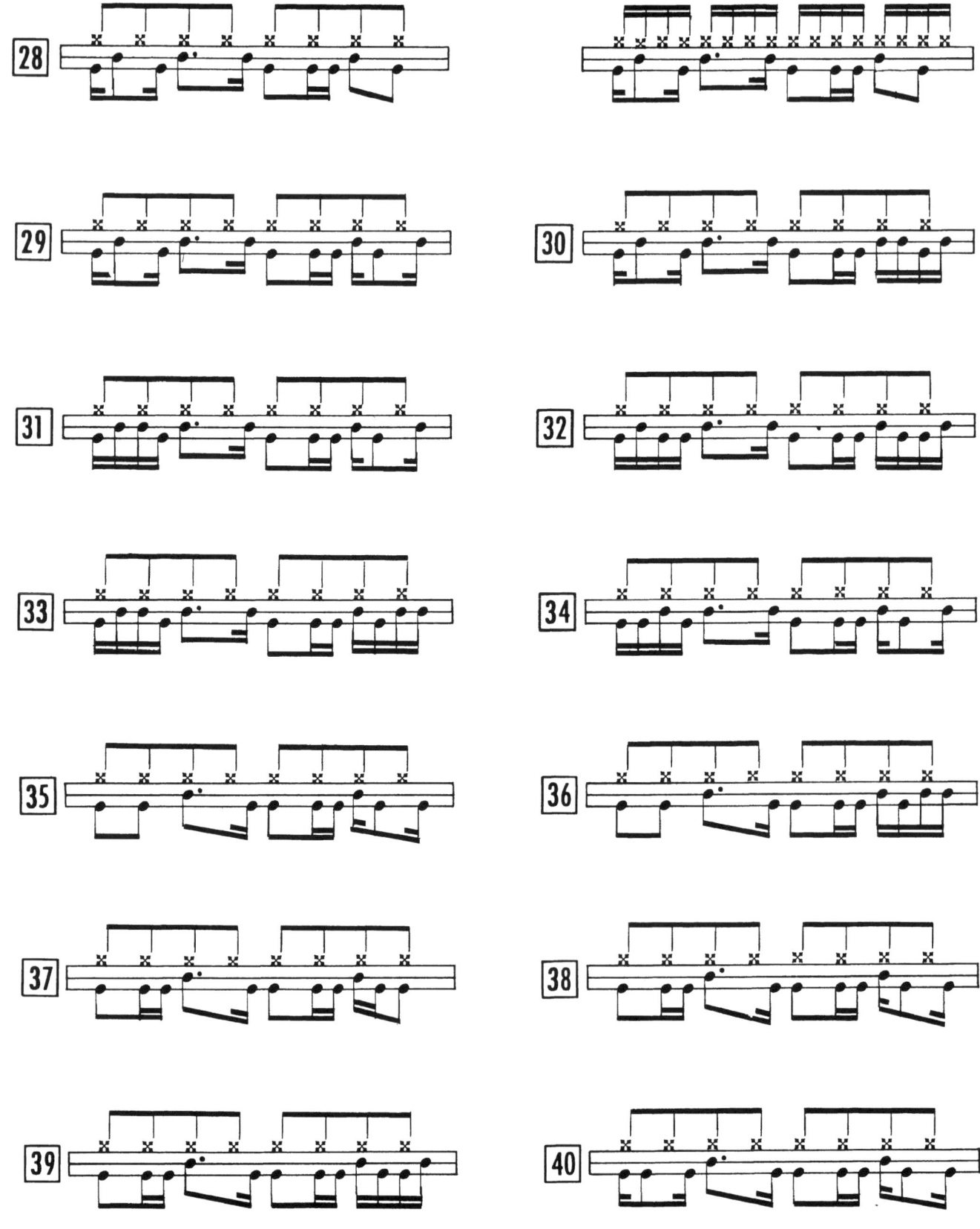

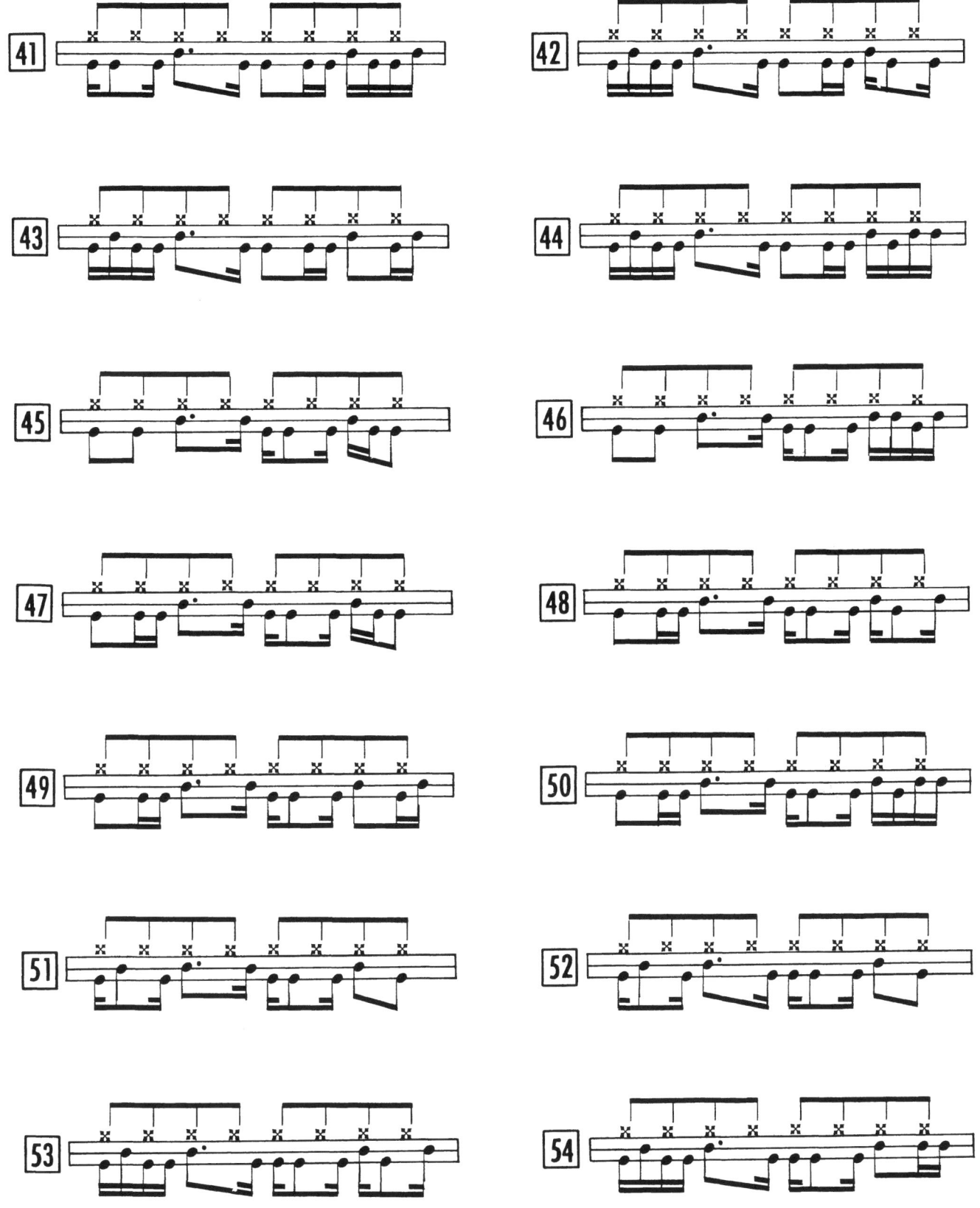

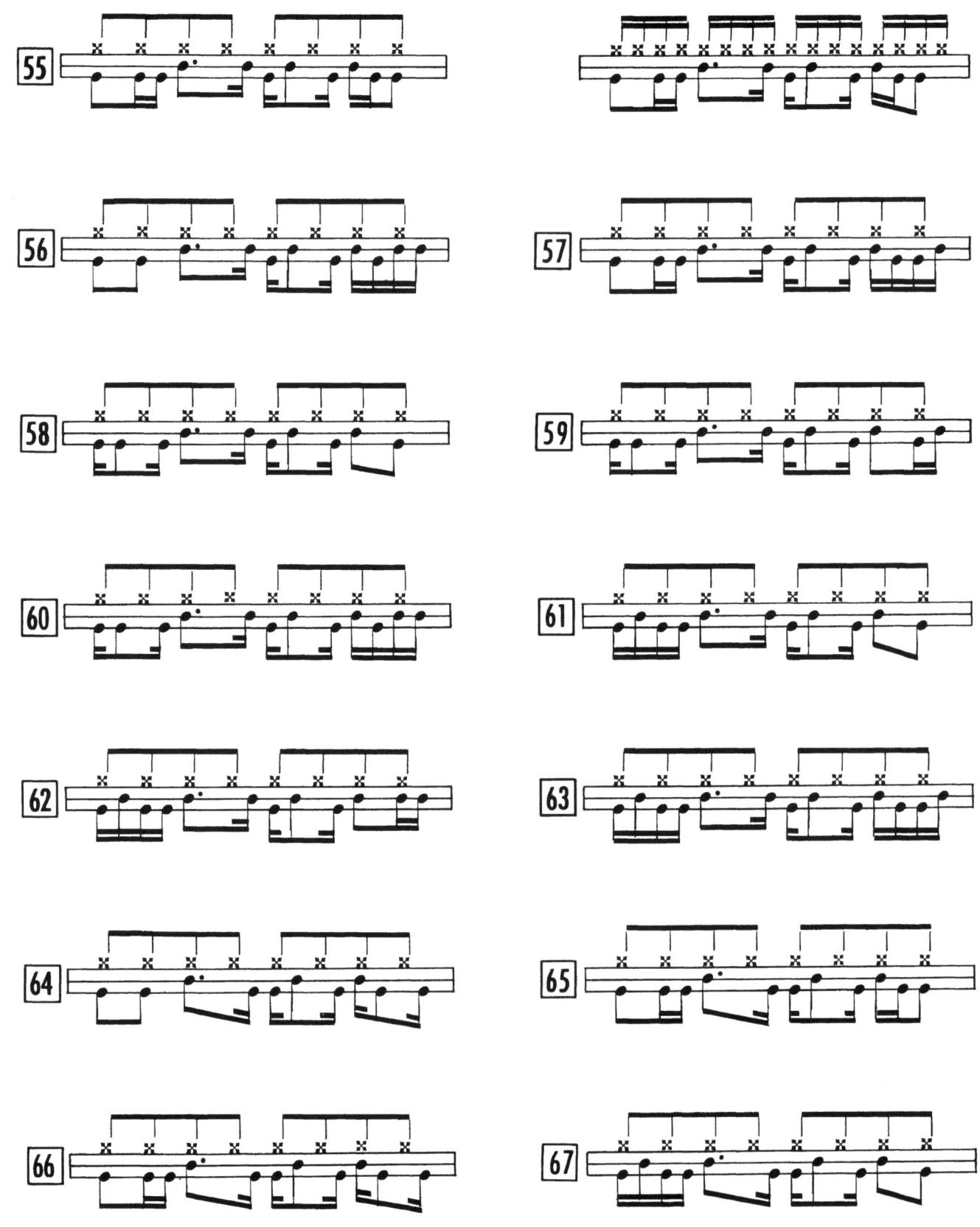

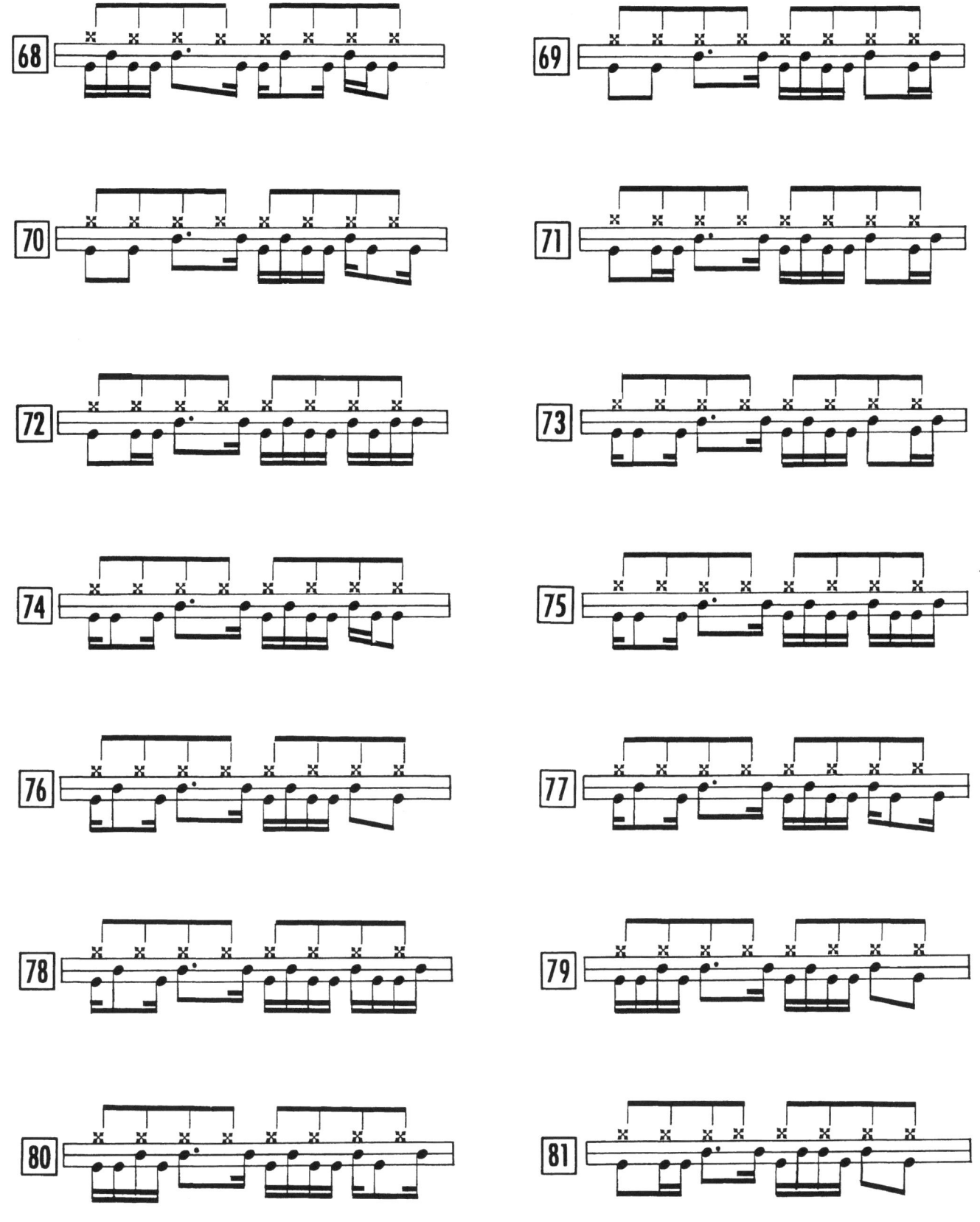

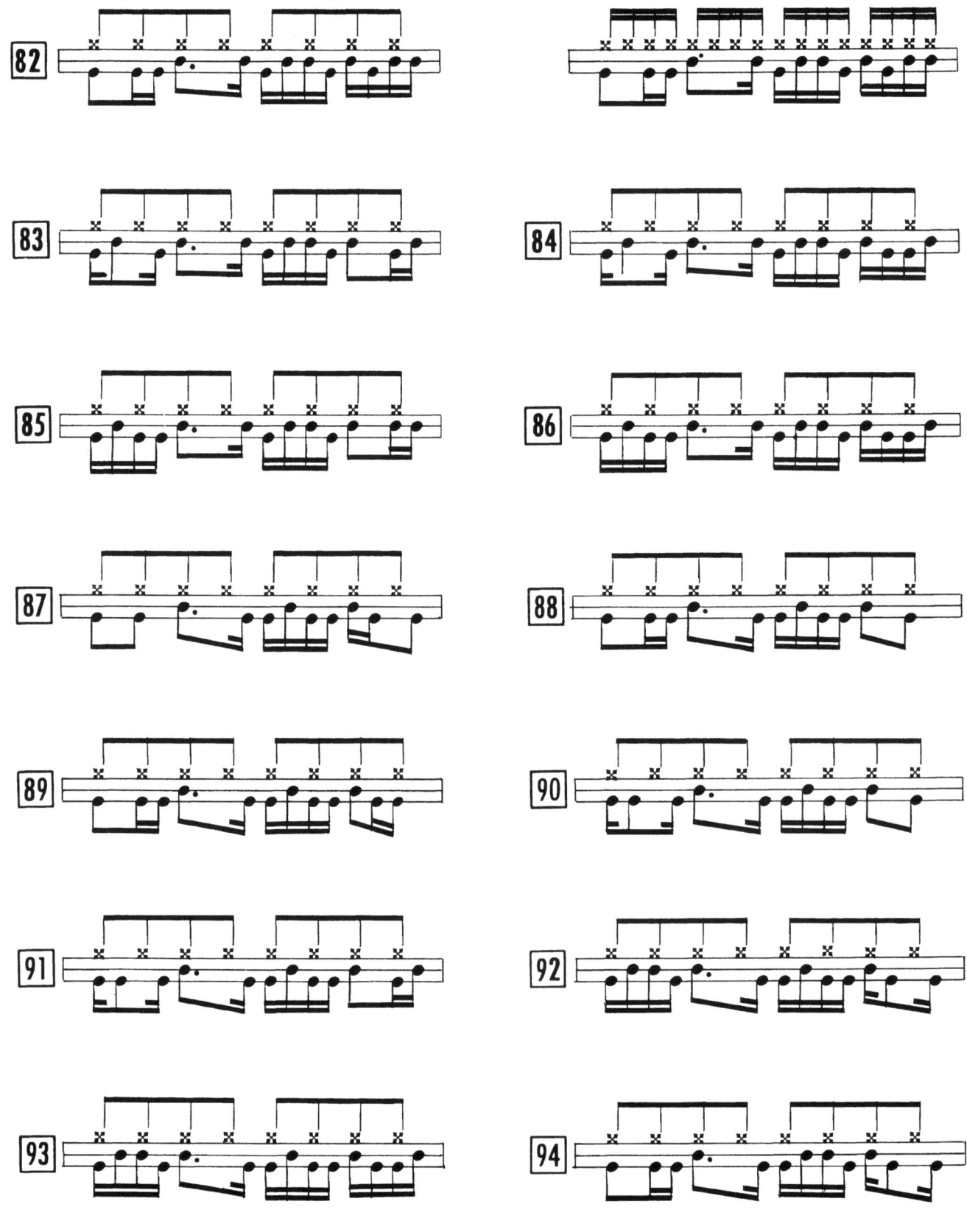

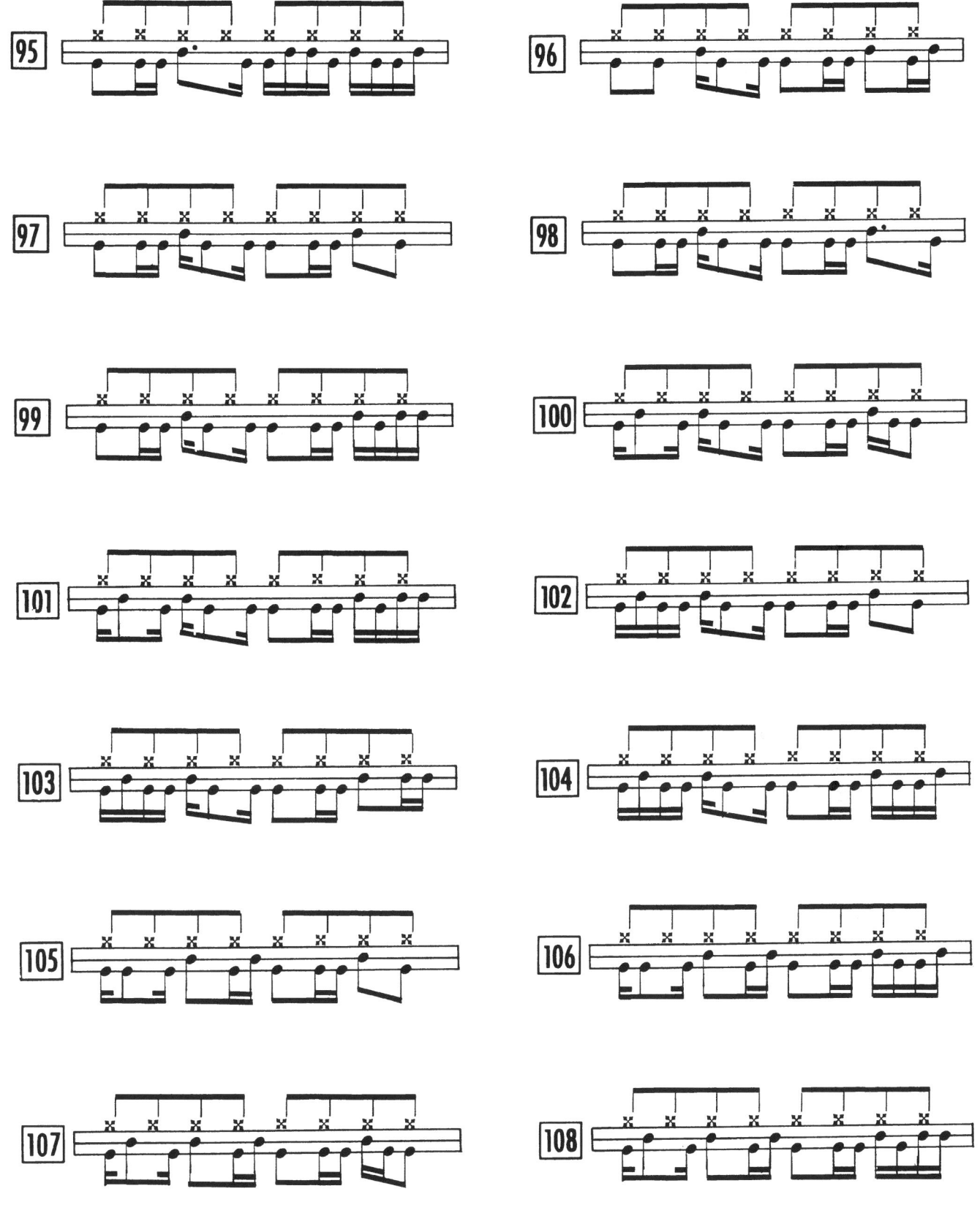

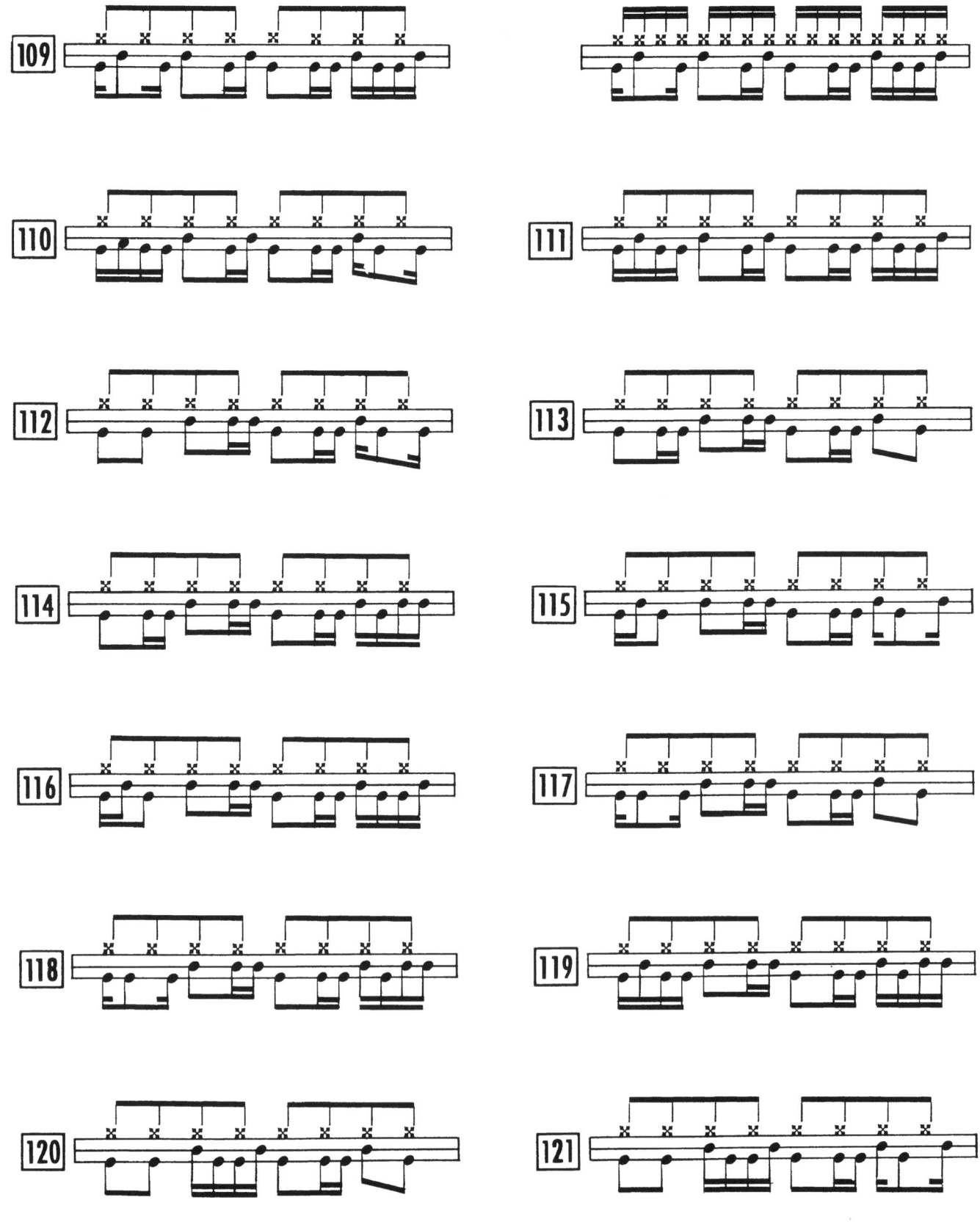

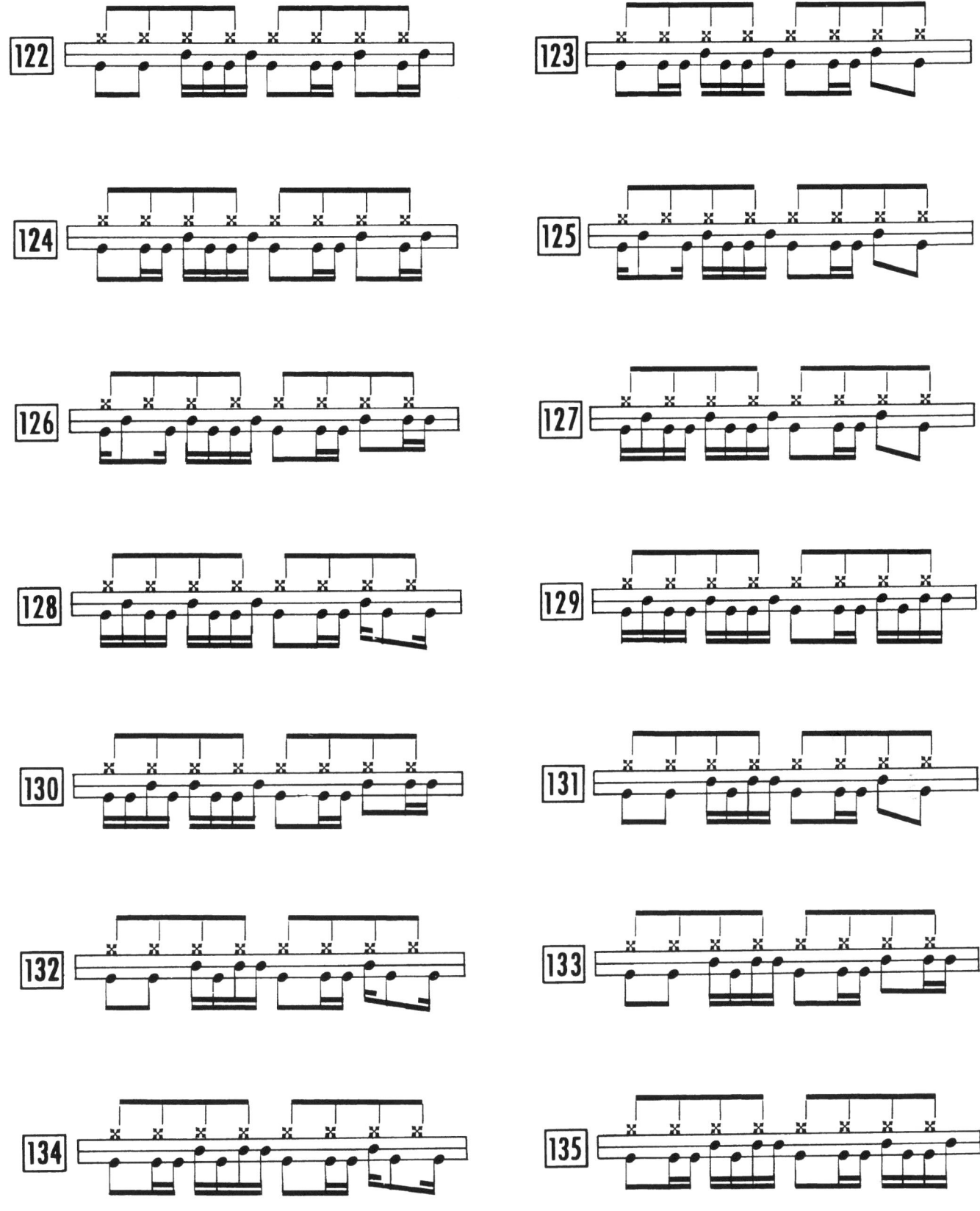

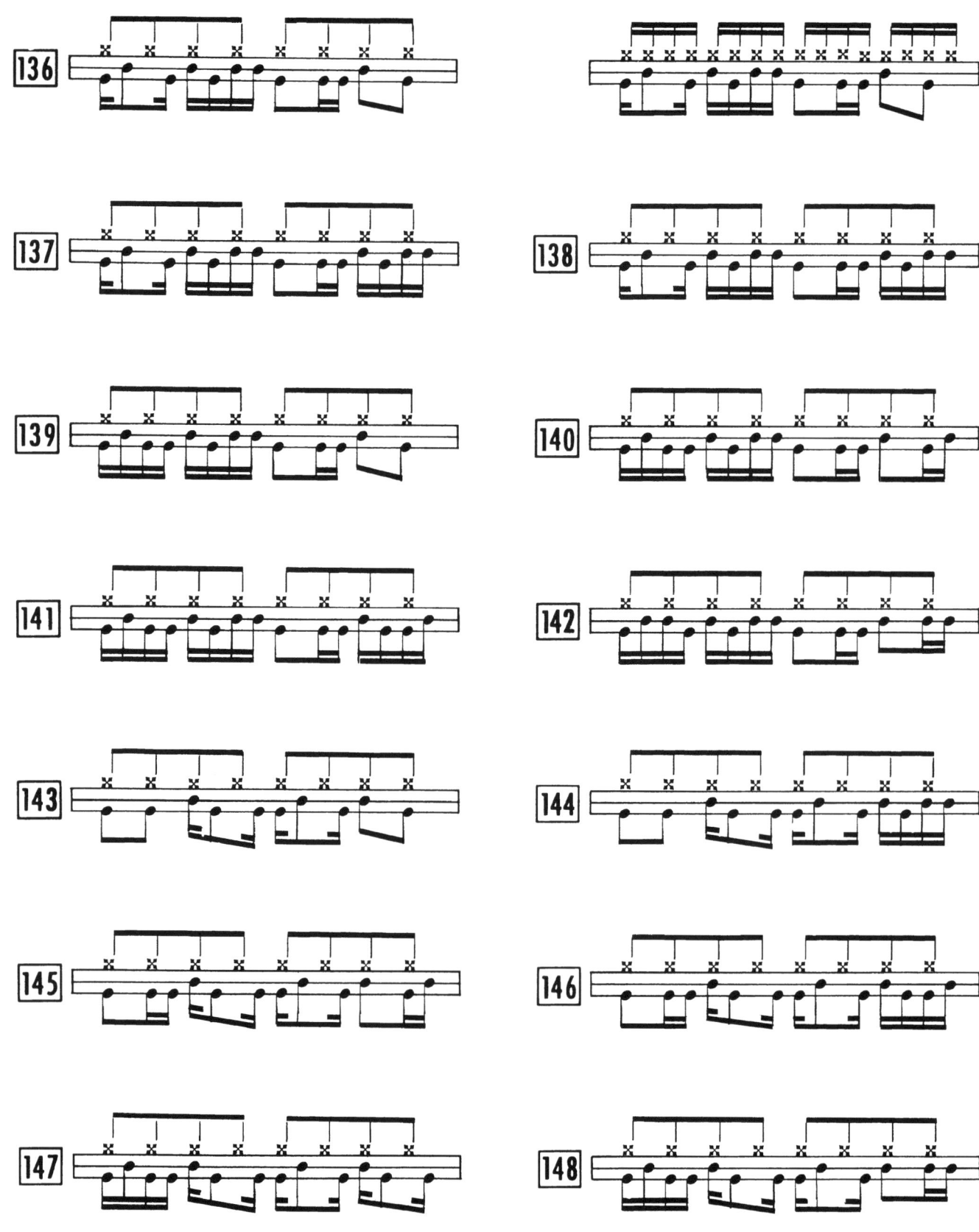

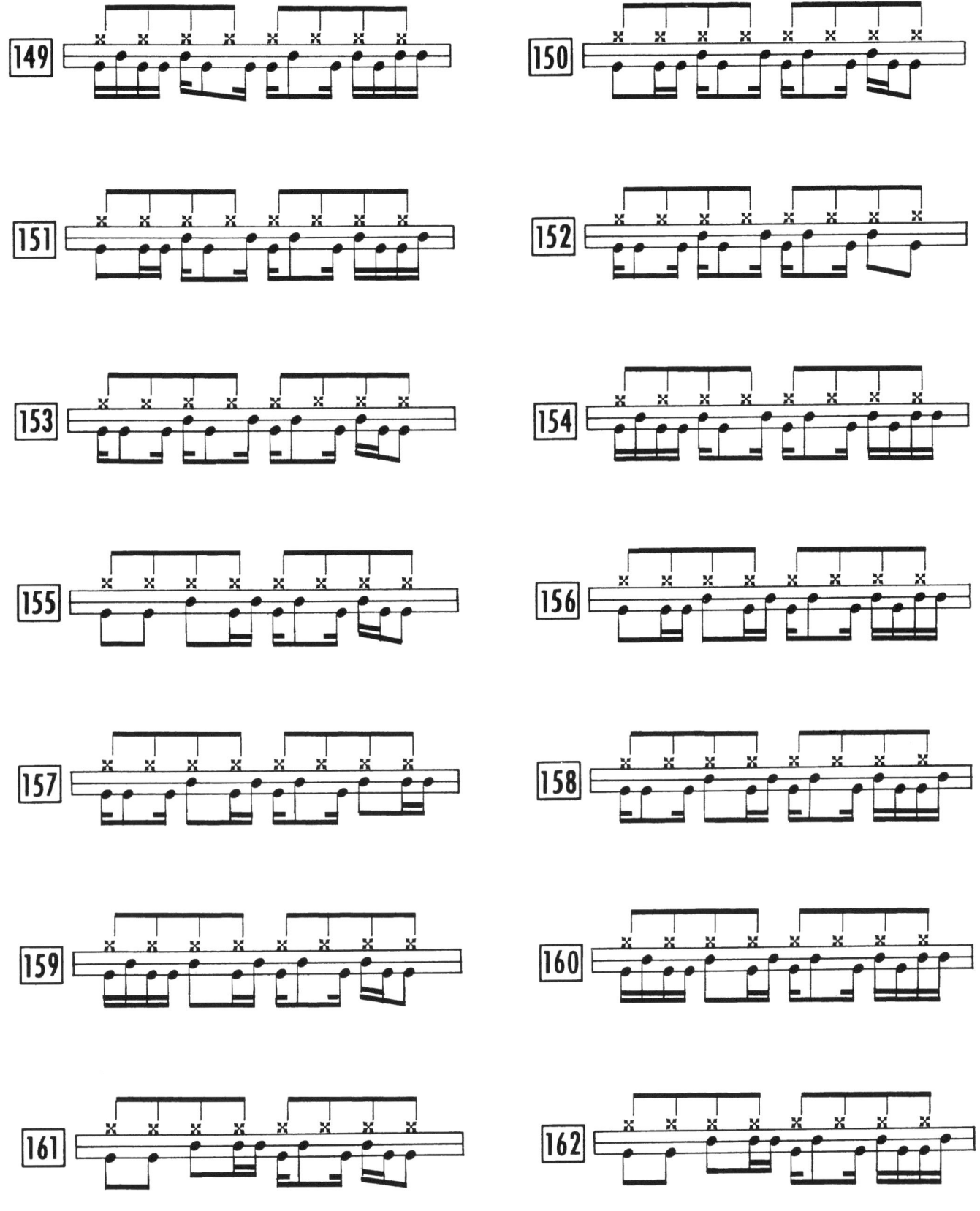

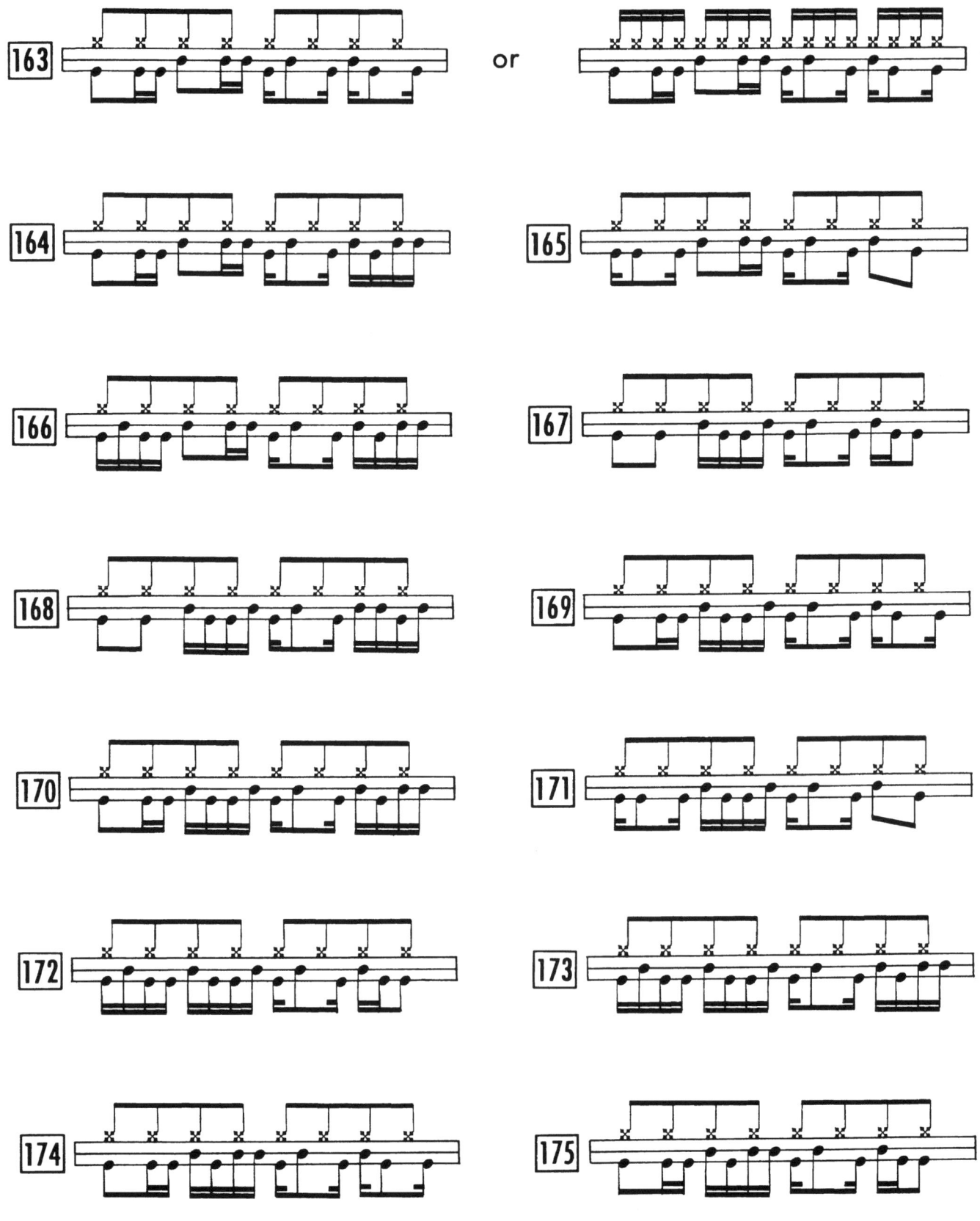

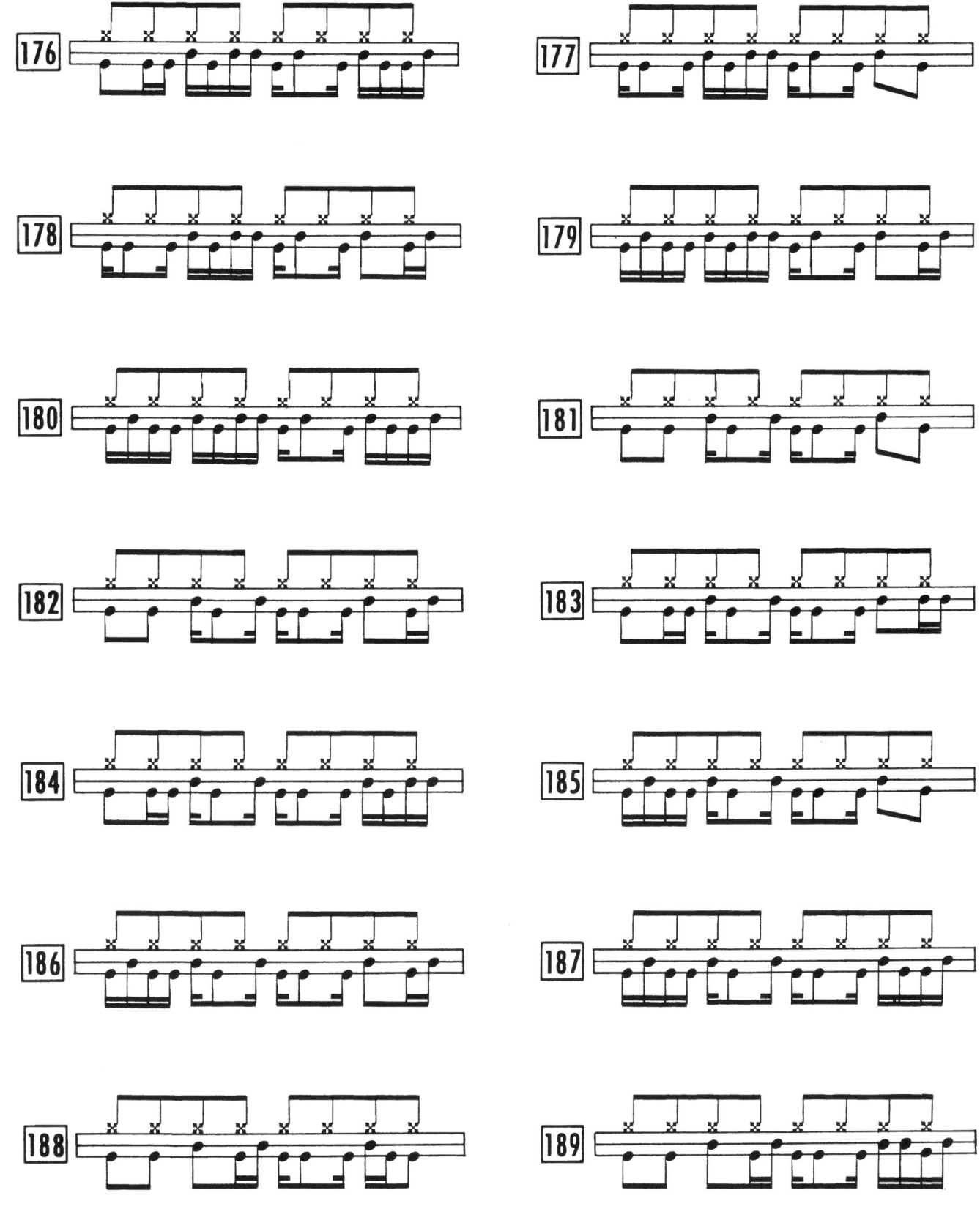

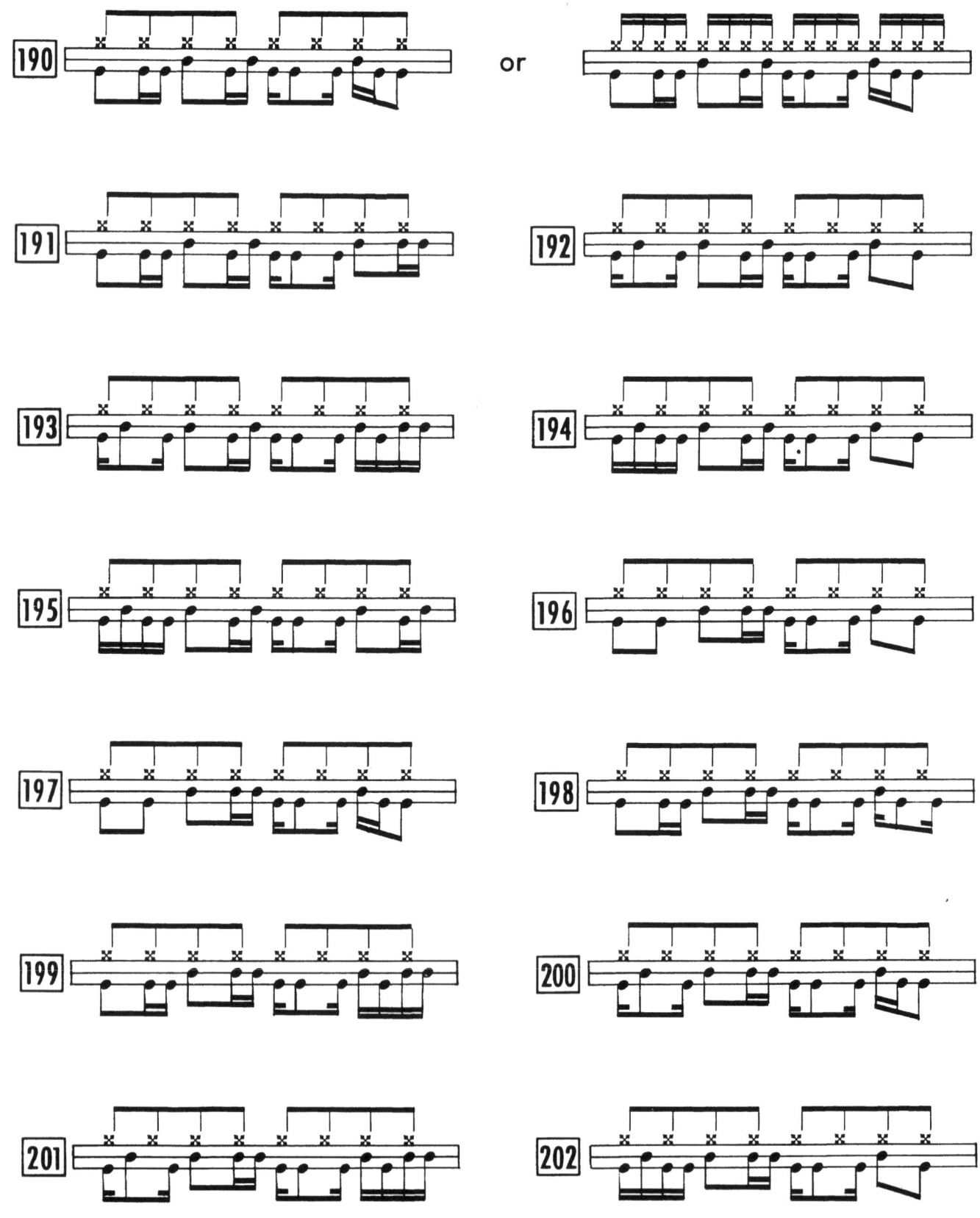

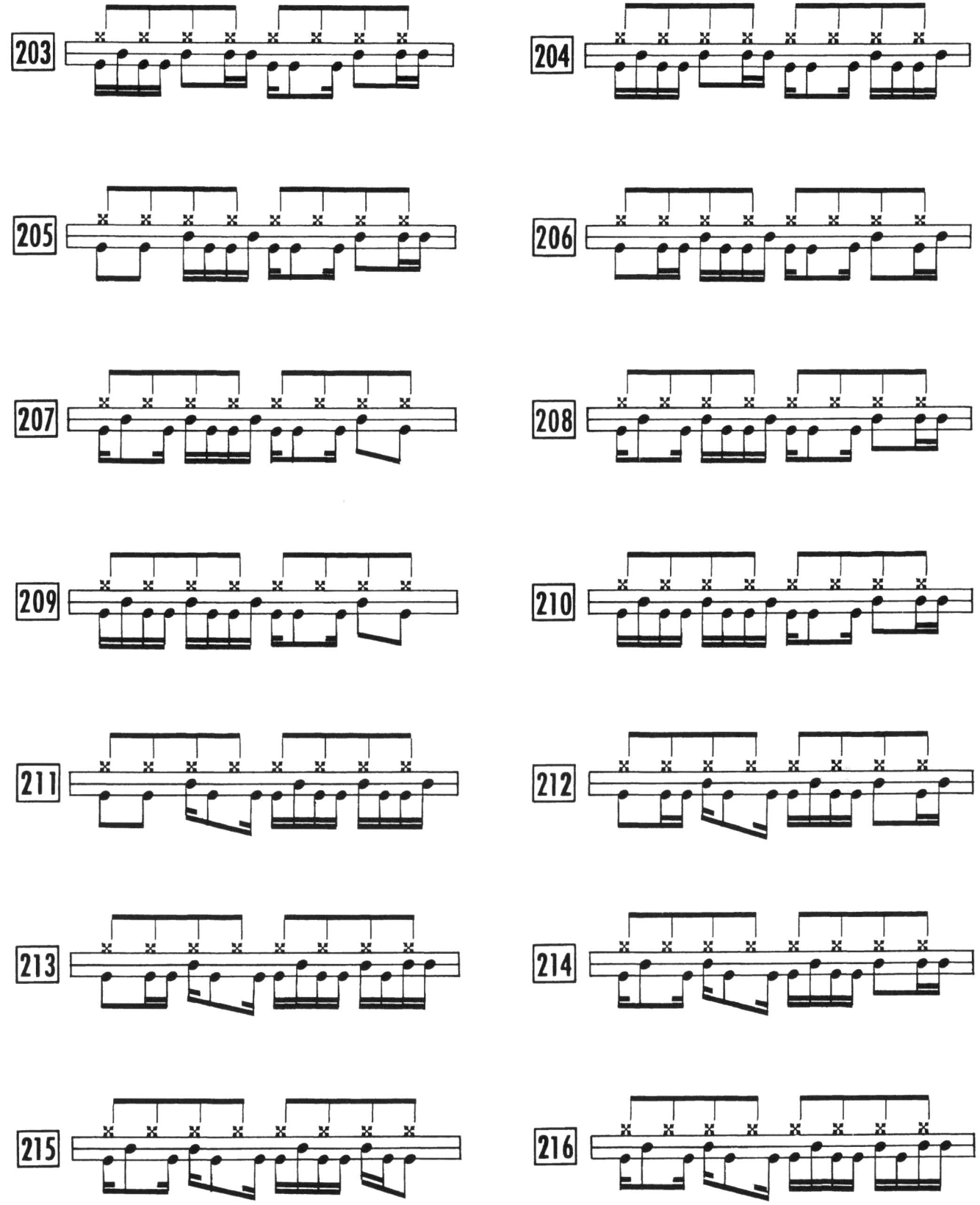

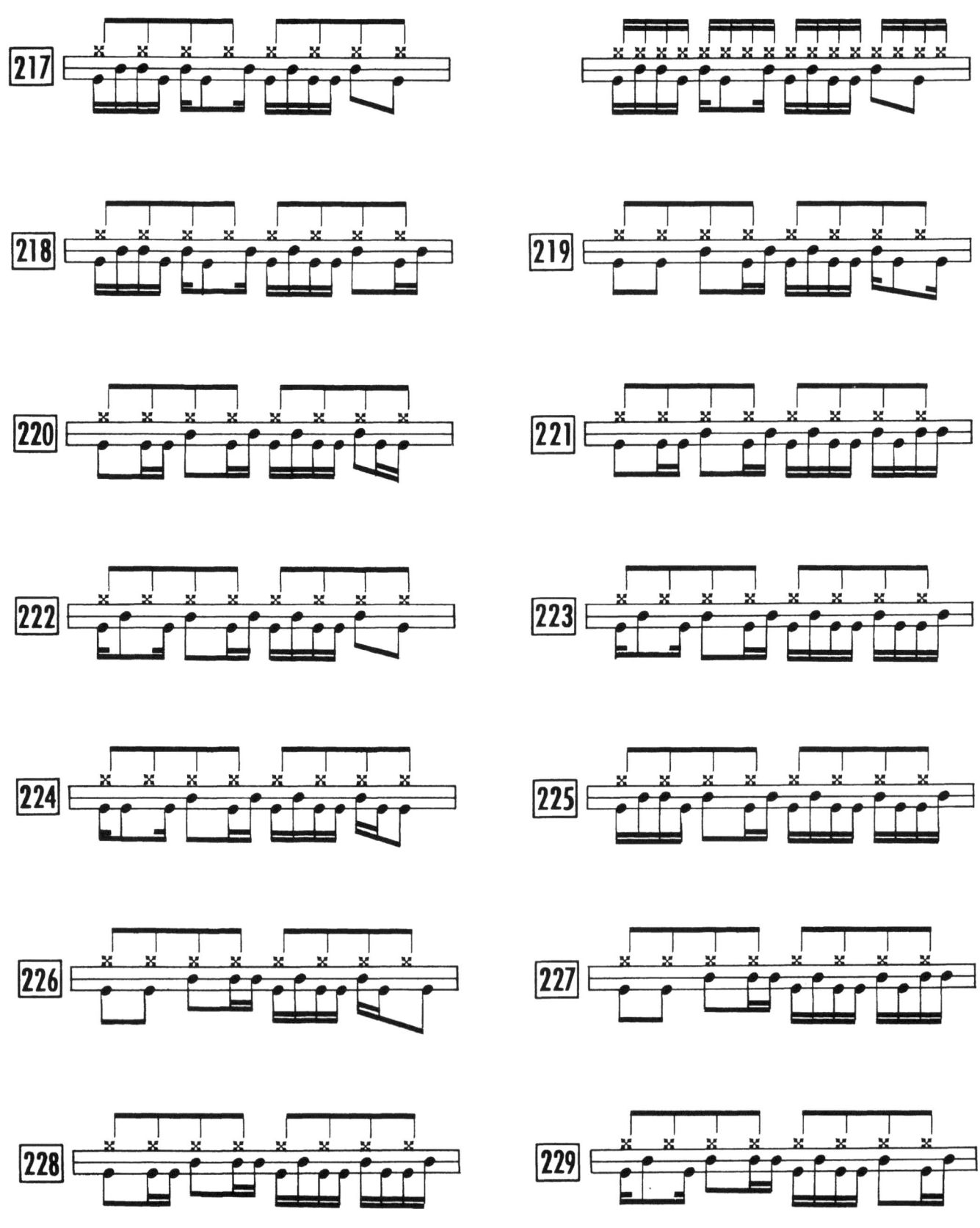

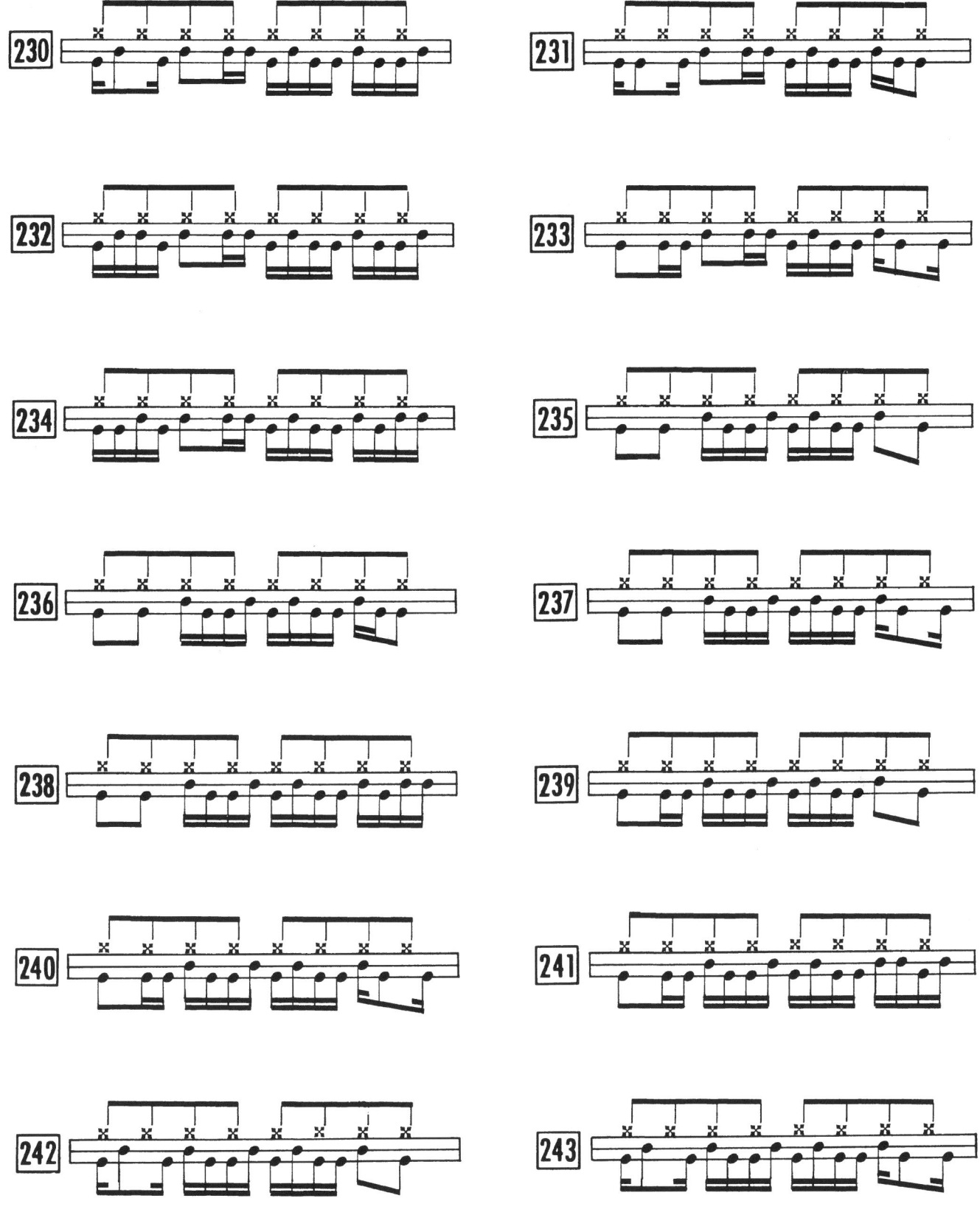

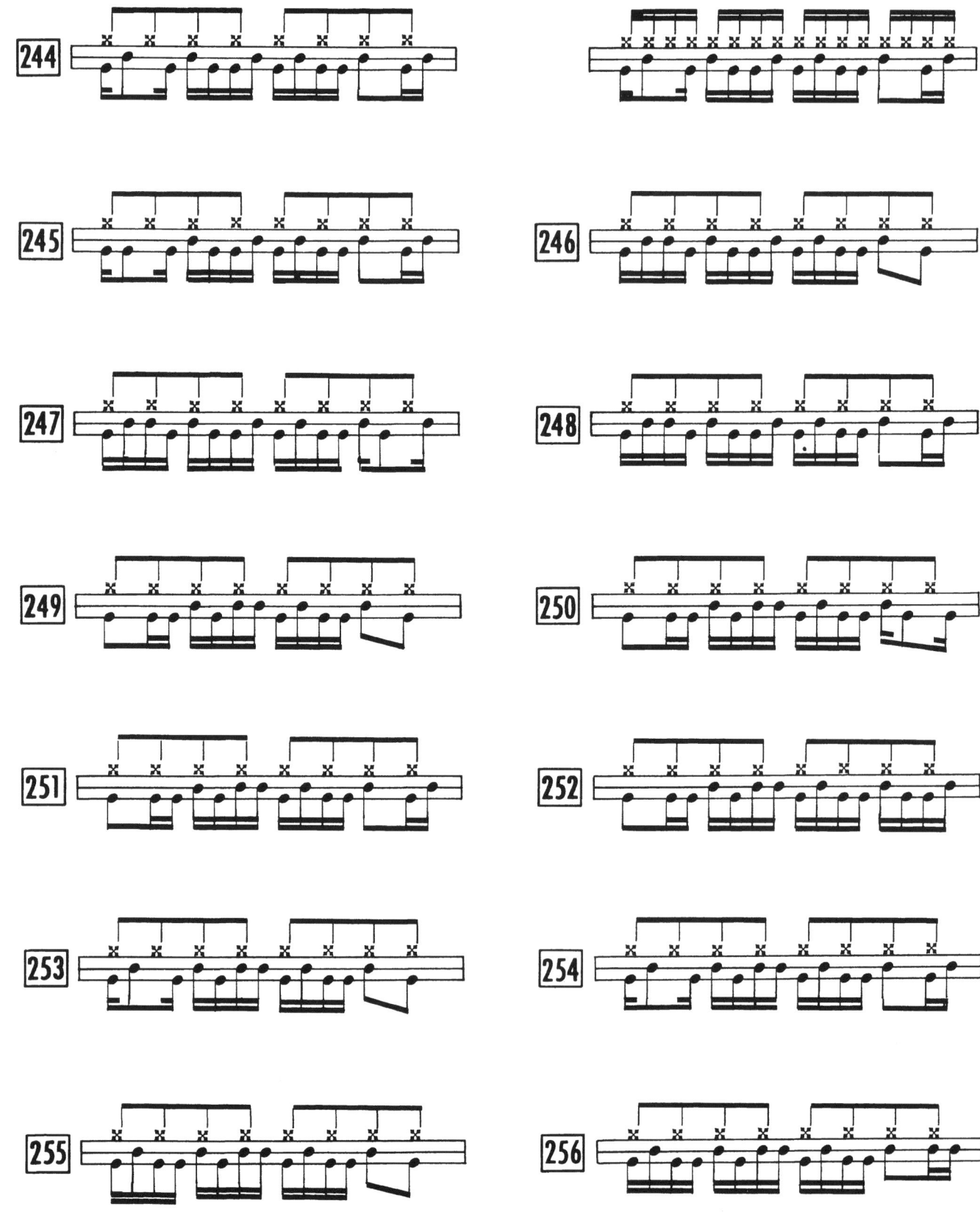

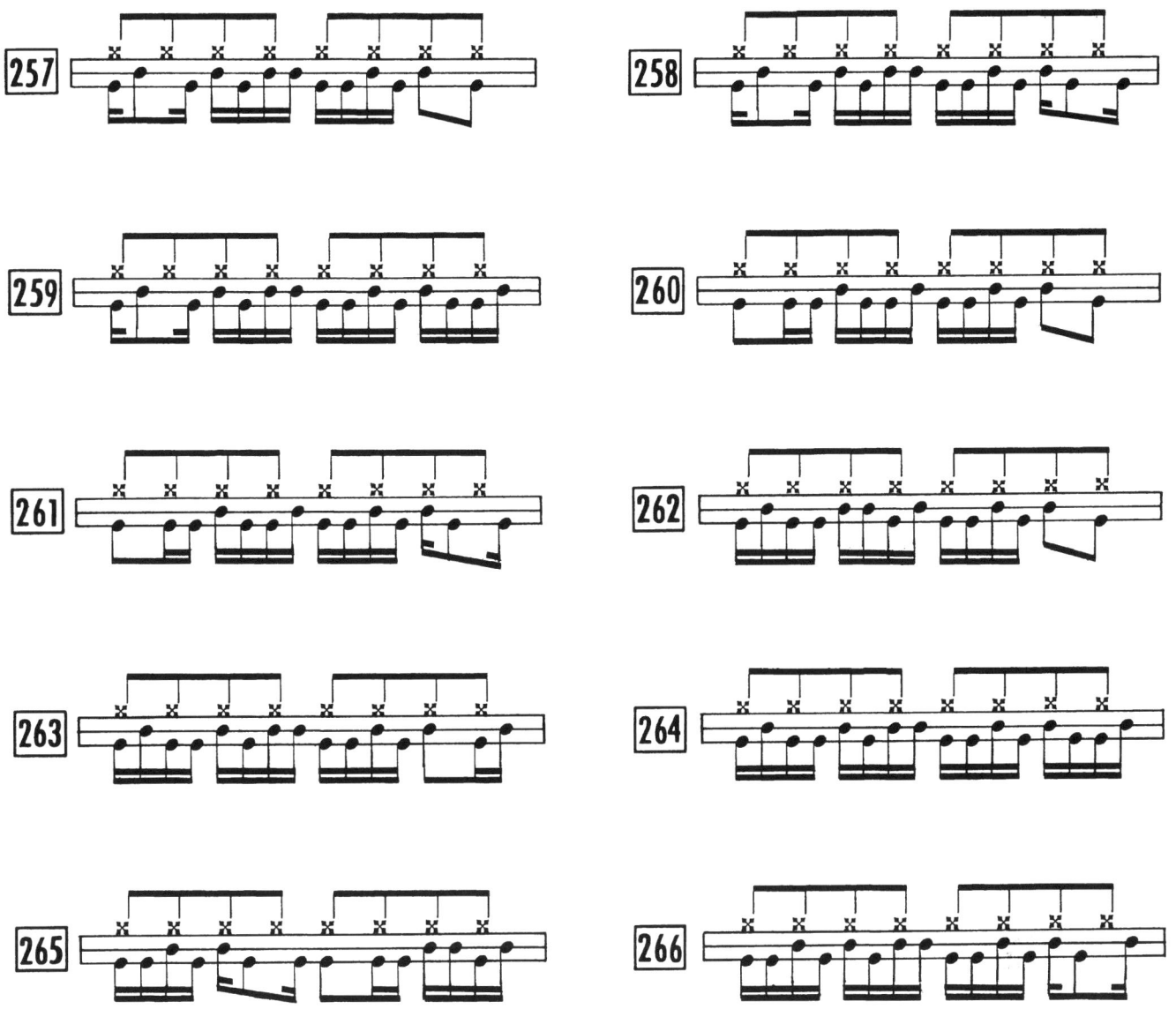

CHAPTER I
PART II

The following are a few eight bar solos designed to demonstrate, in practice, the theory of improvising rhythmically. Most of the figures used are the variations shown in parts one and two. They are connected together in solos in an effort to show how a one or two bar figure can be turned into a longer phrase.

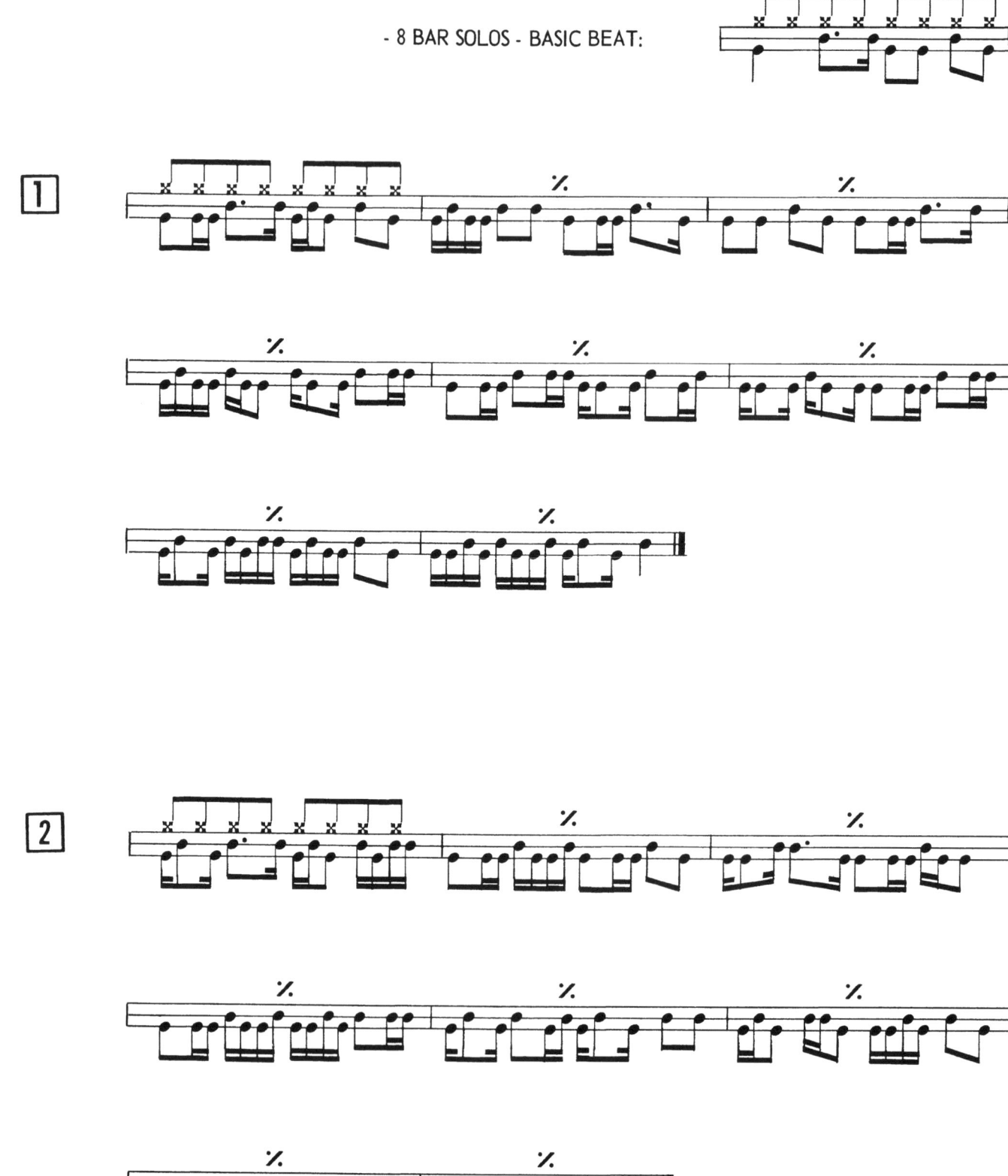

3

4

5

6

37

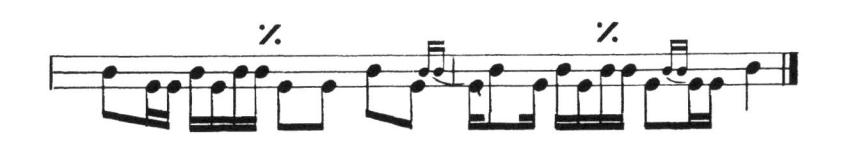

CHAPTER II

BASIC FIGURE:

The figure represented in Chapter Two is perhaps a little more up to date than the figure in Chapter One. It is used quite frequently in modern rock arrangements.

The variations shown here are by no means the only ones. They are merely samples chosen at random. The number of variations possible from a basic pattern are almost infinite. The student must be encouraged to develop his own variations.

ALL FIGURES ARE TO BE PLAYED AGAINST AN EIGHTH NOTE AND A SIXTEENTH NOTE RIDE!

CHAPTER II

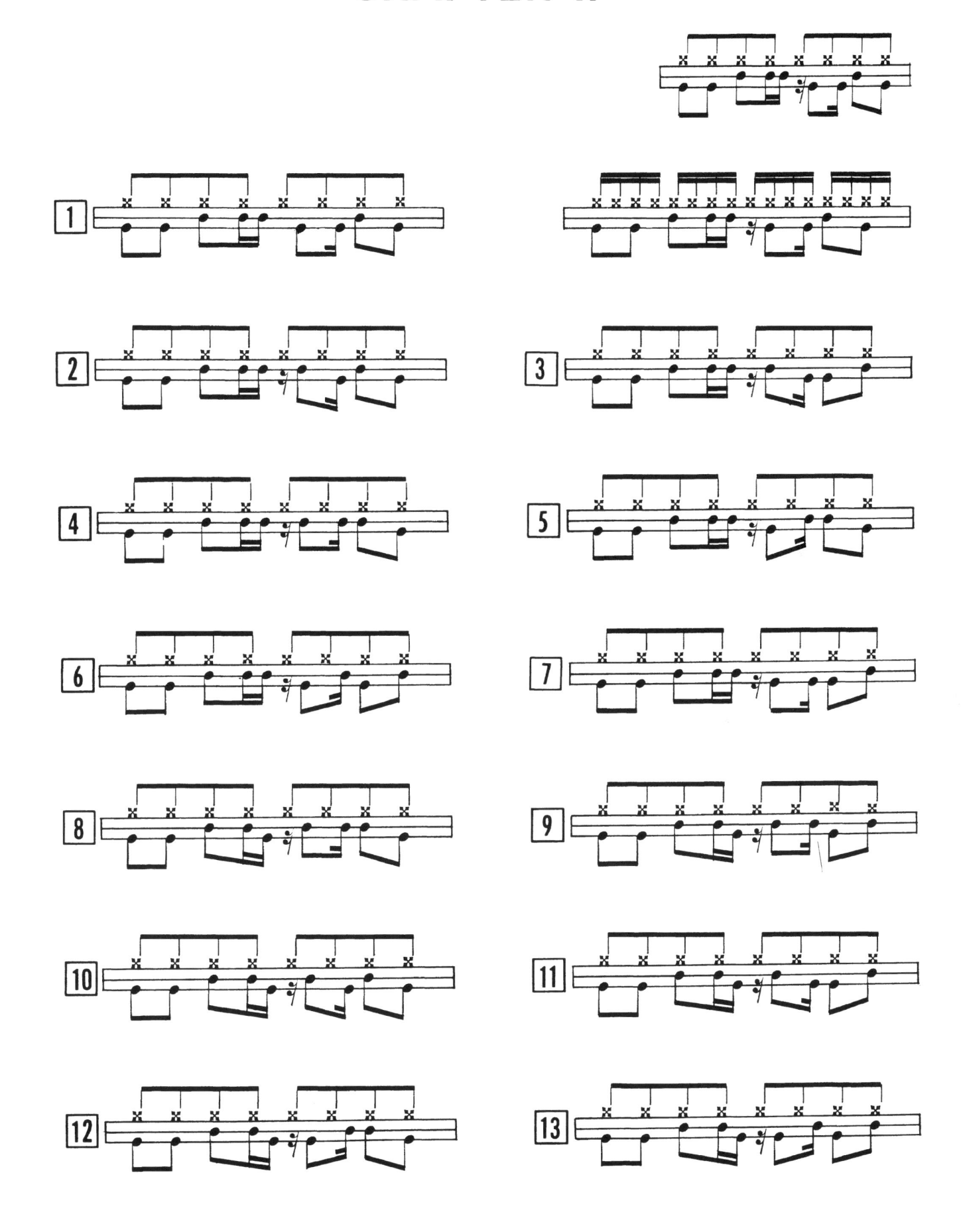

40

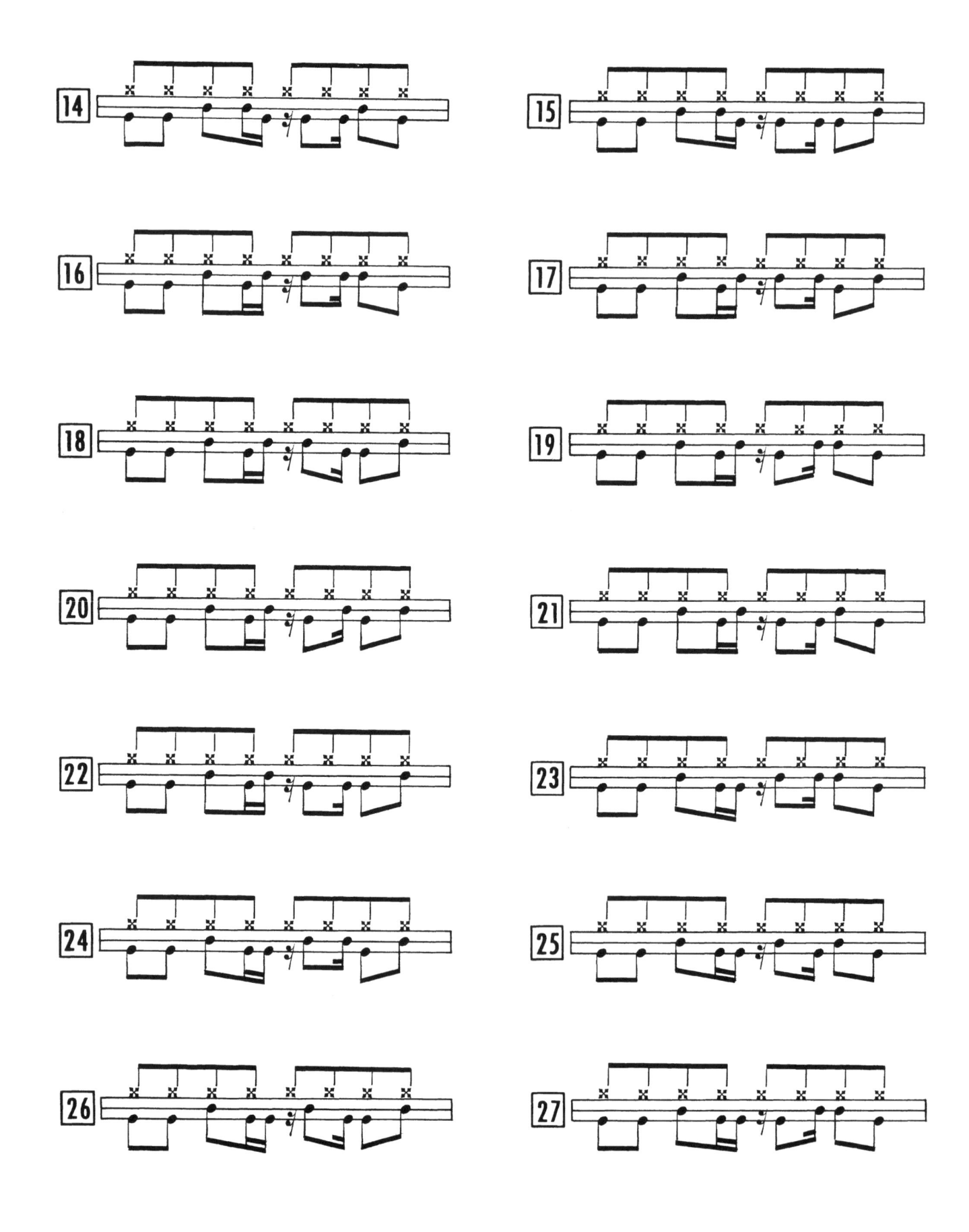

41

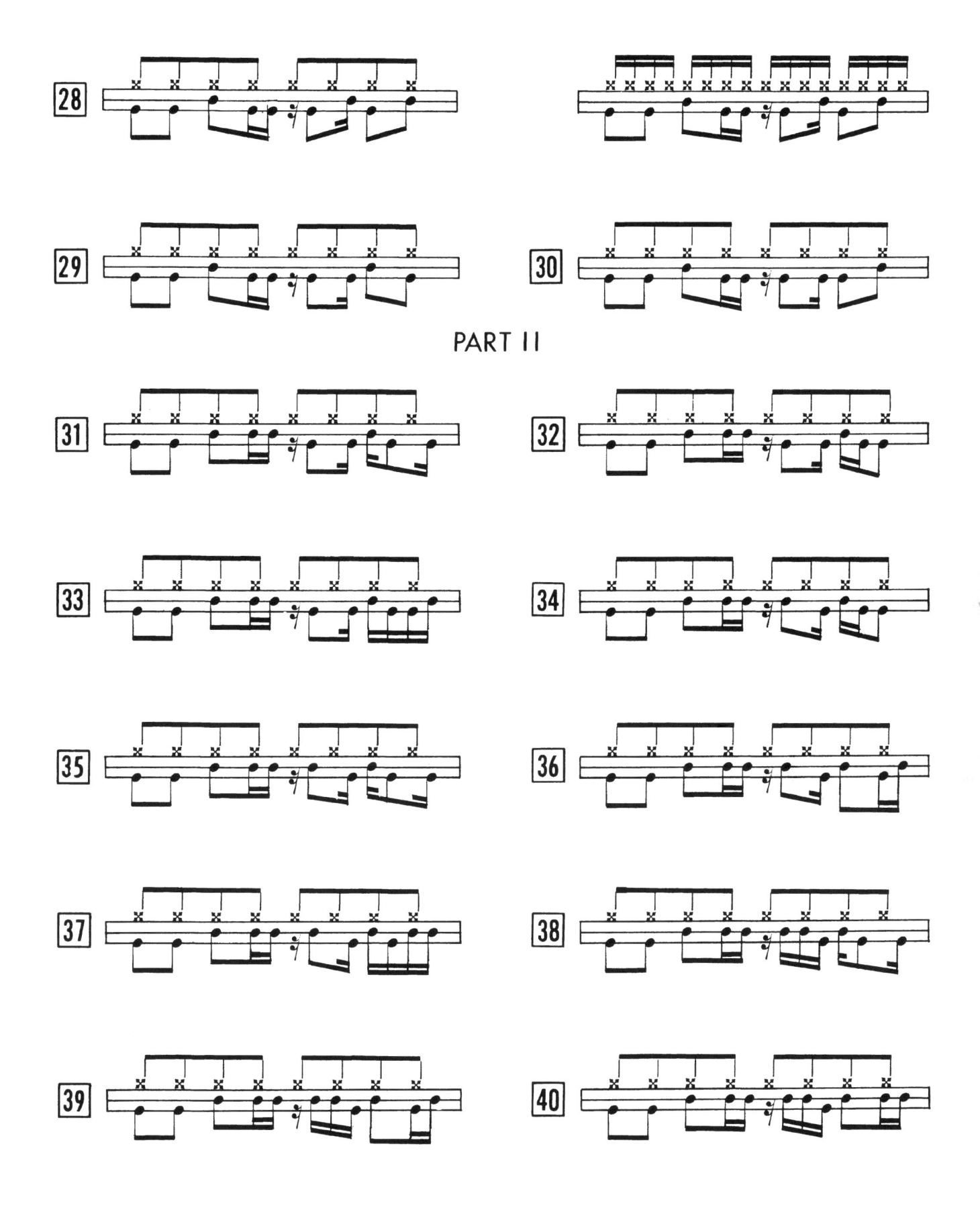

PART II

41

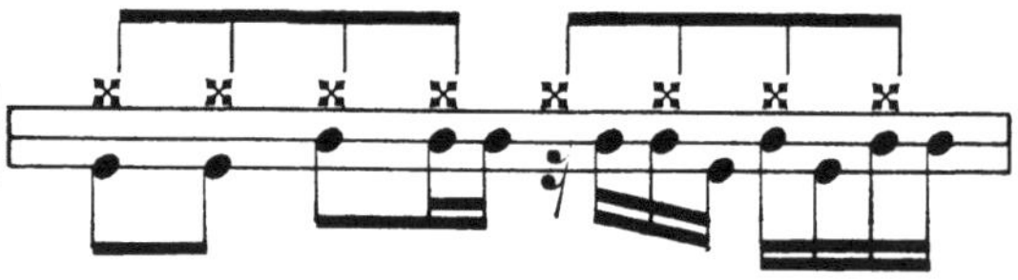

42

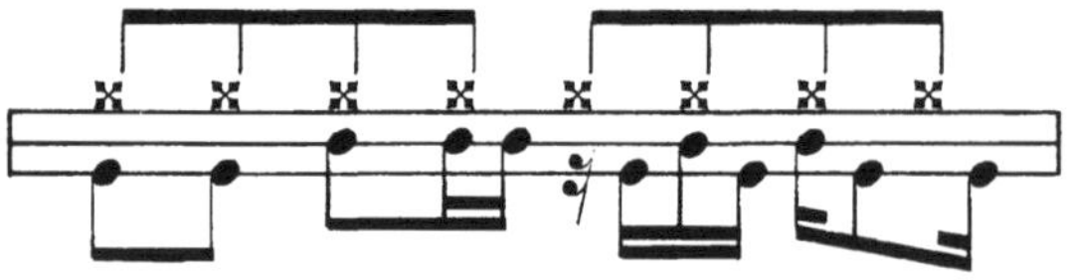

43

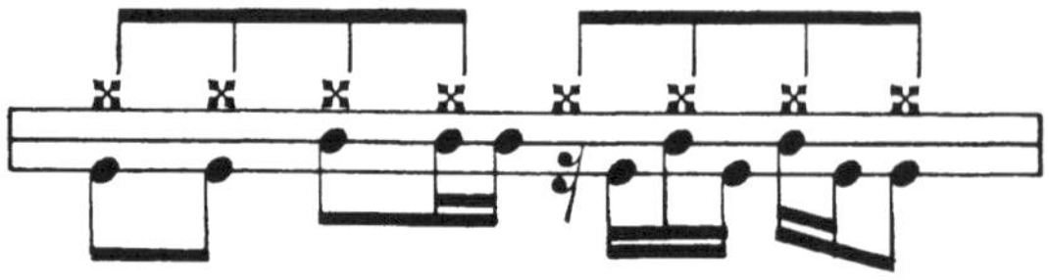

44

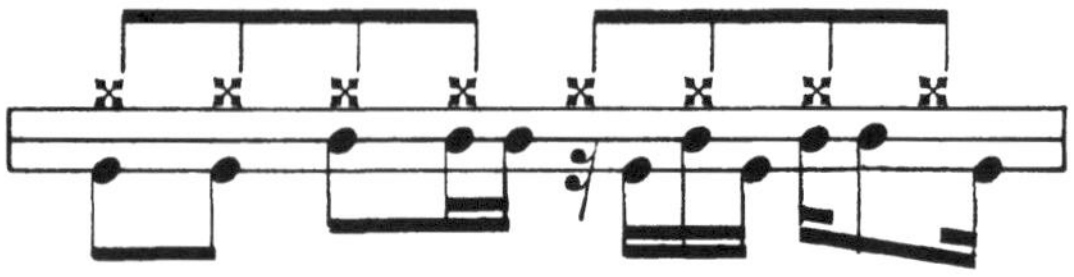

45

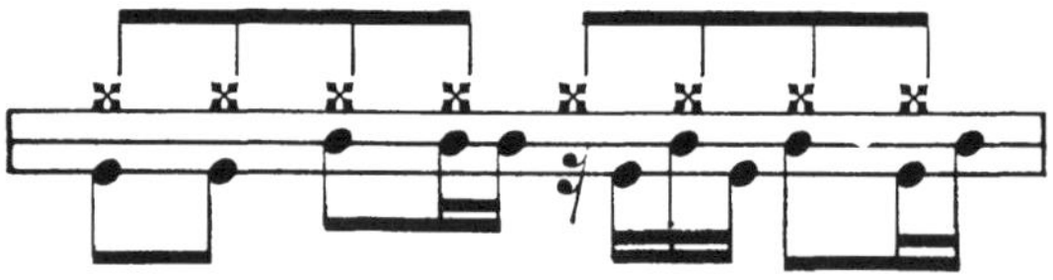

46

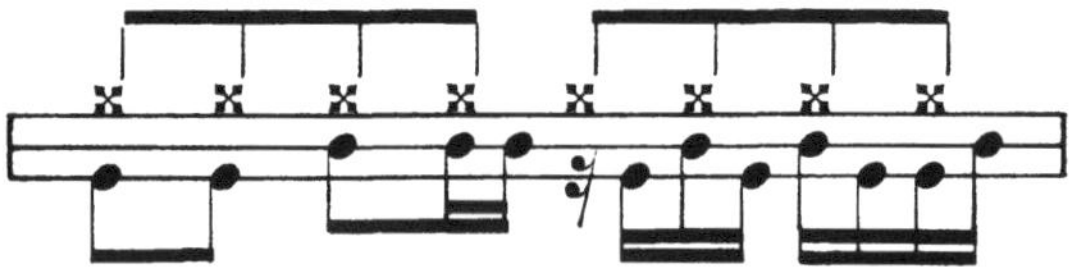

47

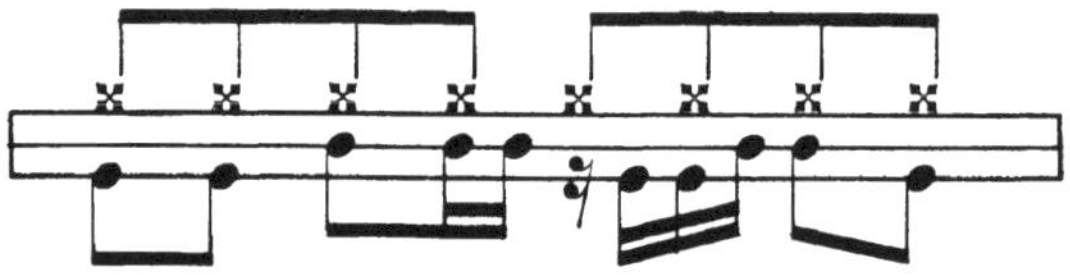

48

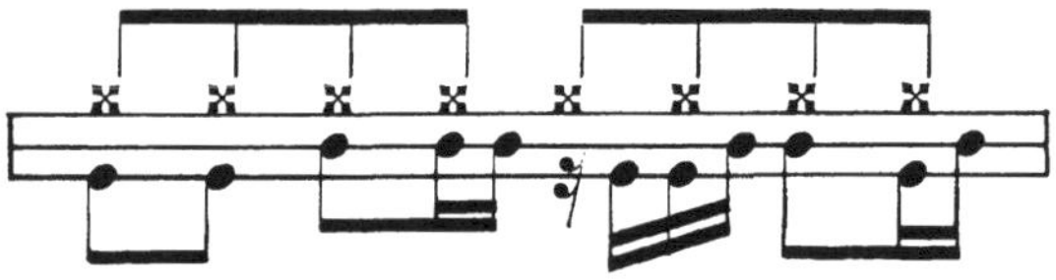

49

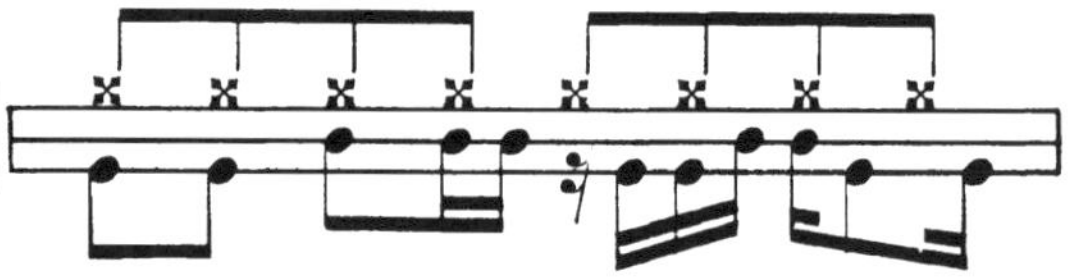

50

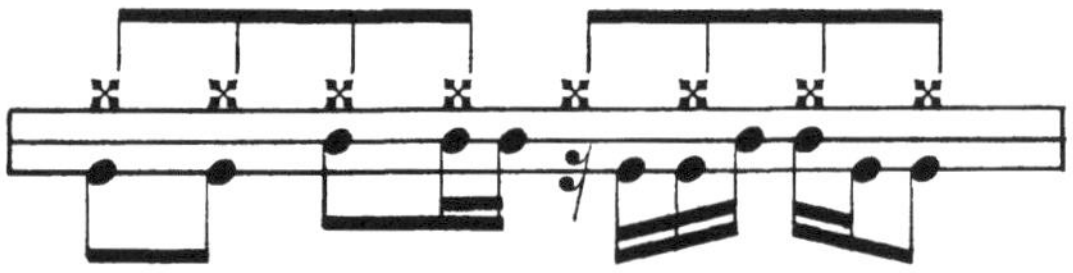

51

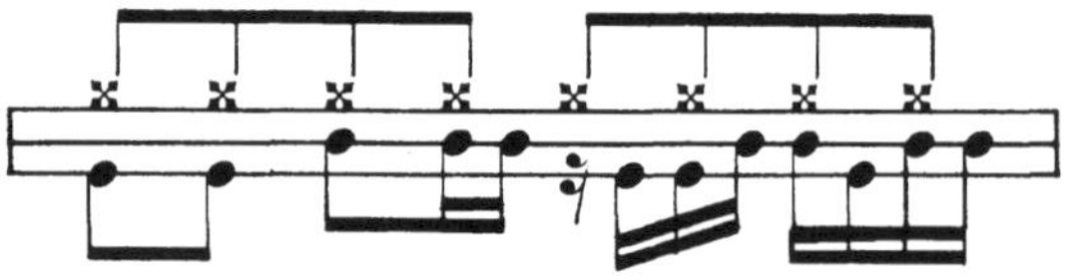

52

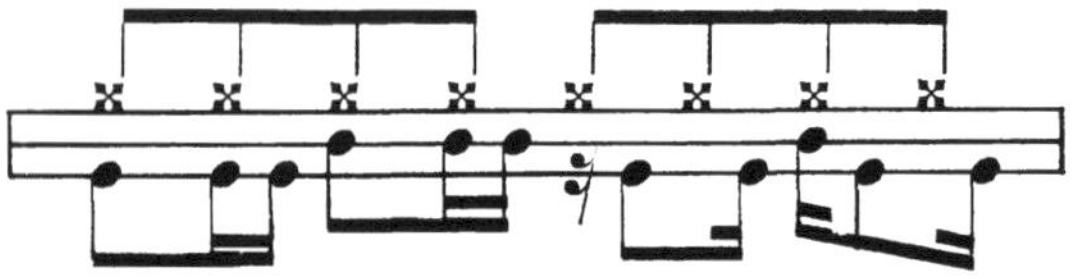

53

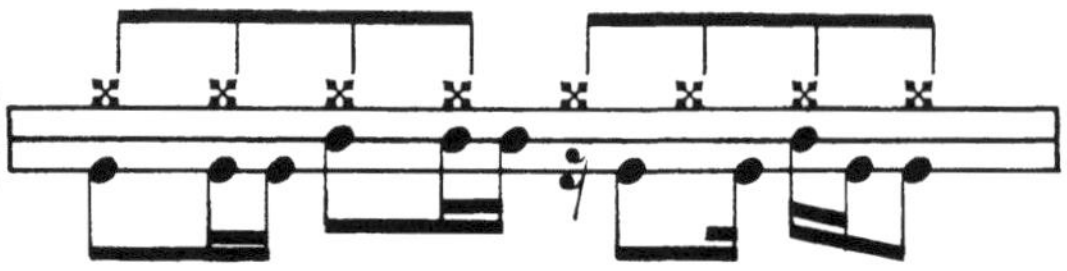

54

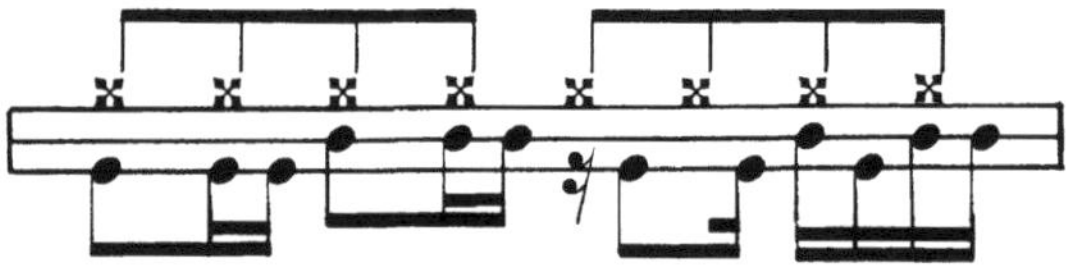

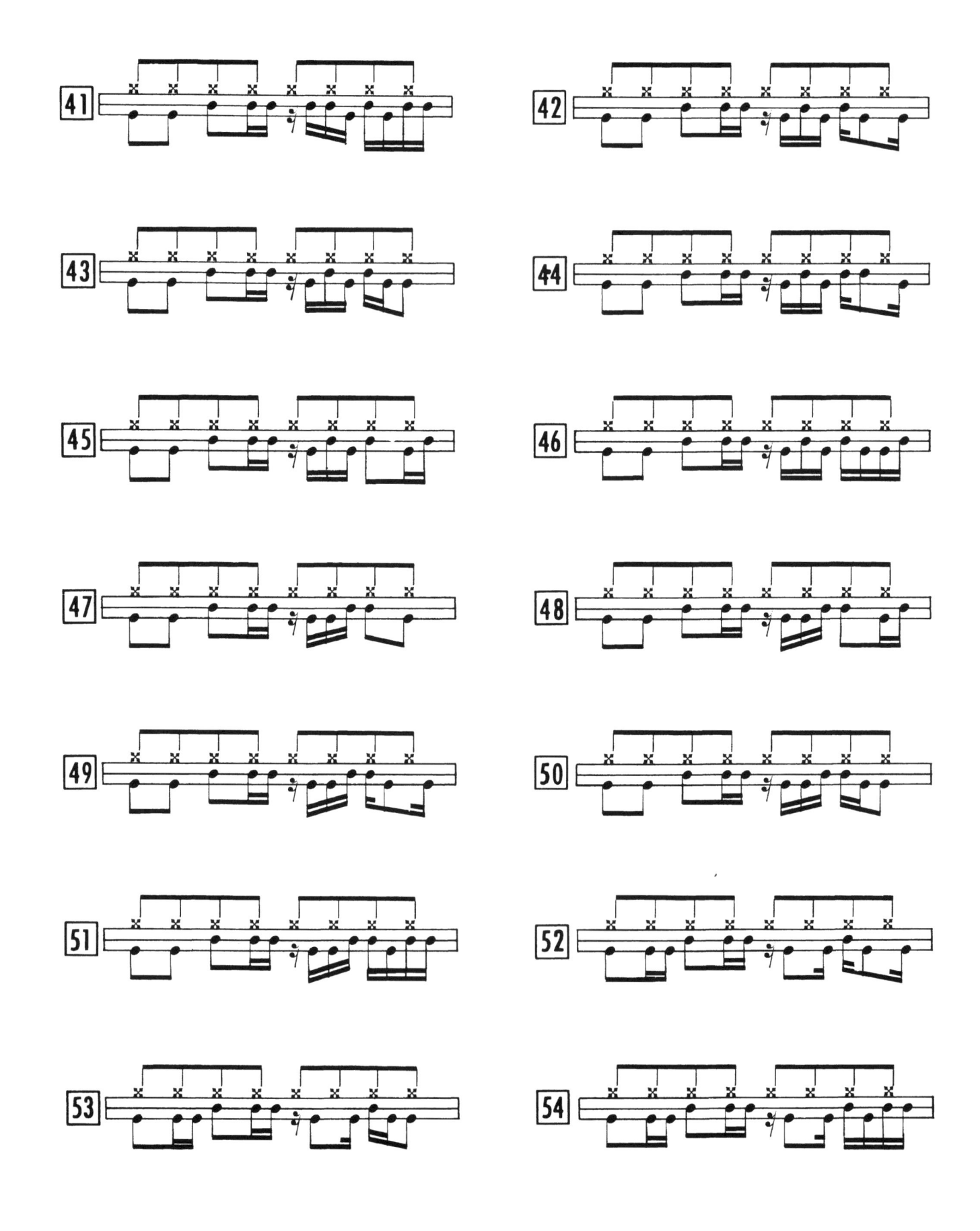

NOTE! USE ♩ ♩ ♩ ♩, ♫♫♫♫, RIDE FOR ALL FIGURES

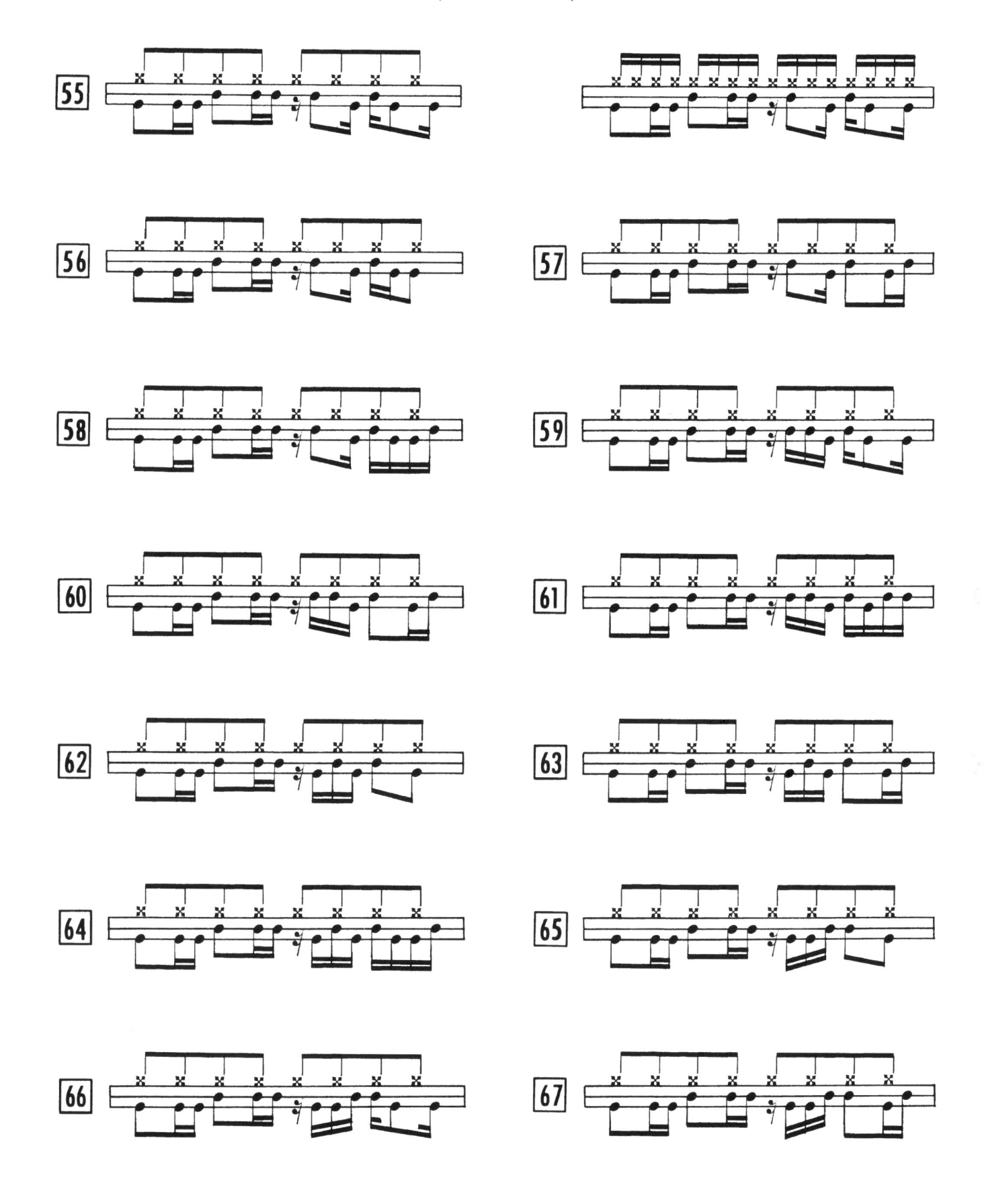

43

44

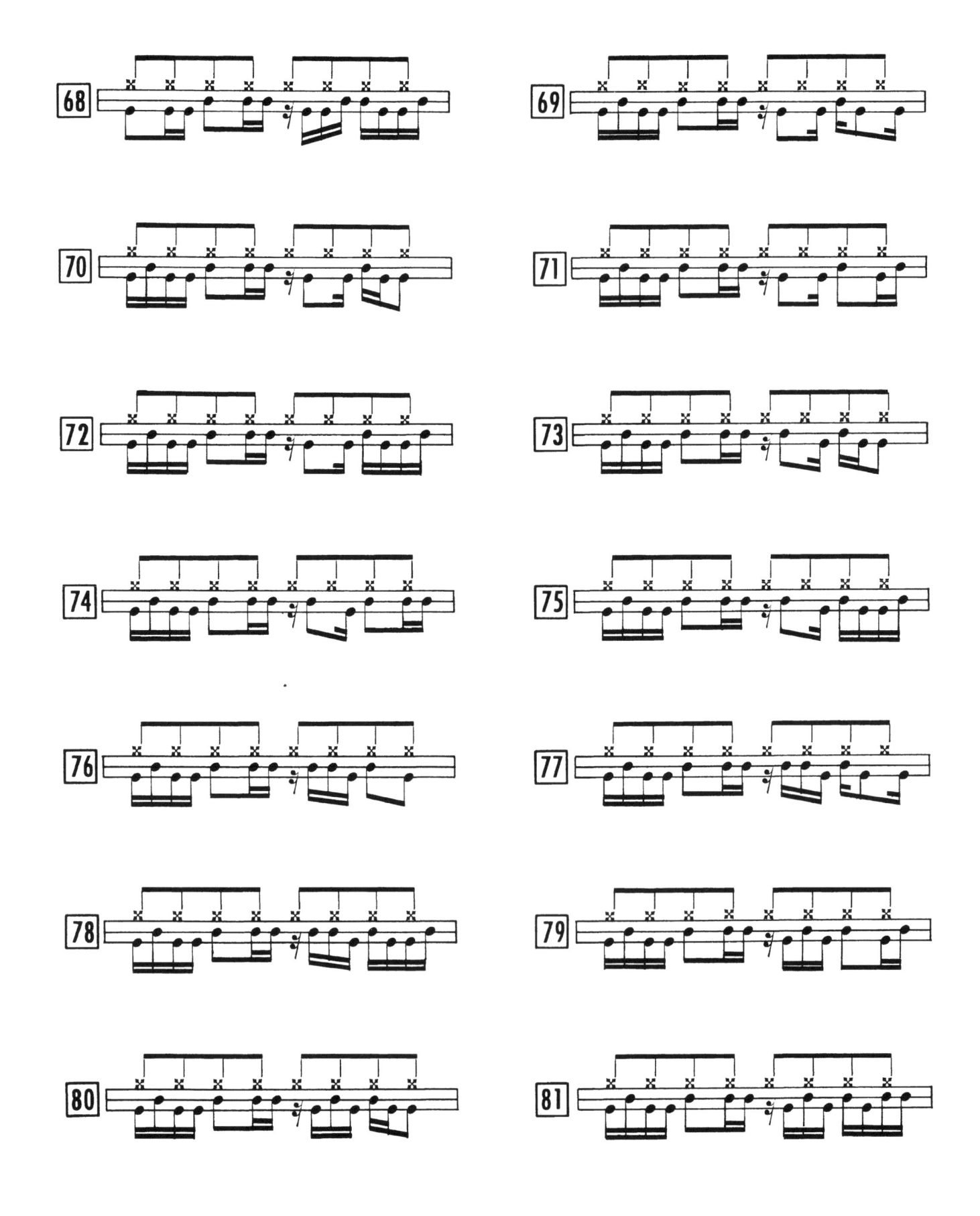

82

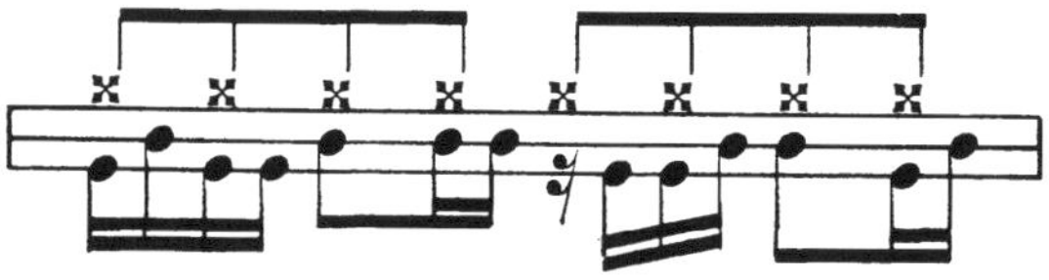

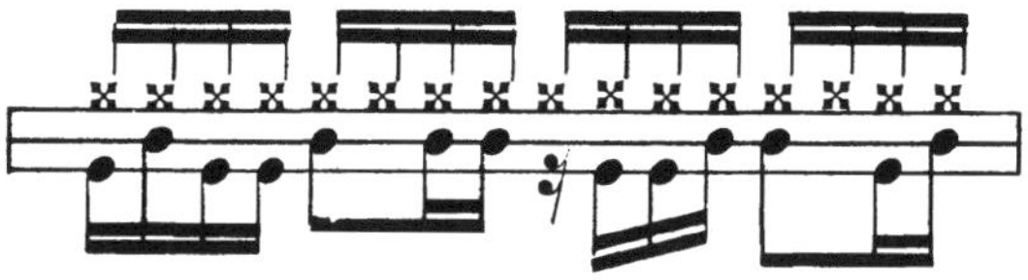

83

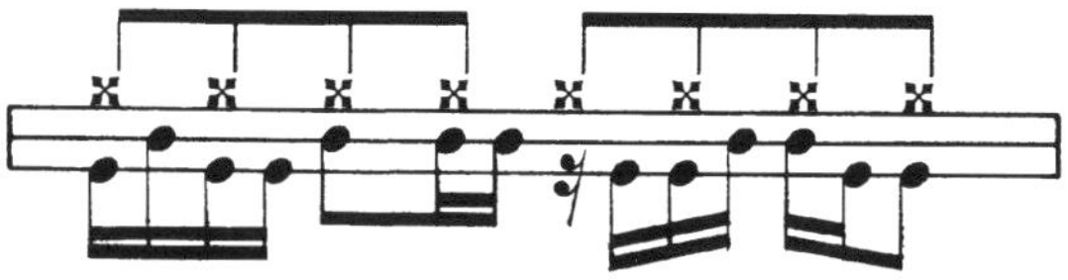

84

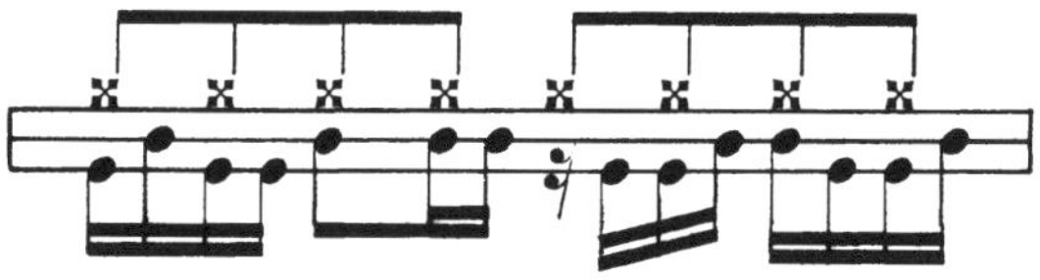

85

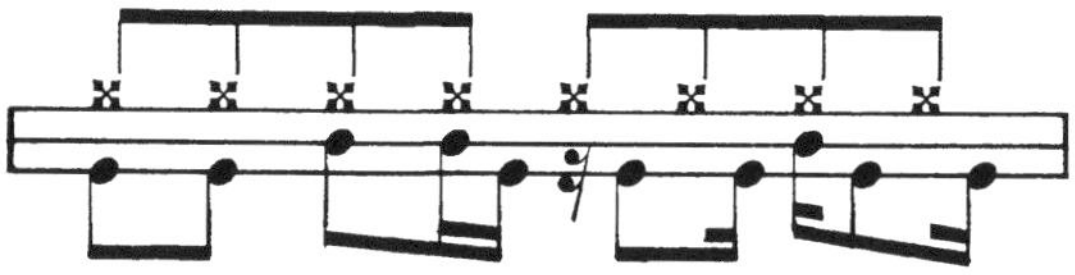

86

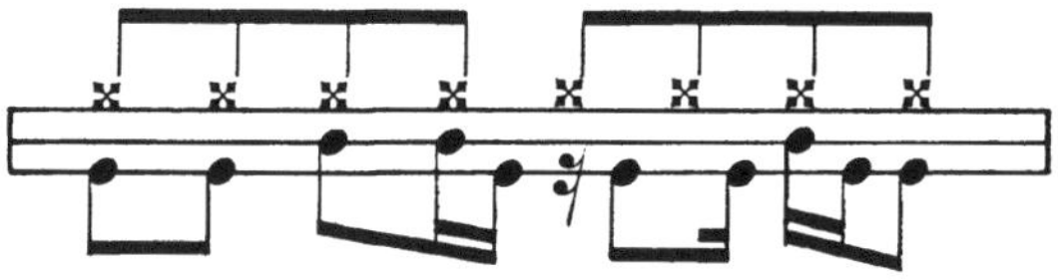

87

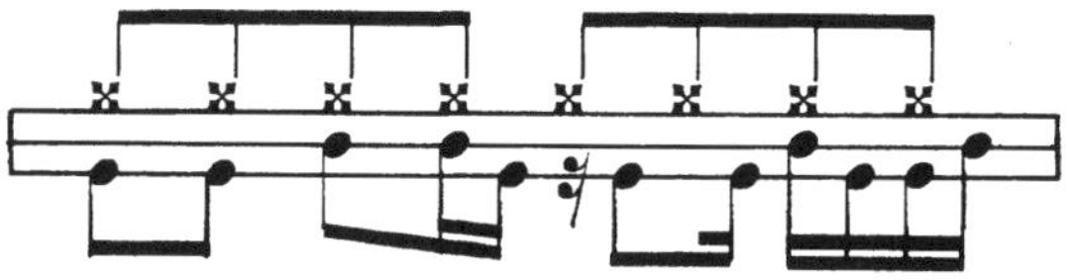

88

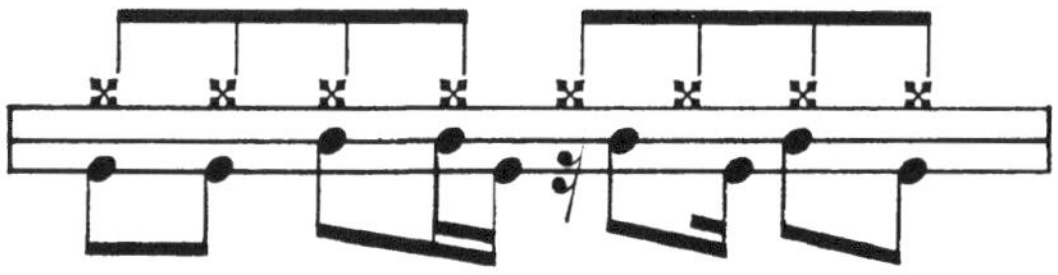

89

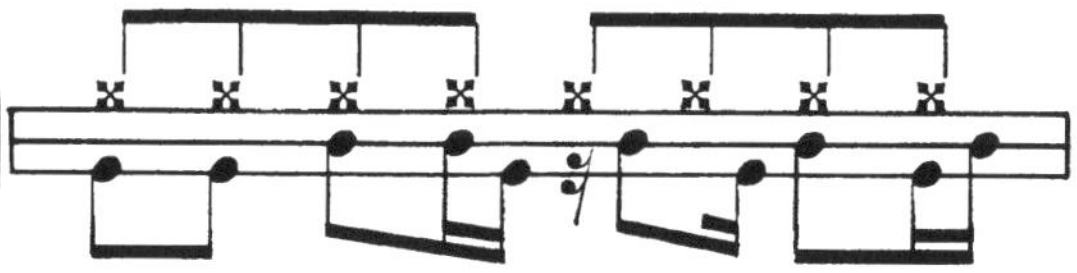

90

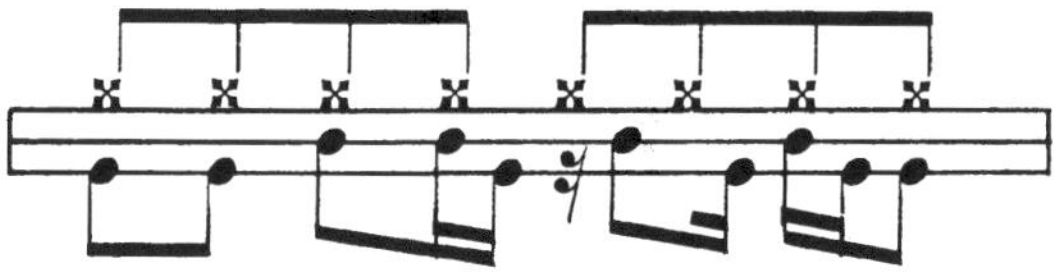

91

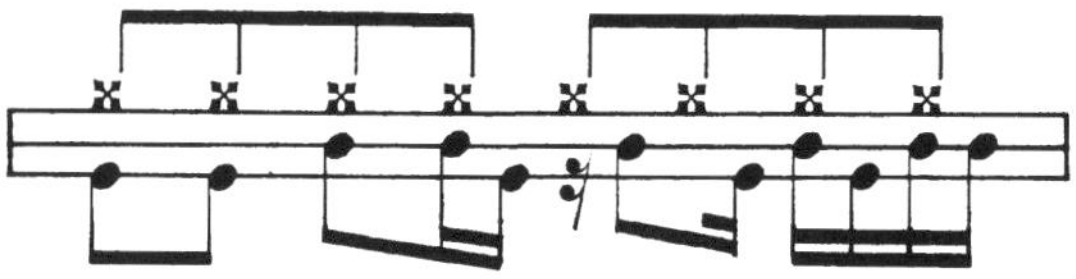

92

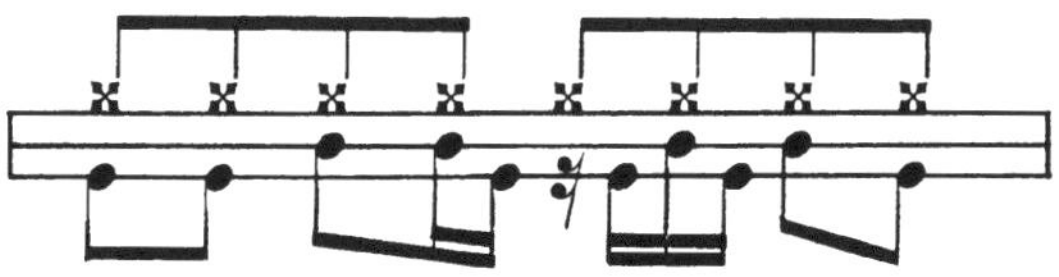

93

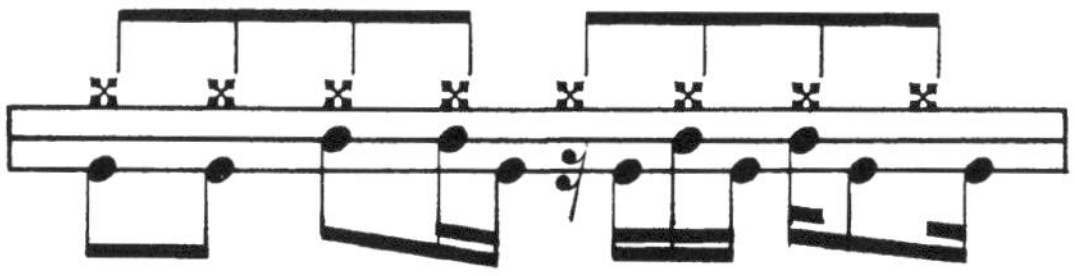

94

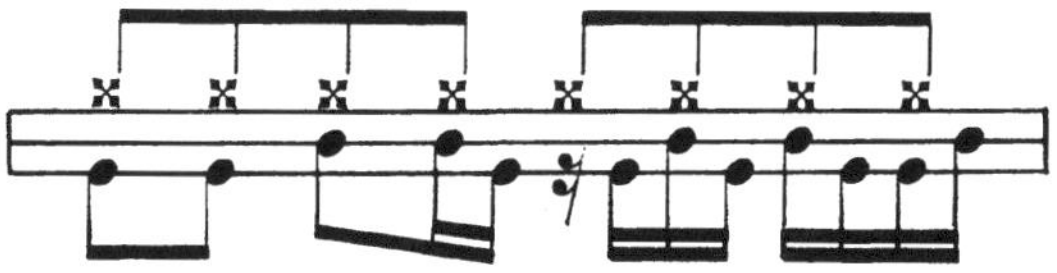

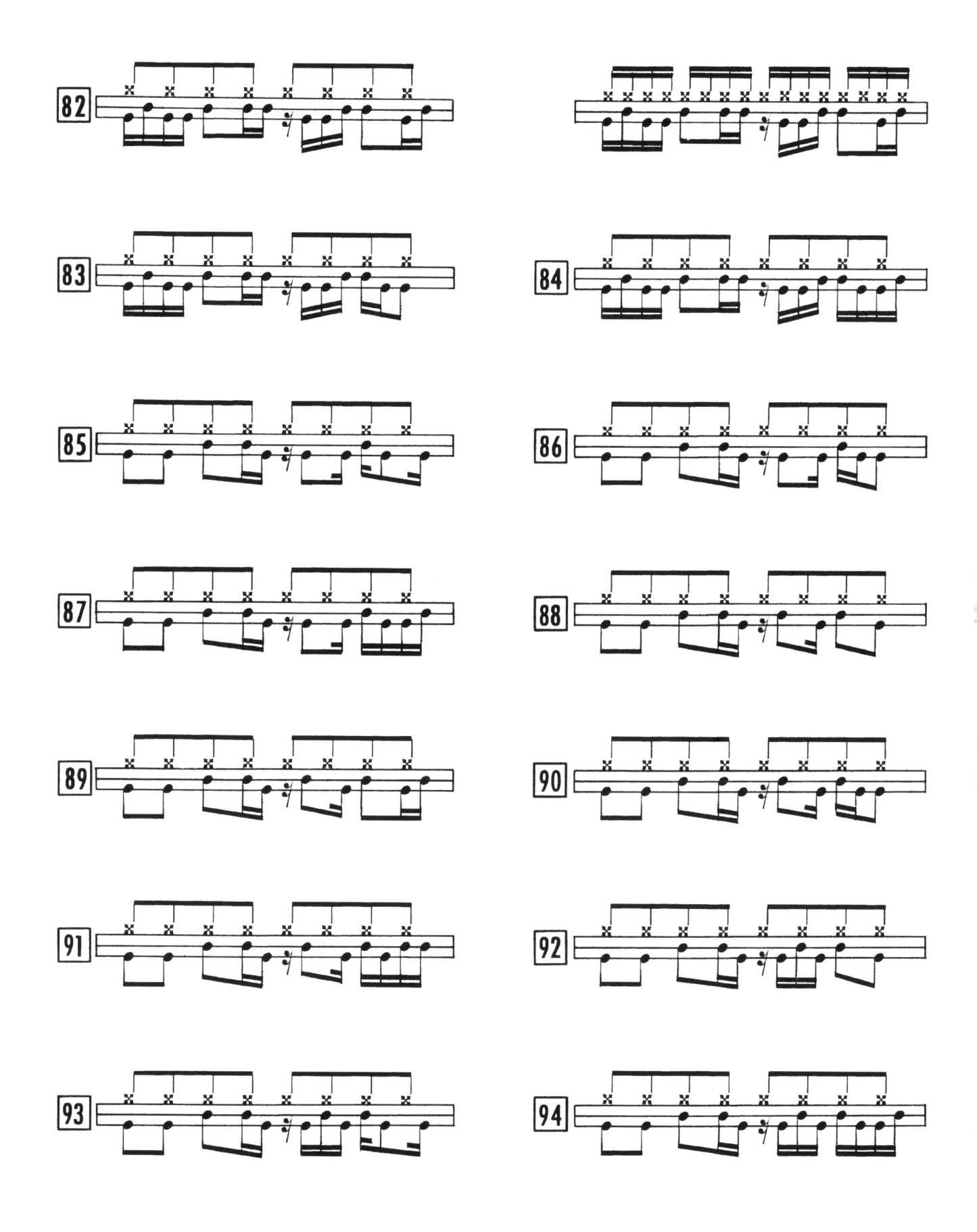

46

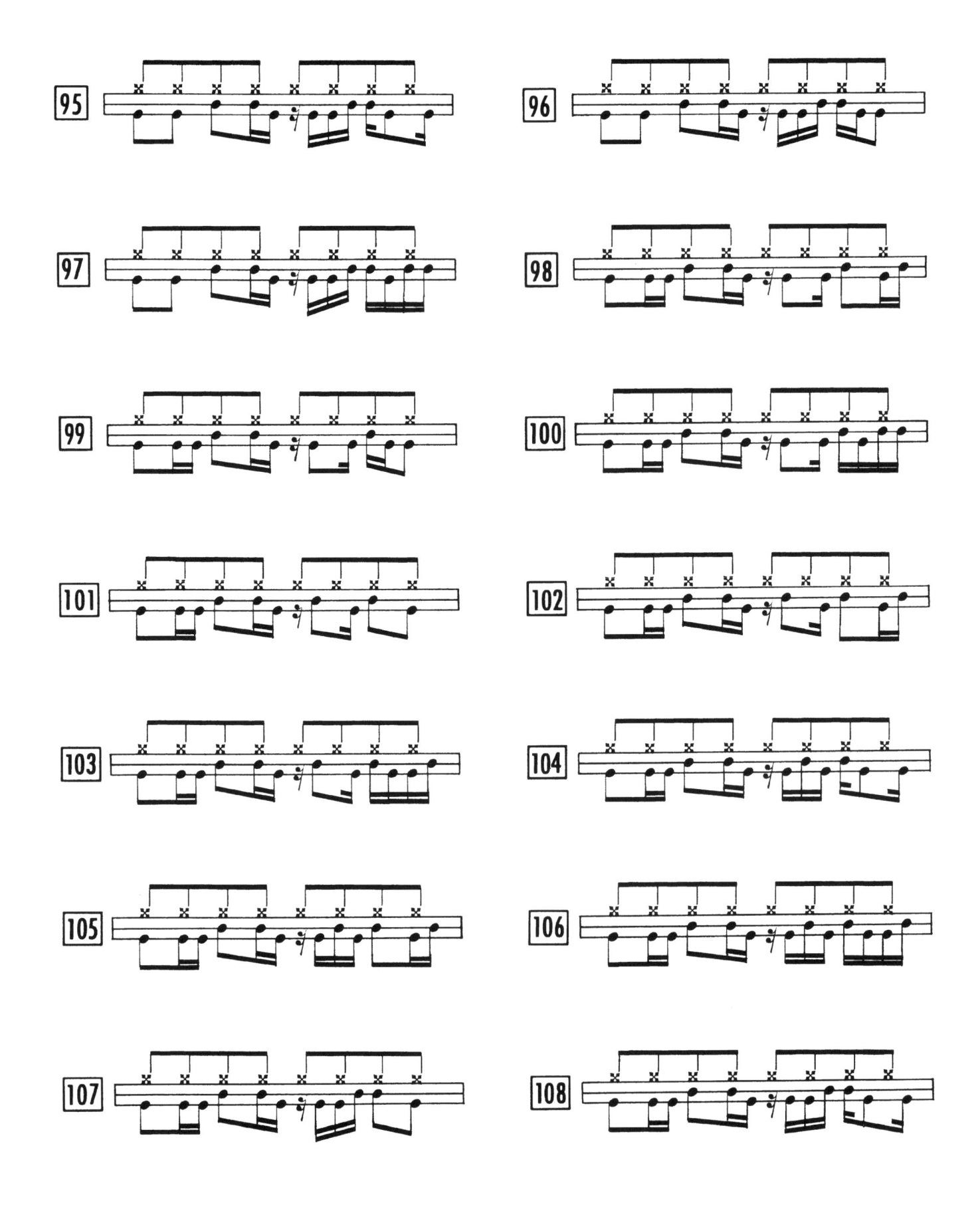

47

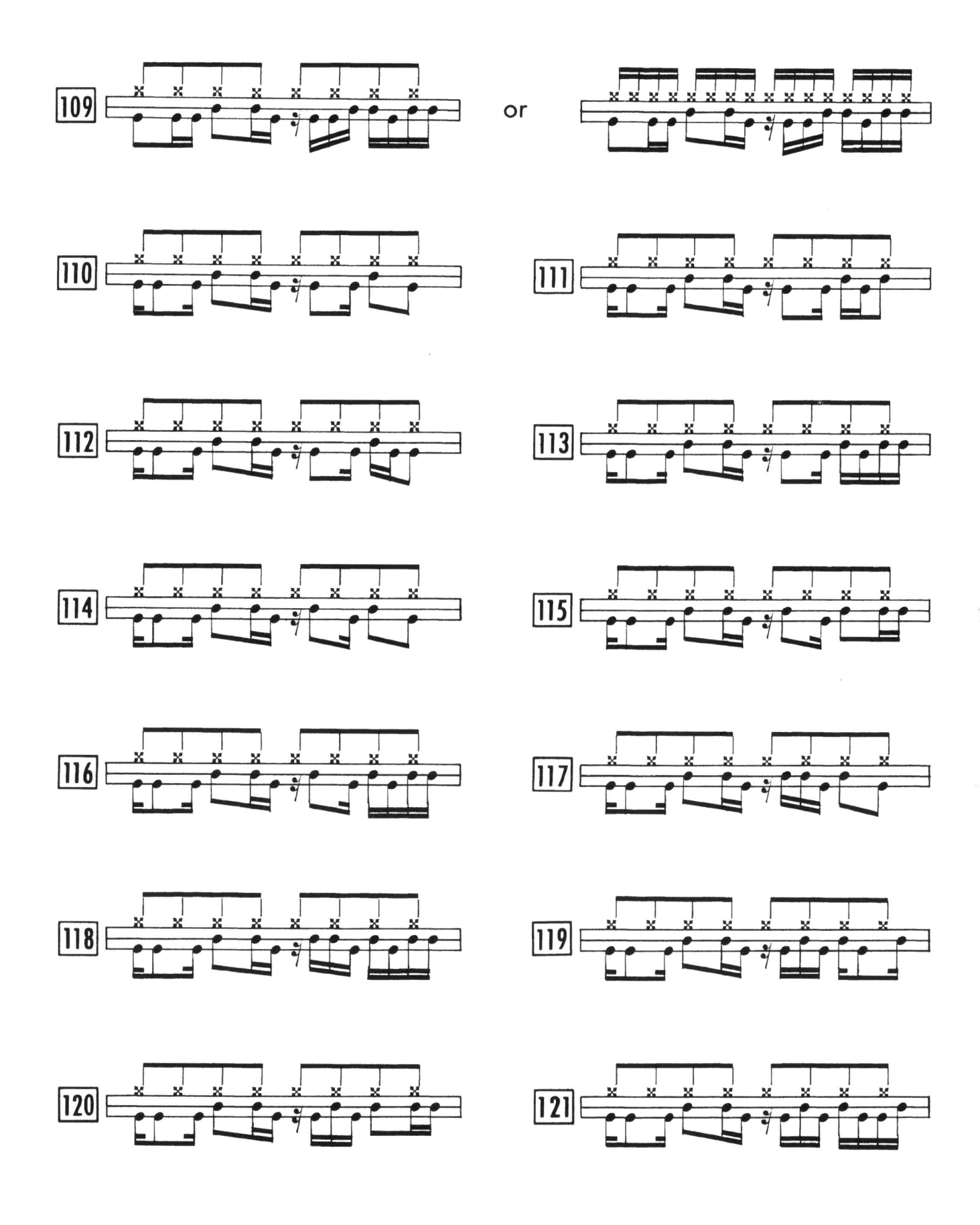

122
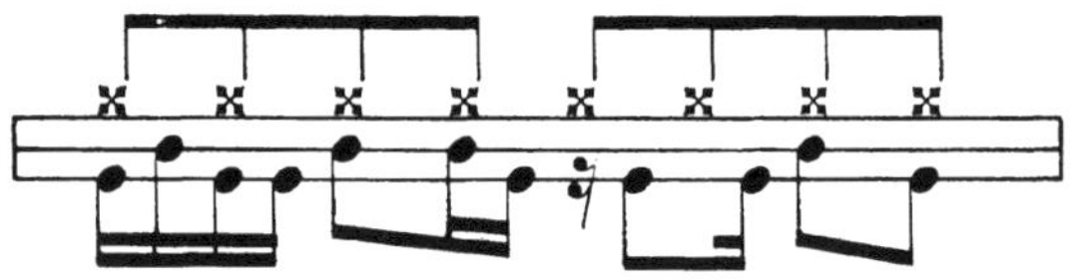

123
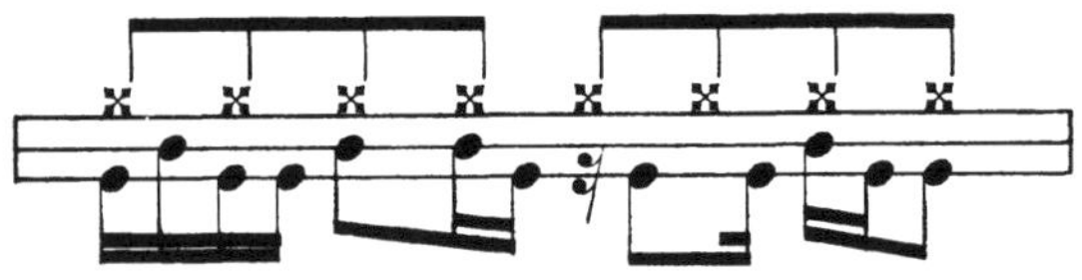

124
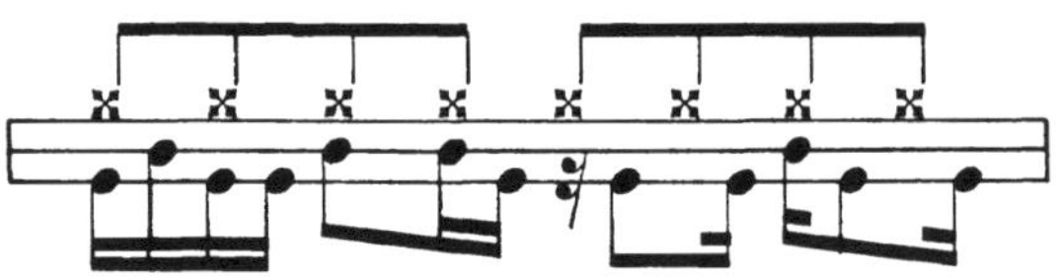

125
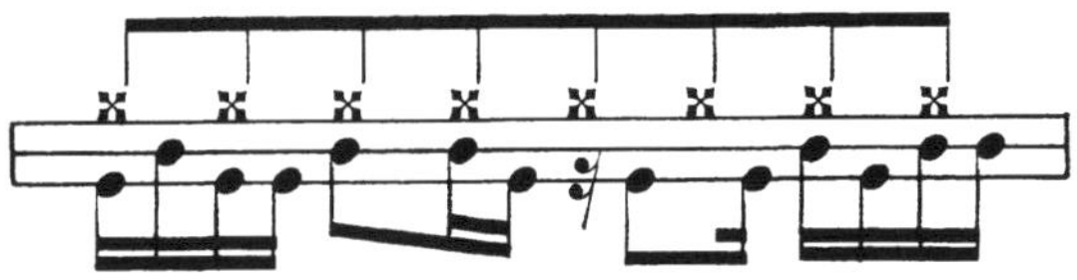

126
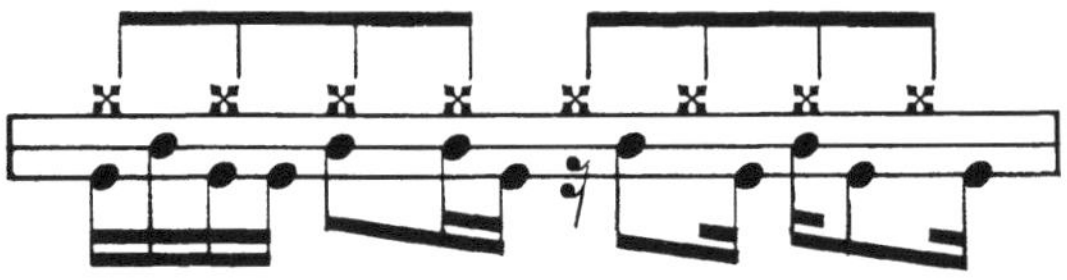

127
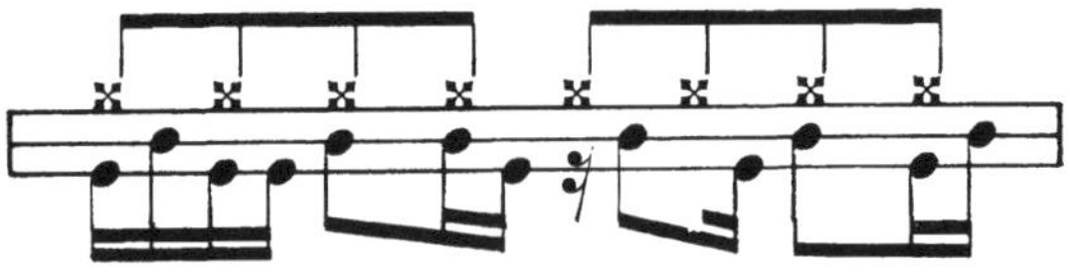

128
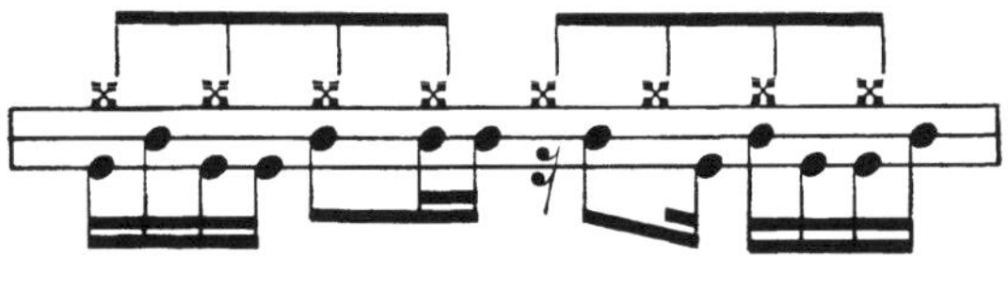

129
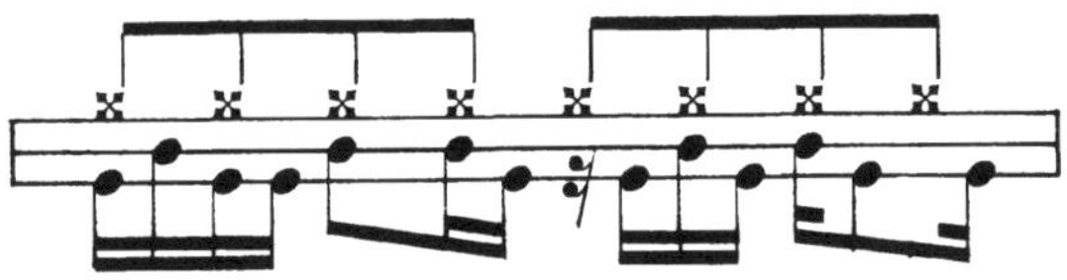

130
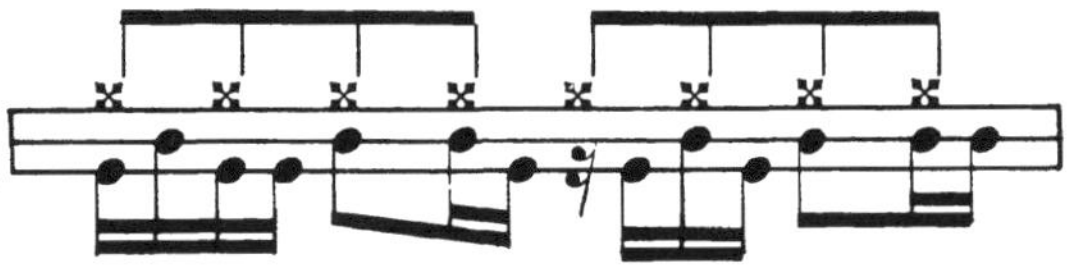

131
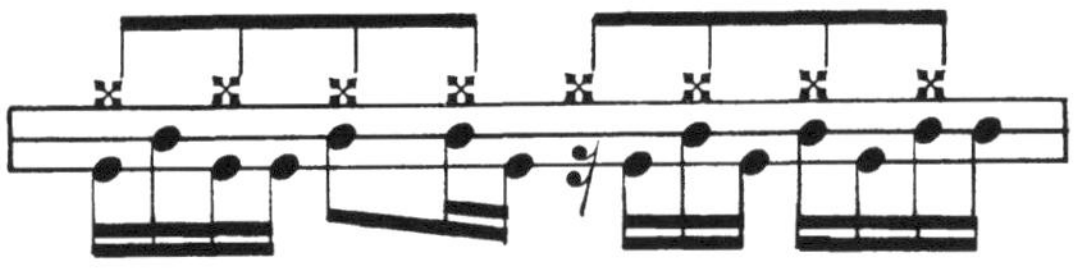

132
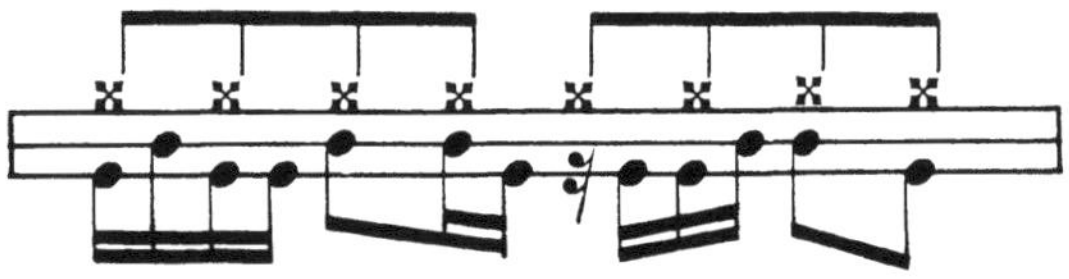

133
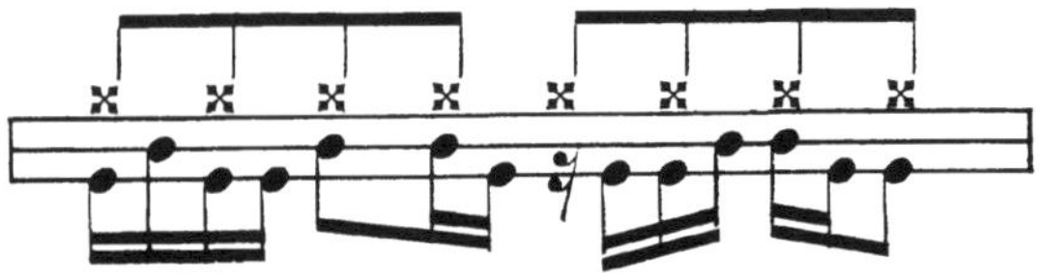

134
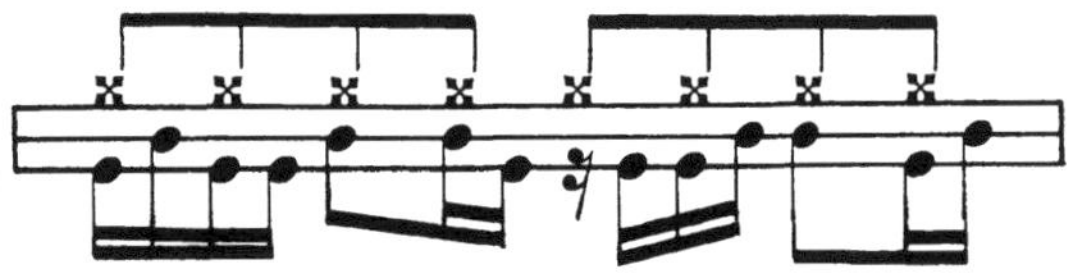

135
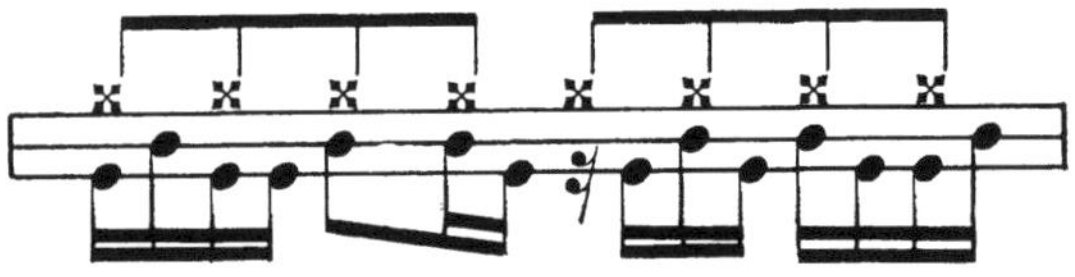

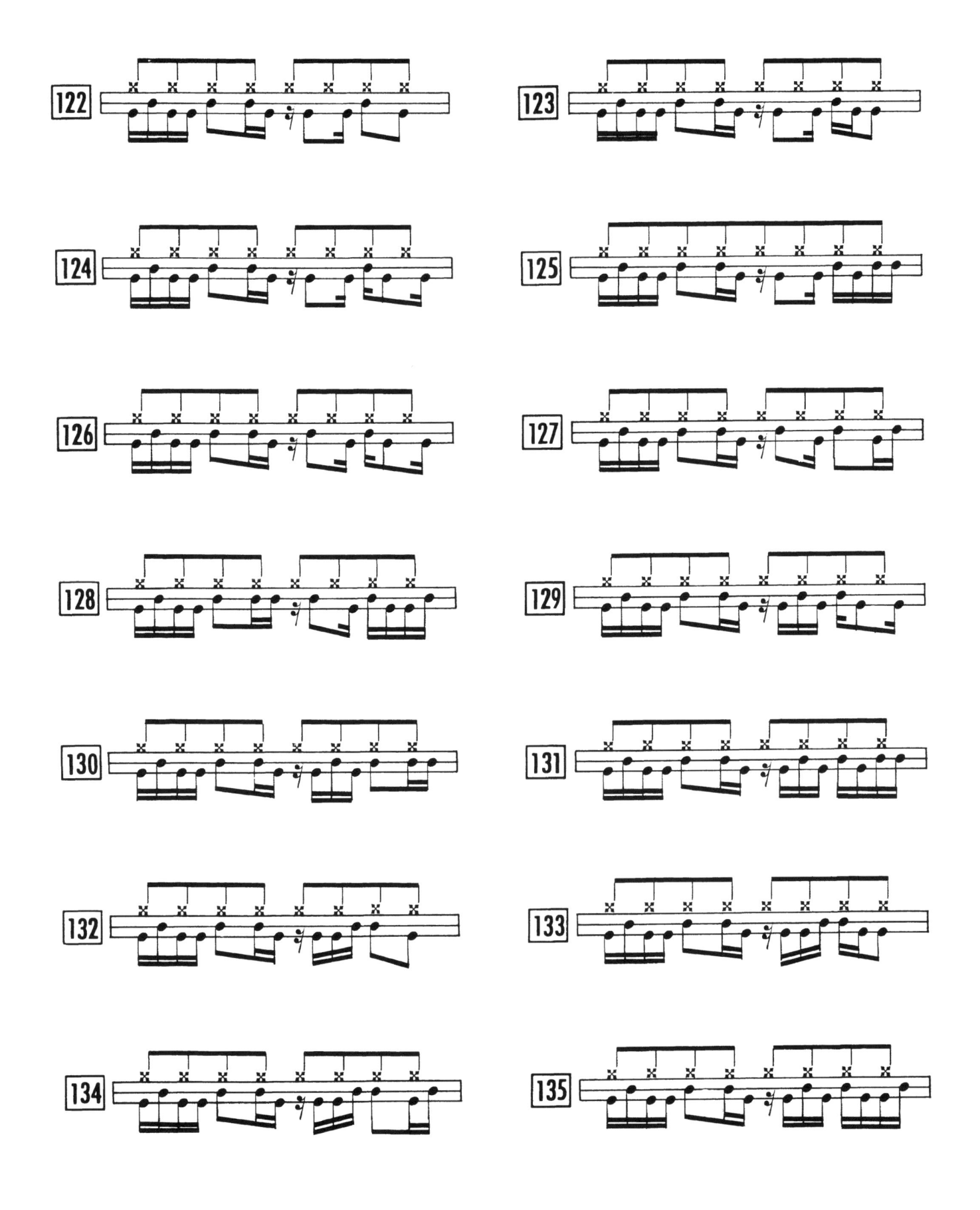

NOTE! USE 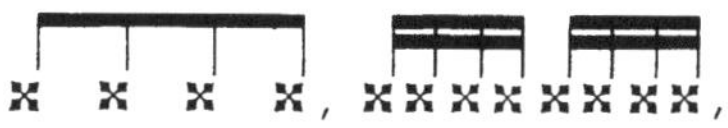 RIDE FOR ALL FIGURES

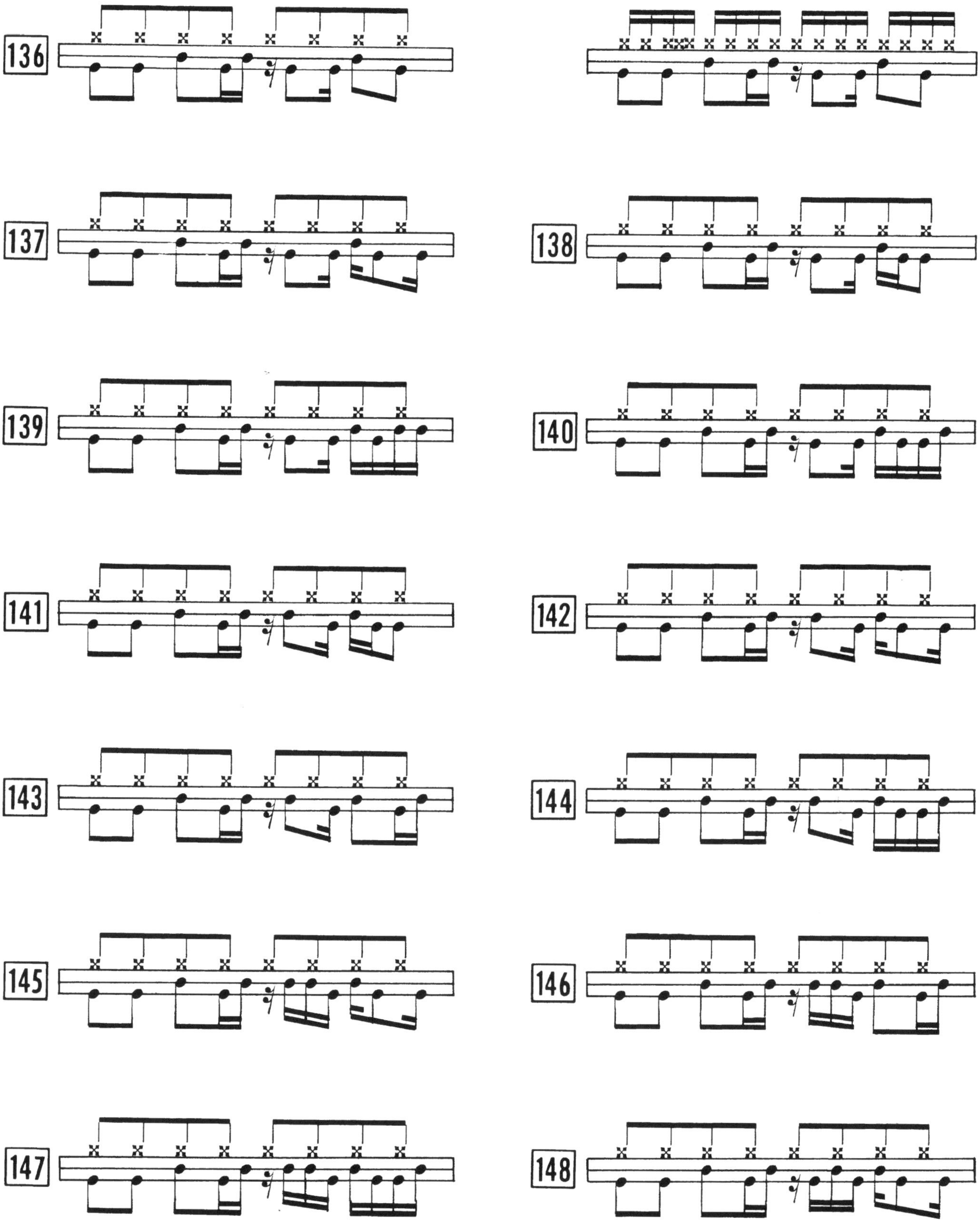

50

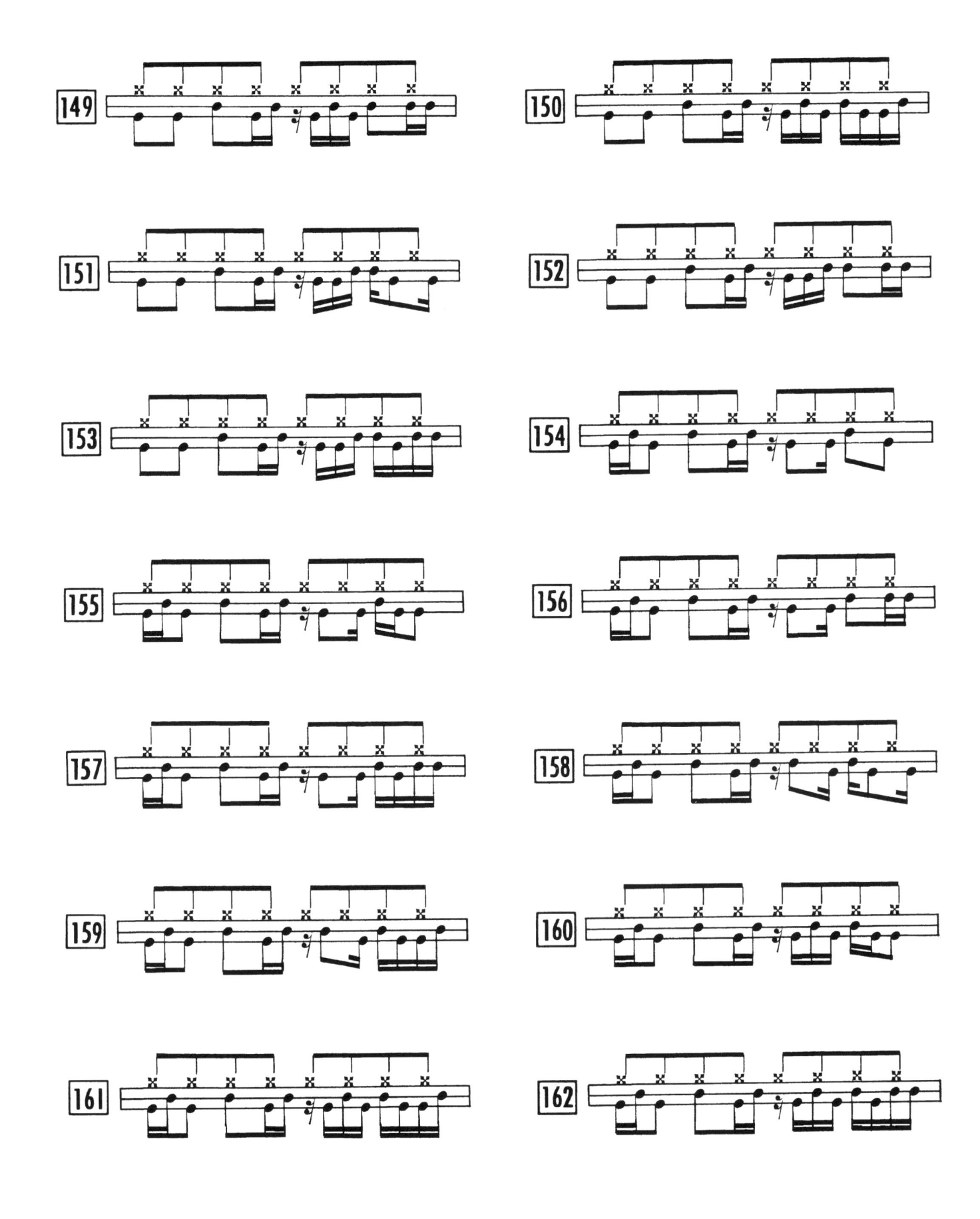

163
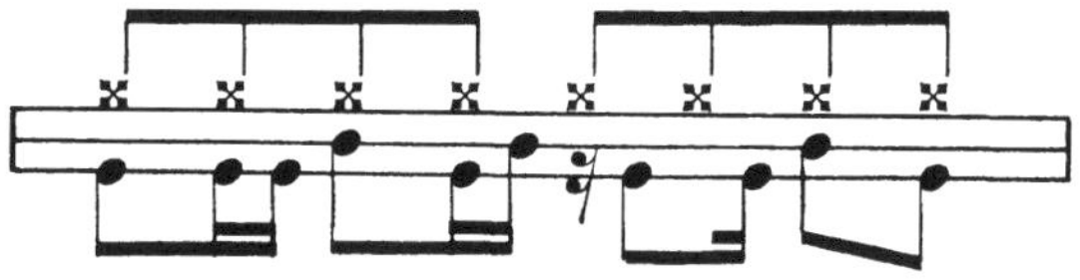
or
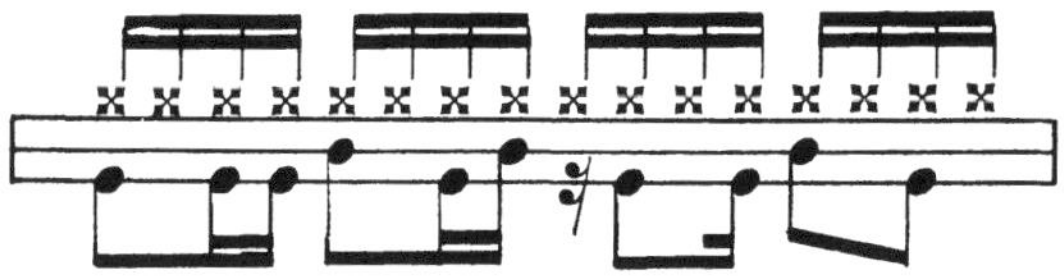

164
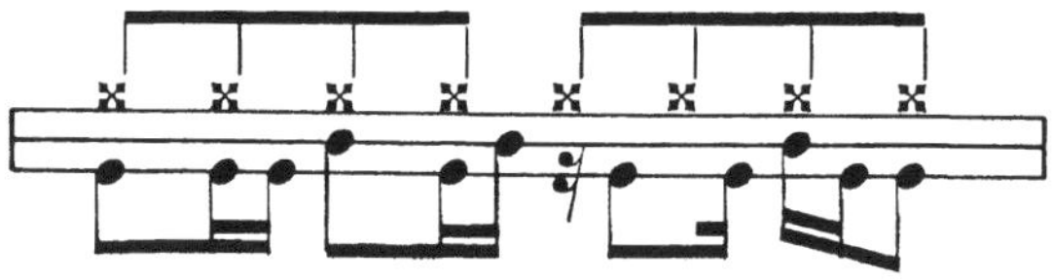

165
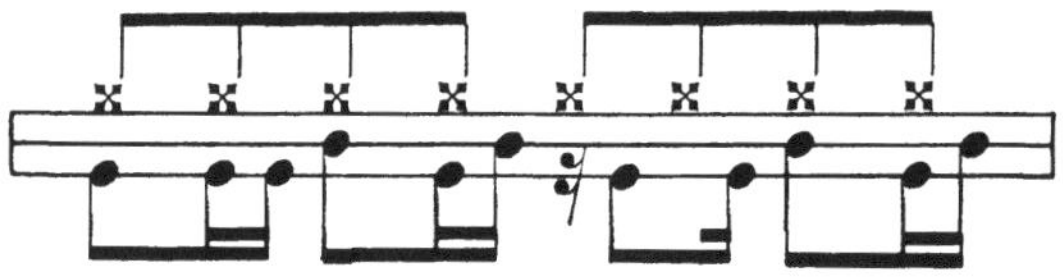

166
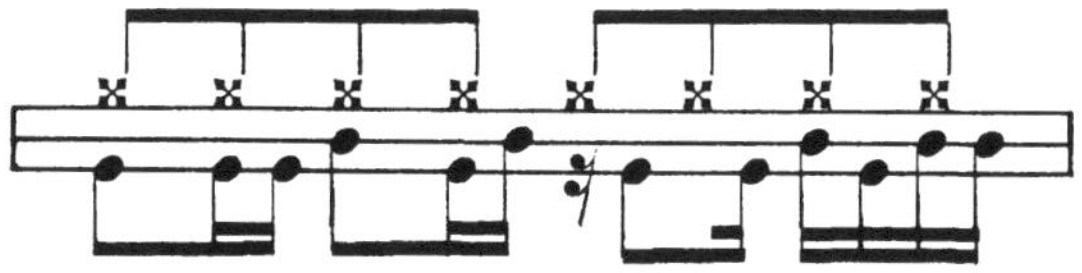

167
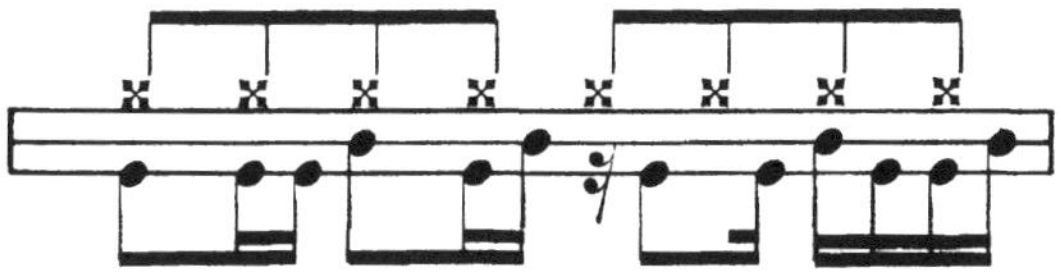

168
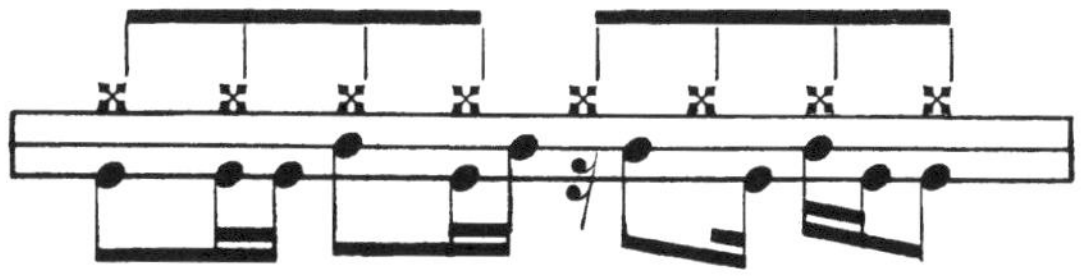

169
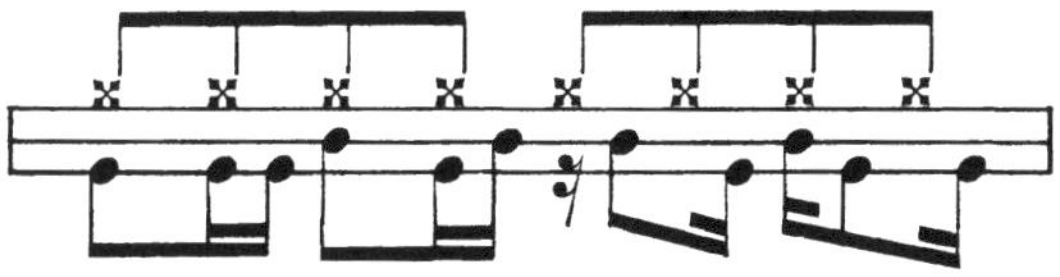

170
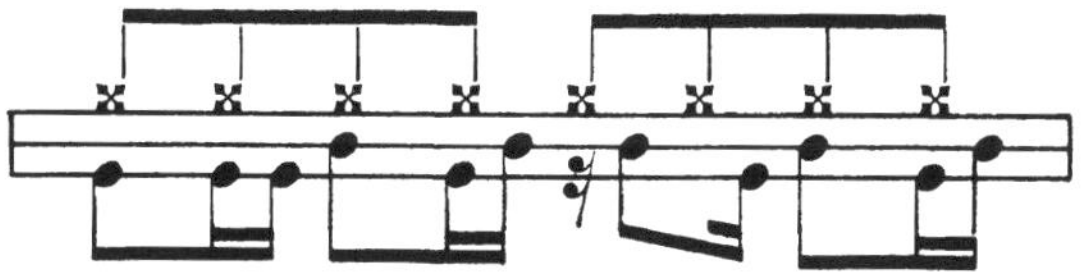

171
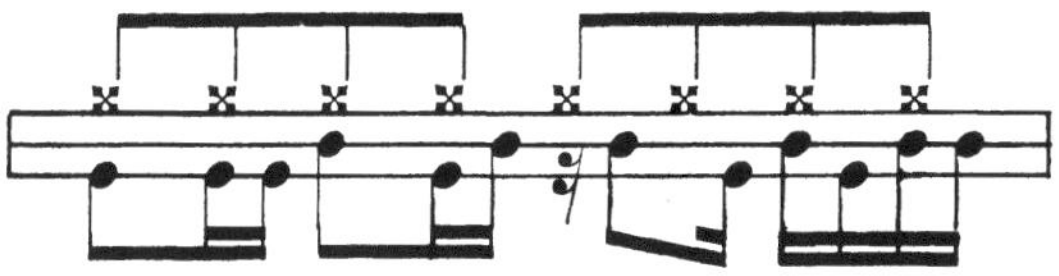

172
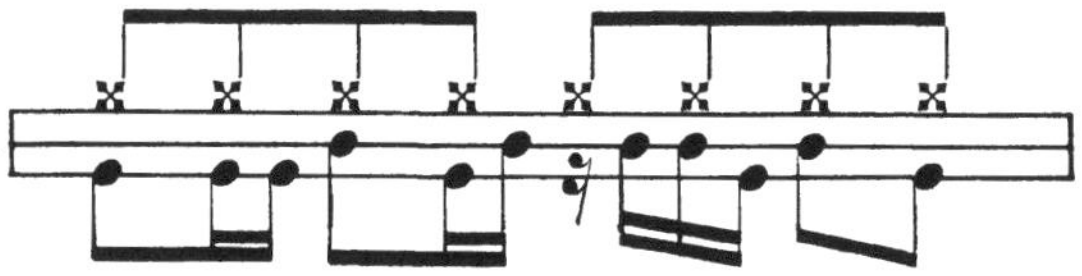

173
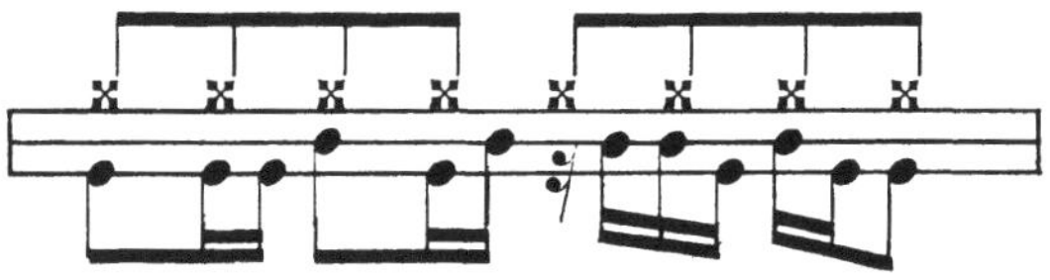

174
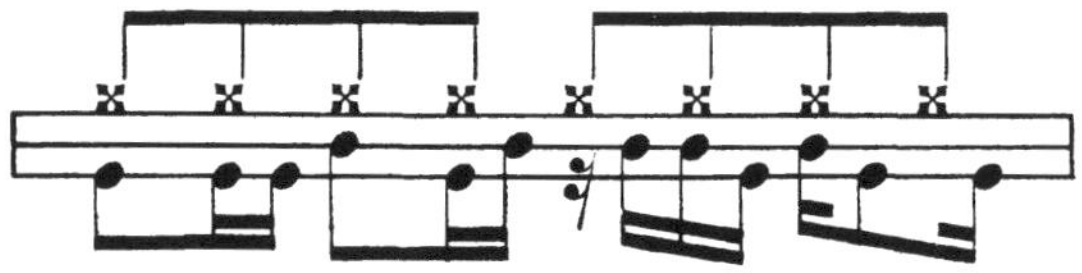

175
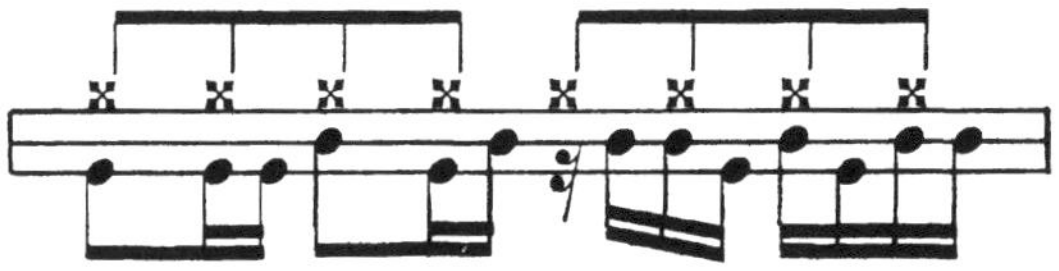

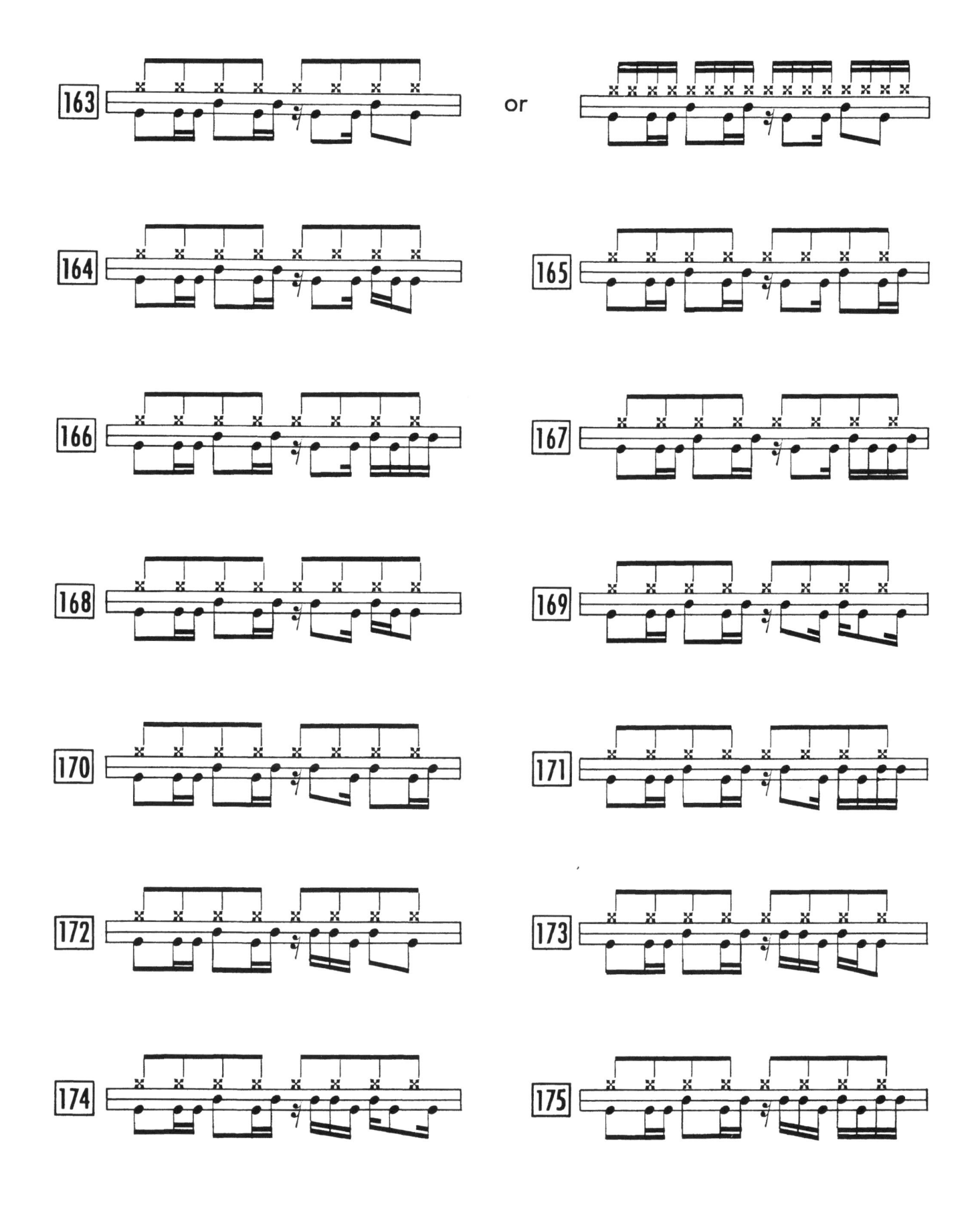

52

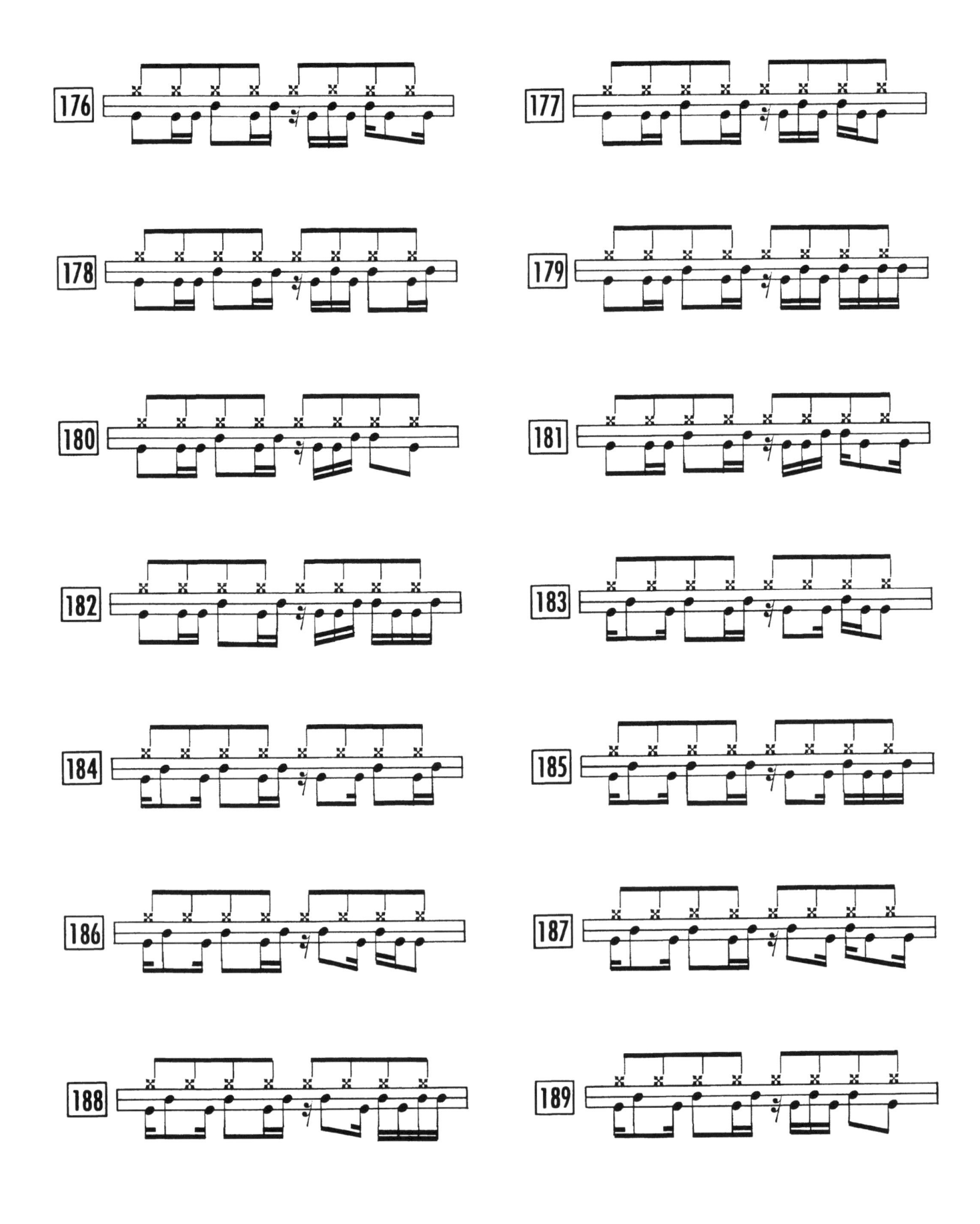

190 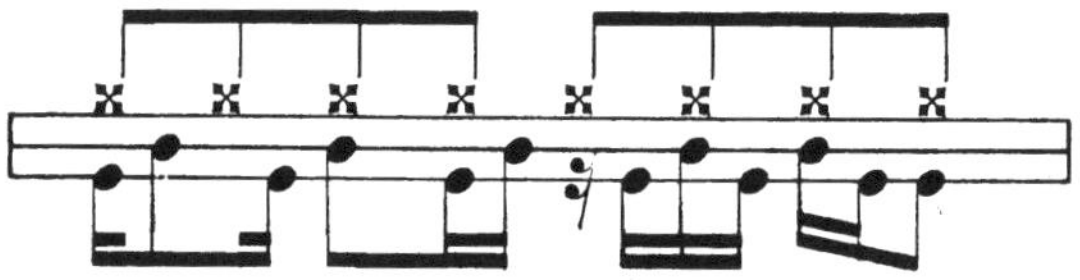

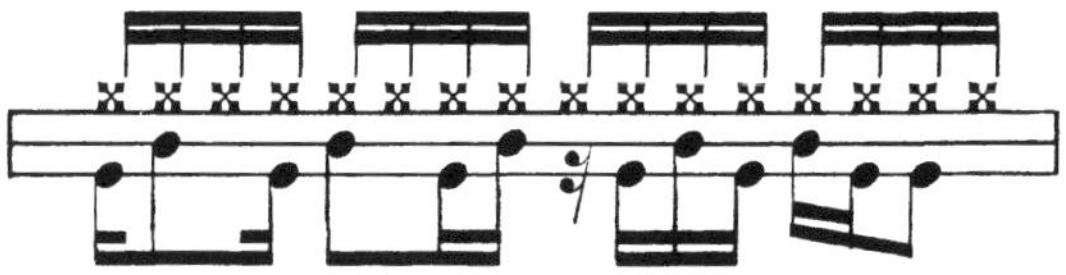

191 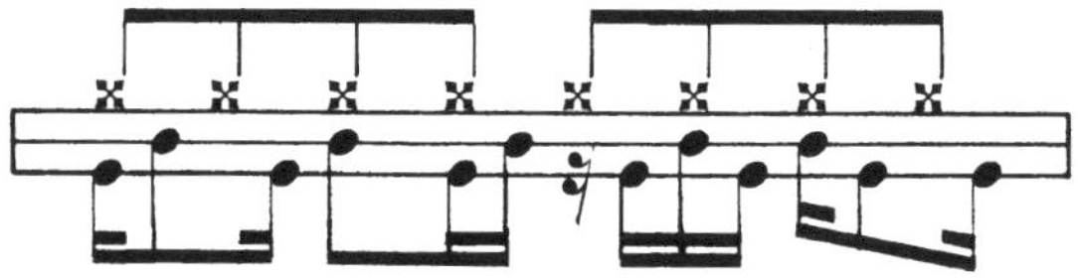

192 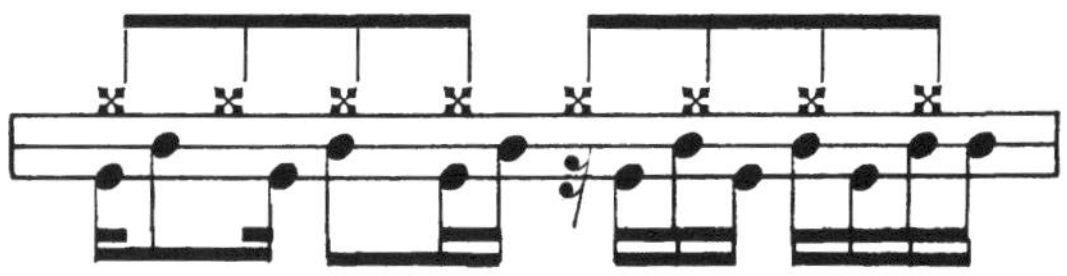

193 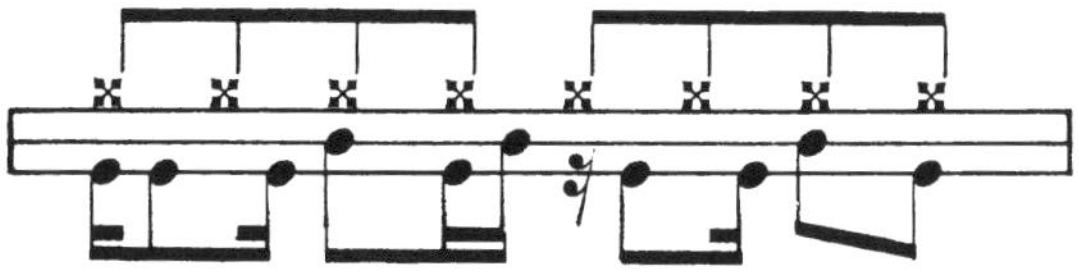

194 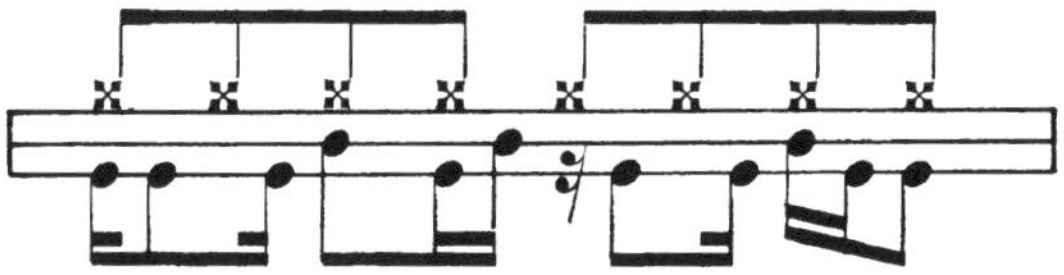

195 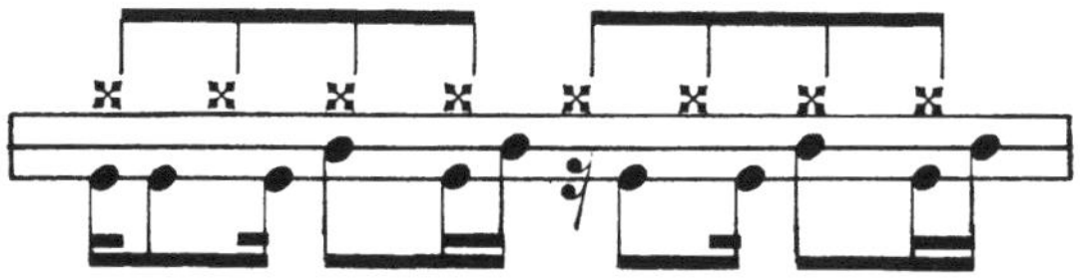

196 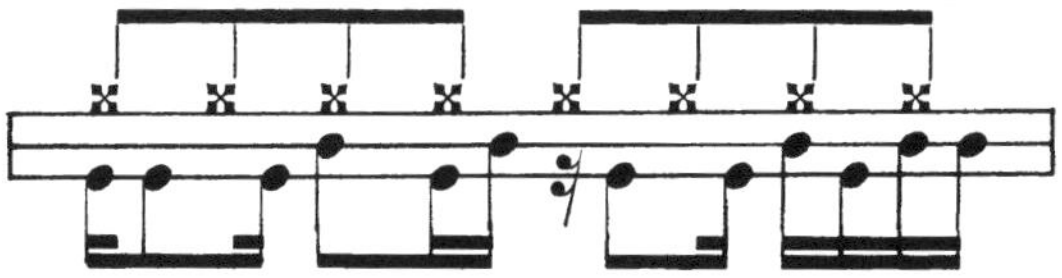

197 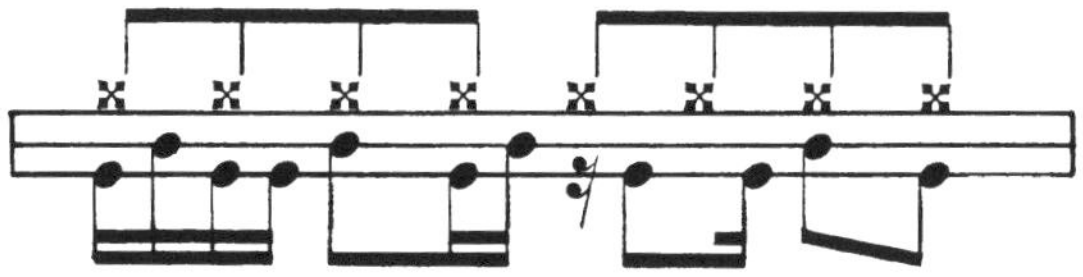

198 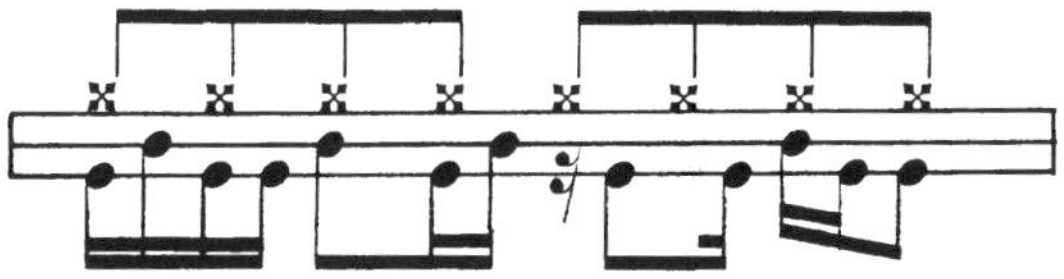

199 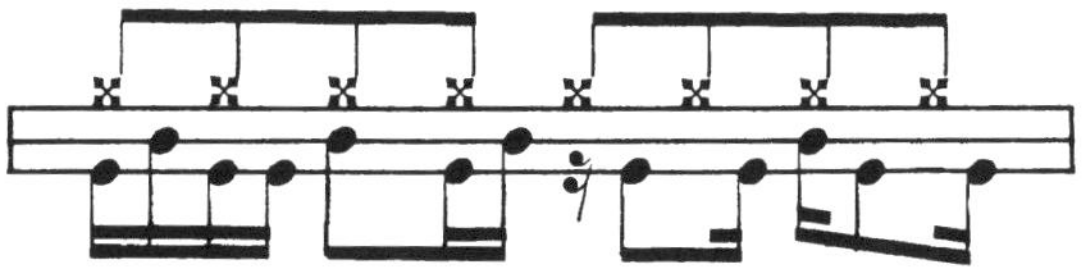

200 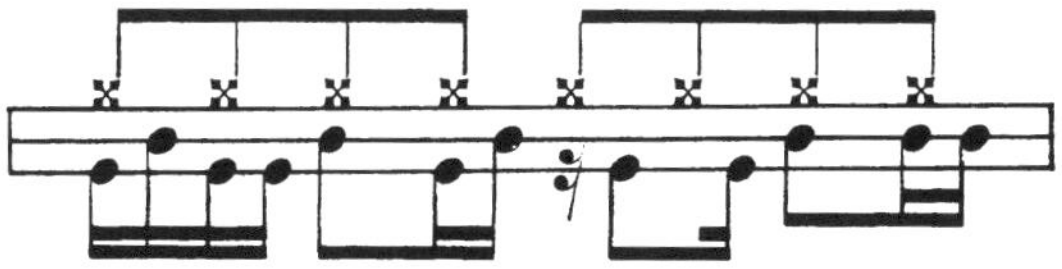

201 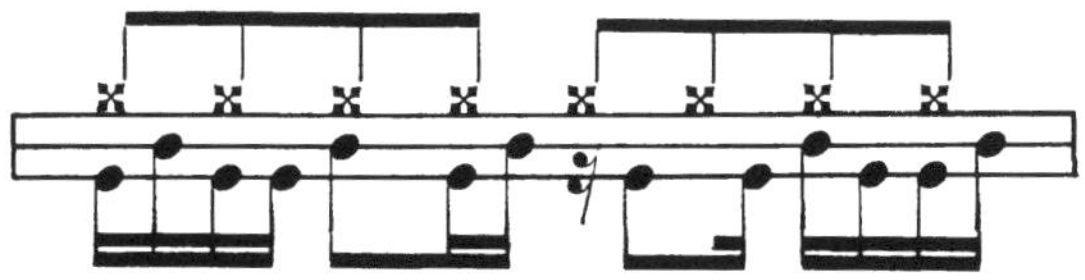

202 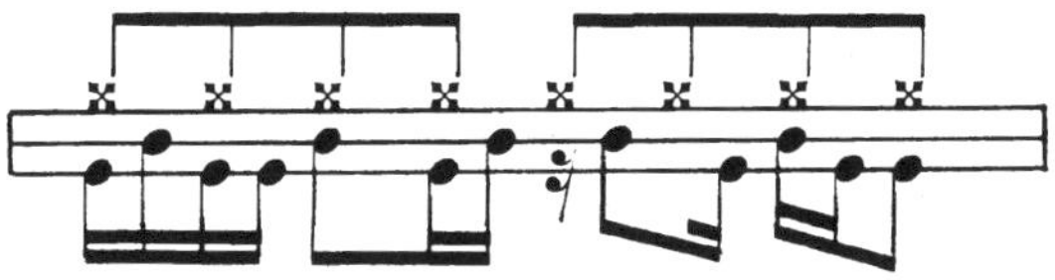

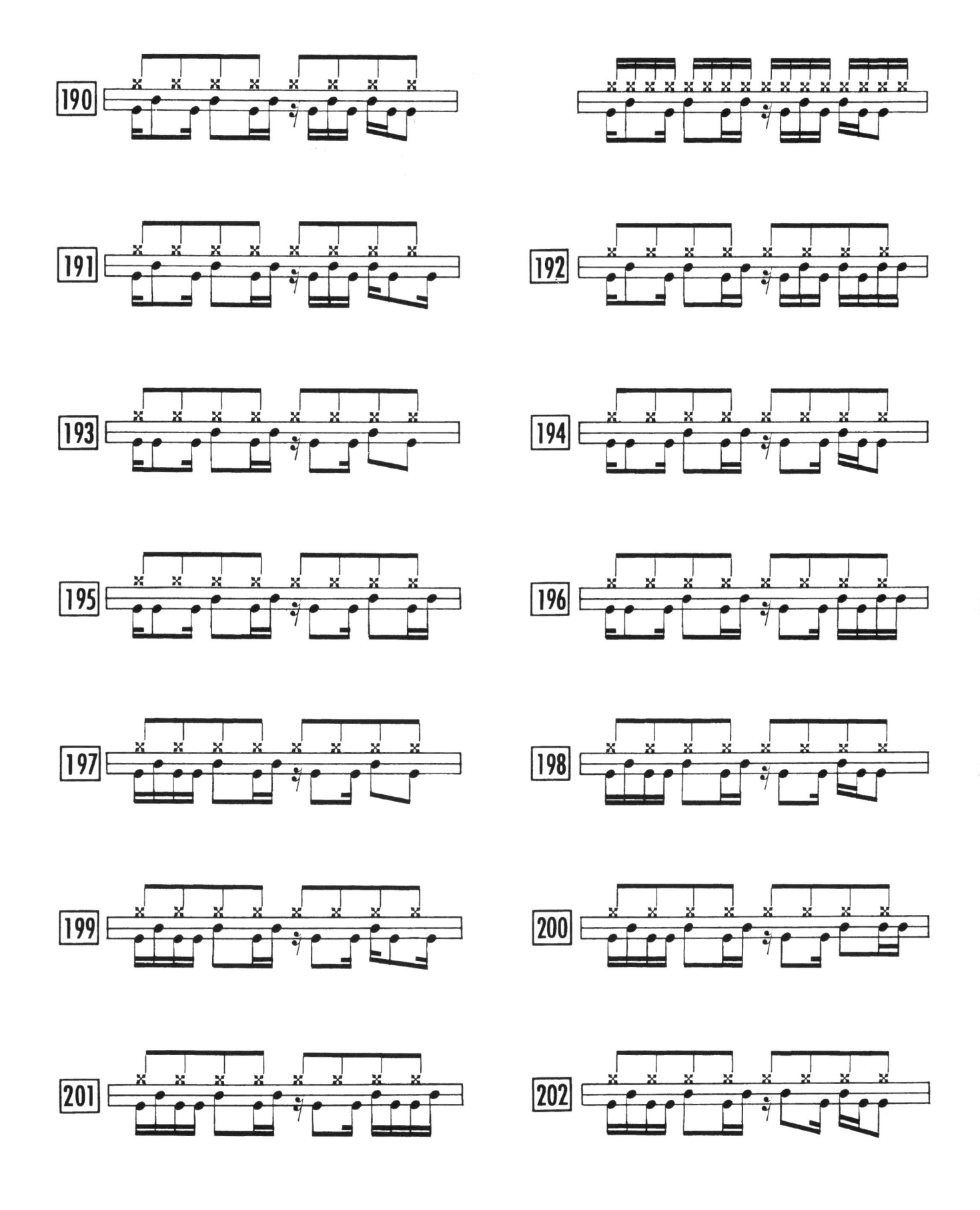

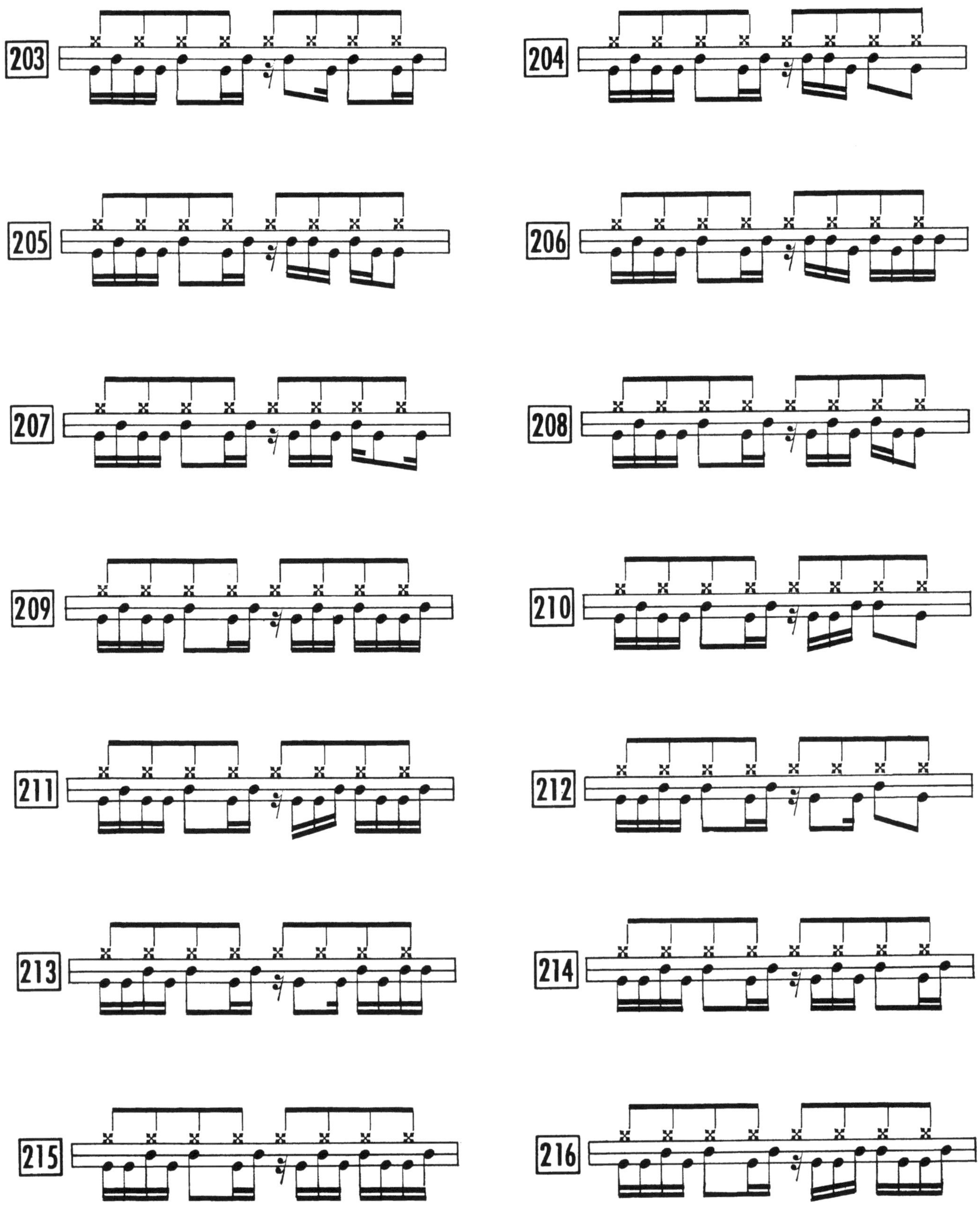
203
204
205
206
207
208
209
210
211
212
213
214
215
216

NOTE! USE ♩ ♩ ♩ ♩, ♫♫♫♫, RIDE FOR ALL FIGURES

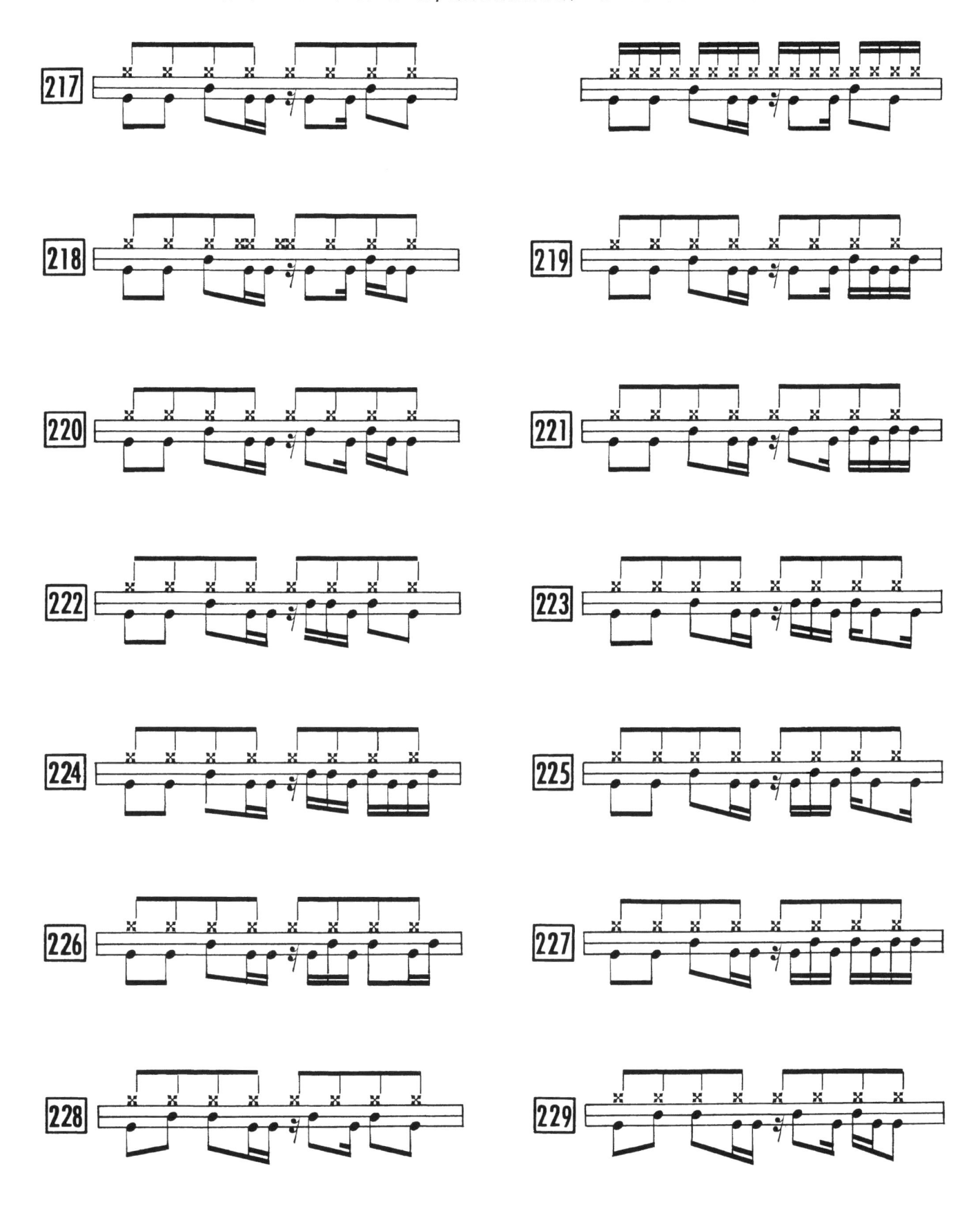

230
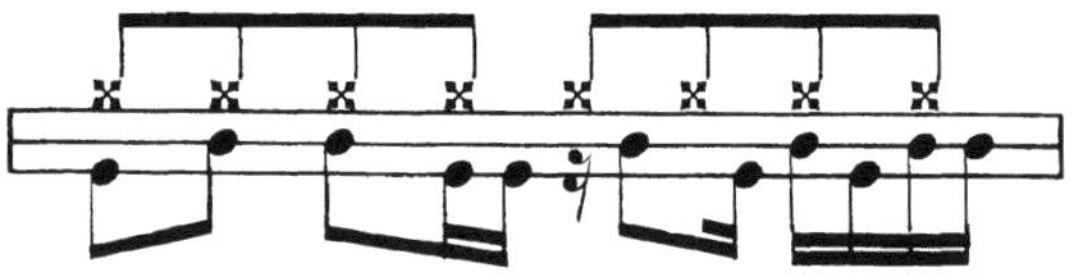

231
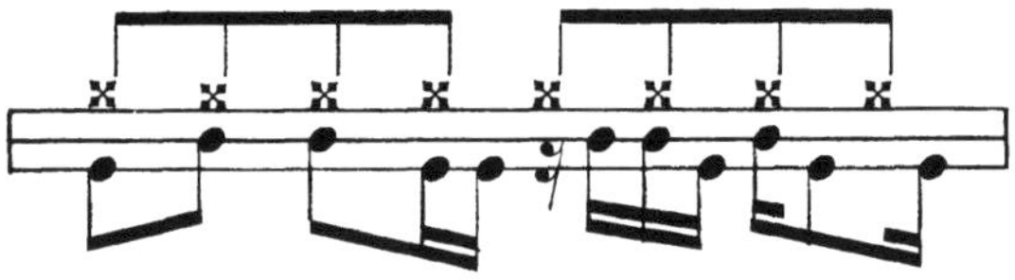

232
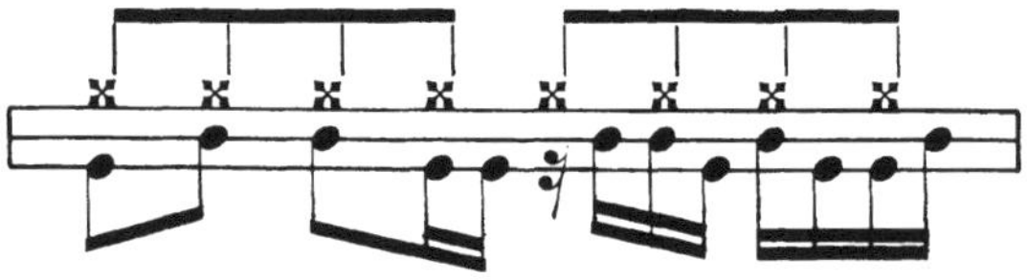

233
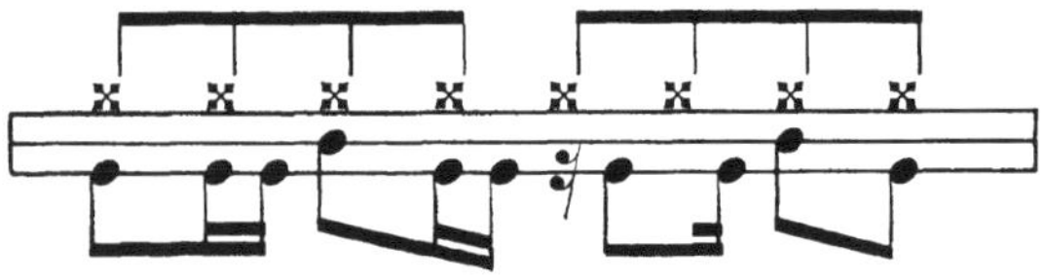

234
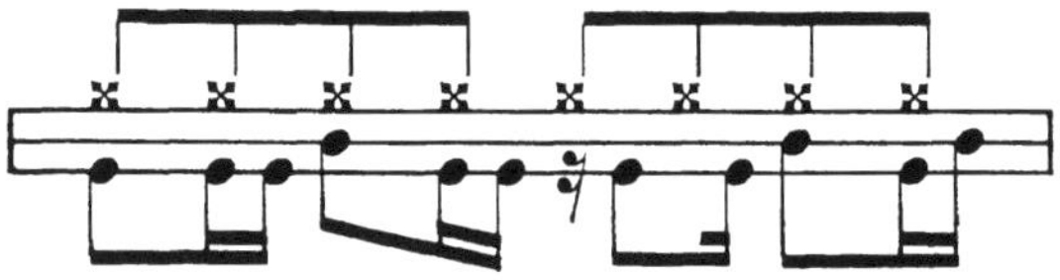

235
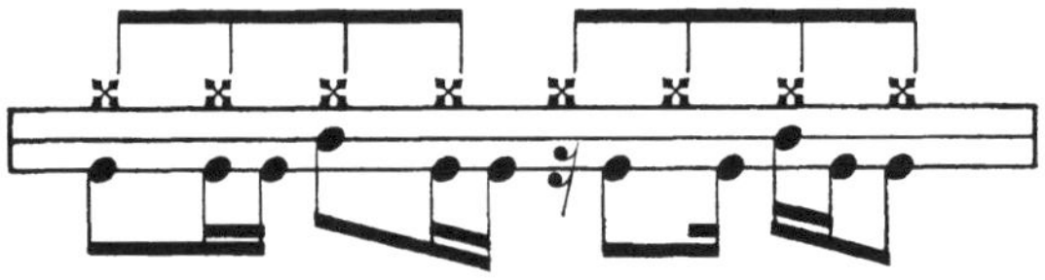

236
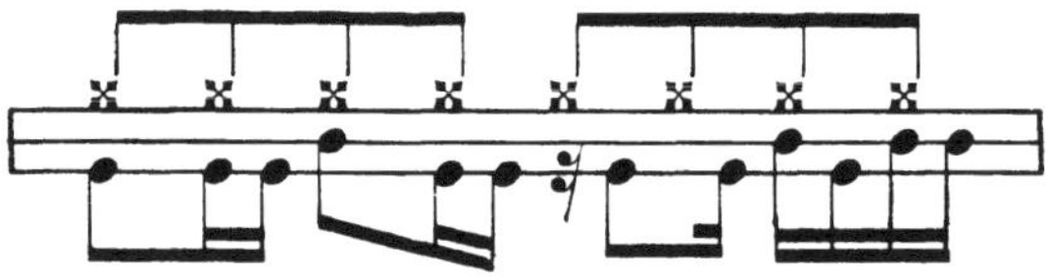

237
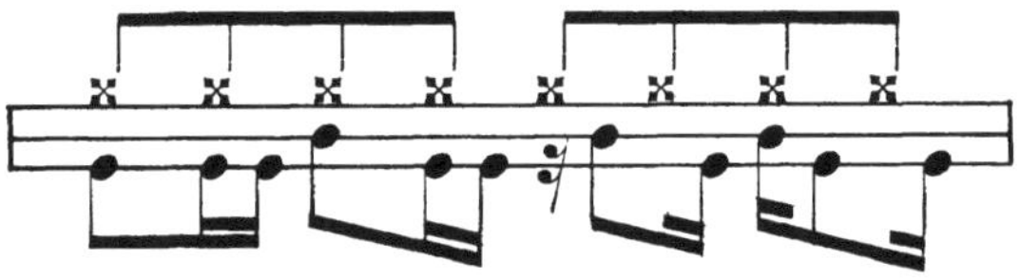

238
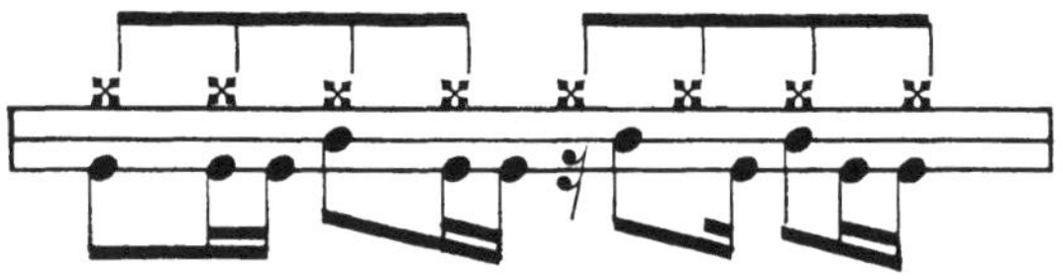

239
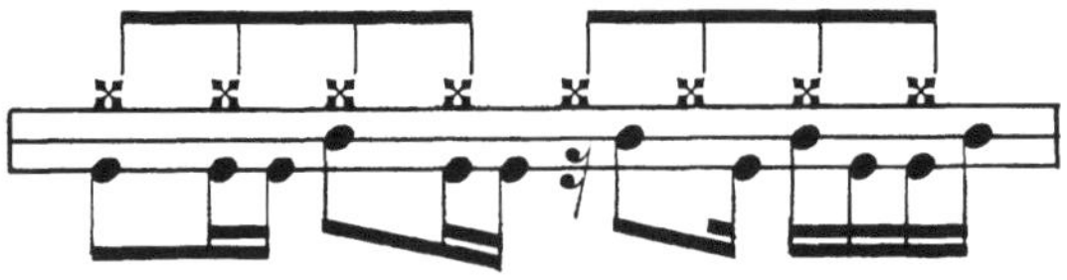

240
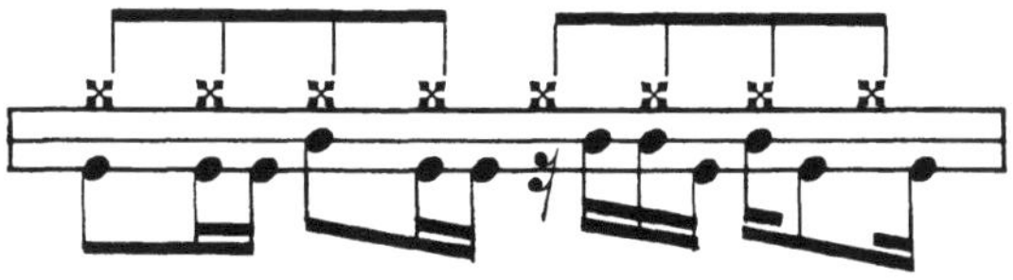

241
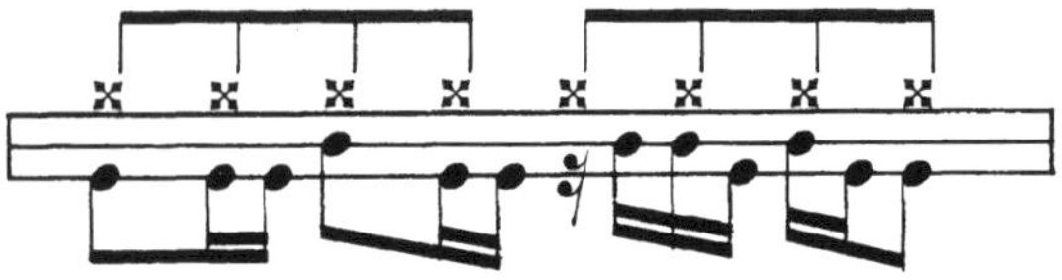

242
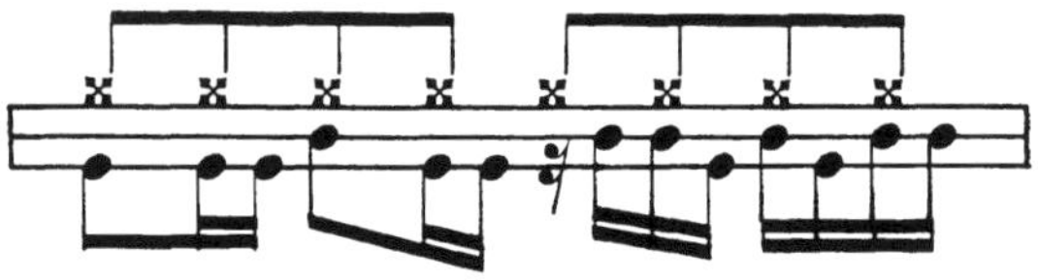

243
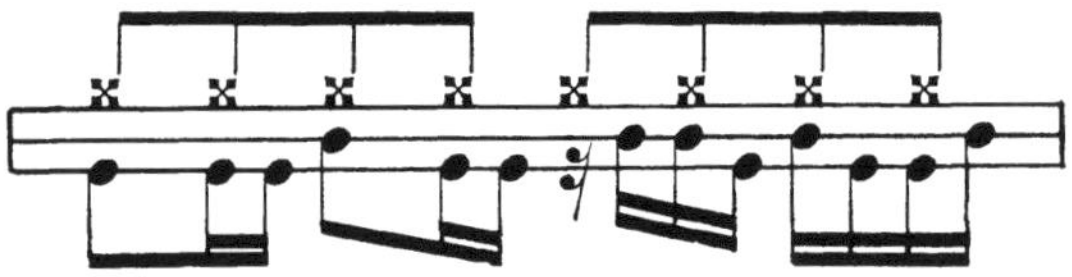

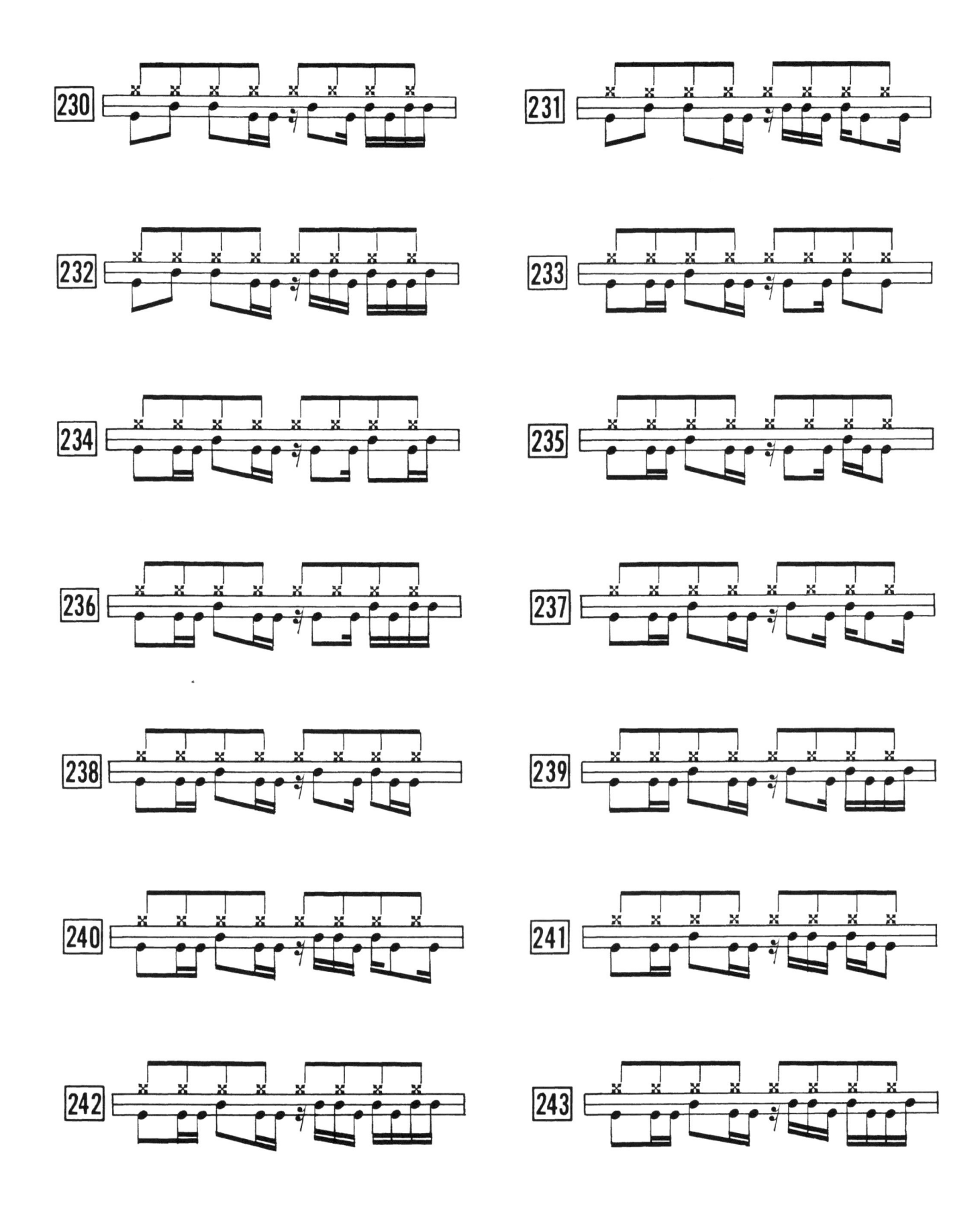

244

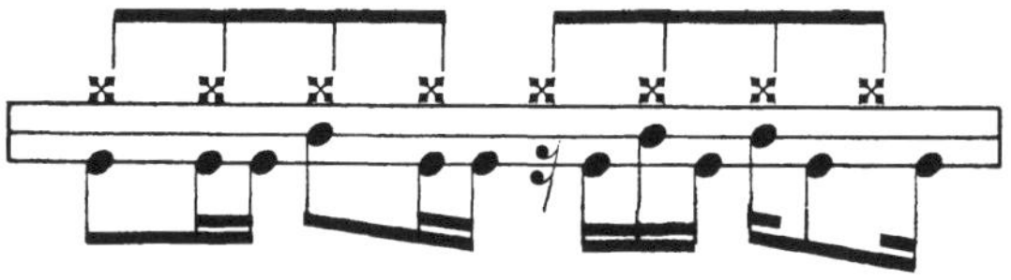

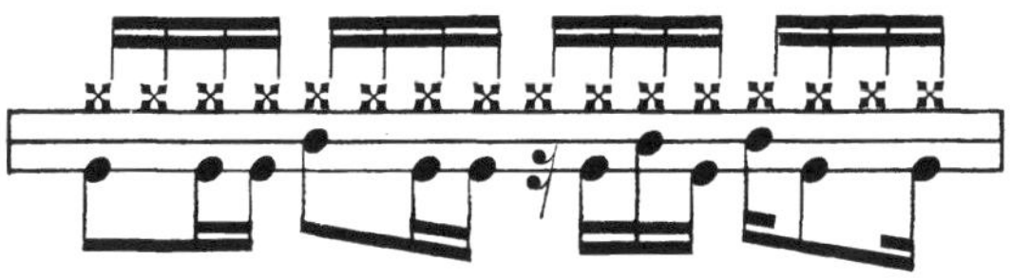

245

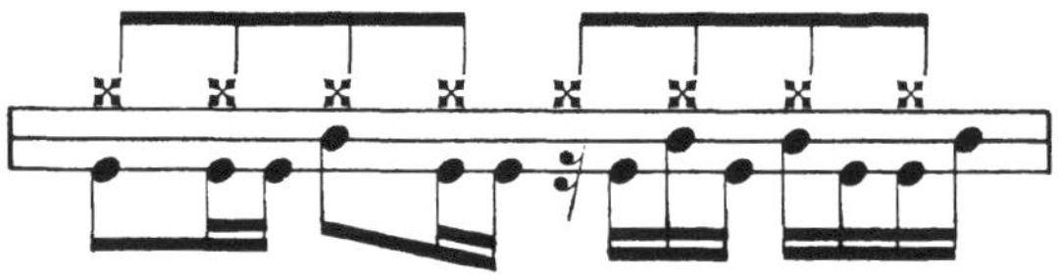

246

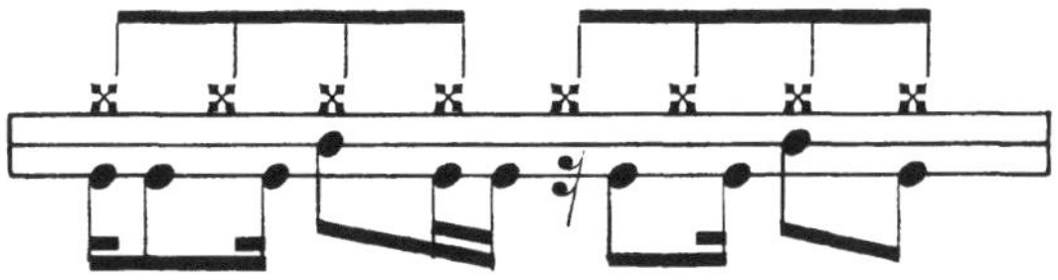

247

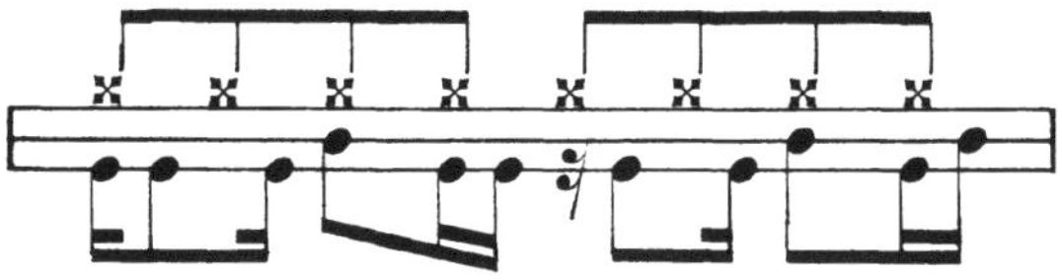

248

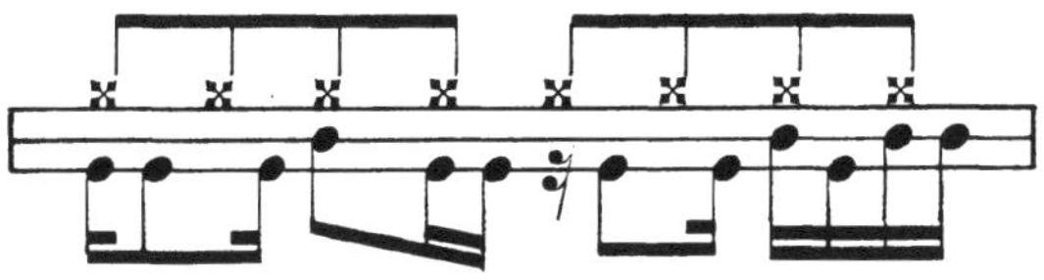

249

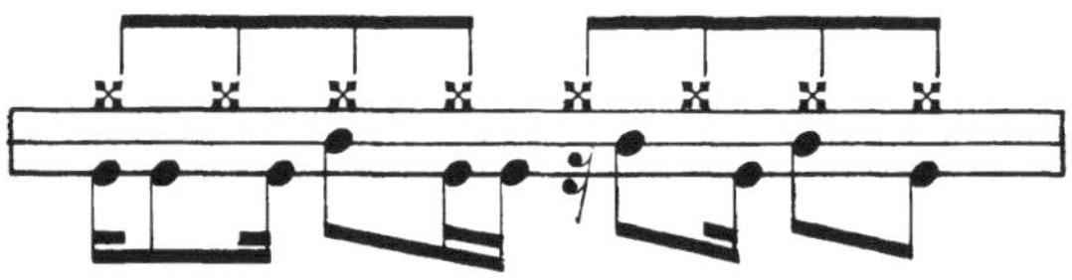

250

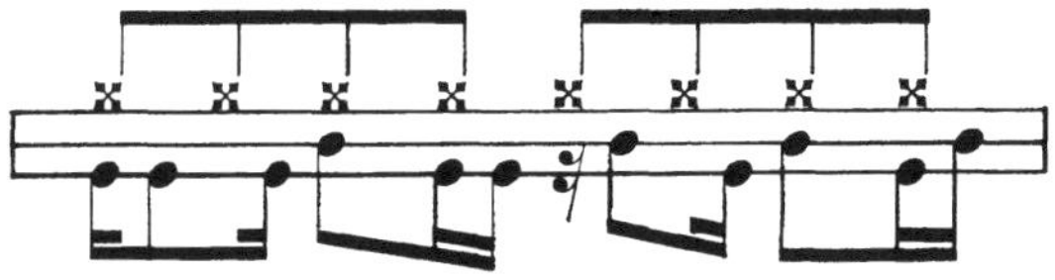

251

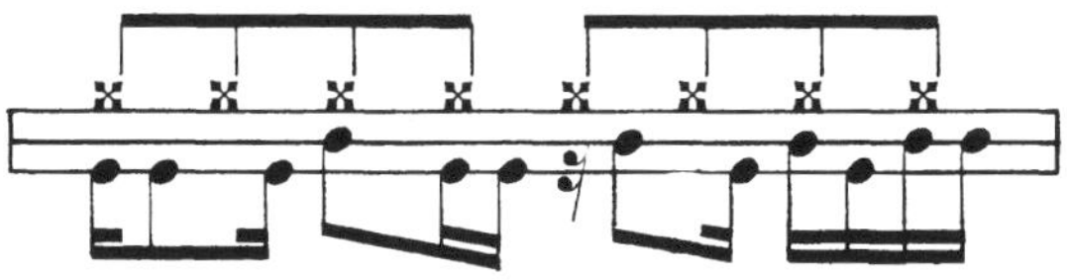

252

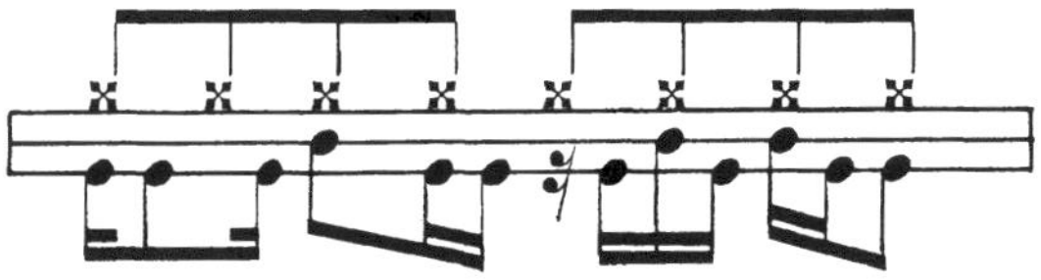

253

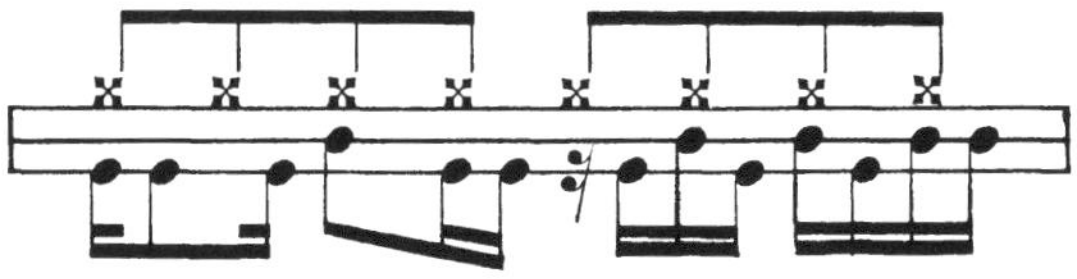

254

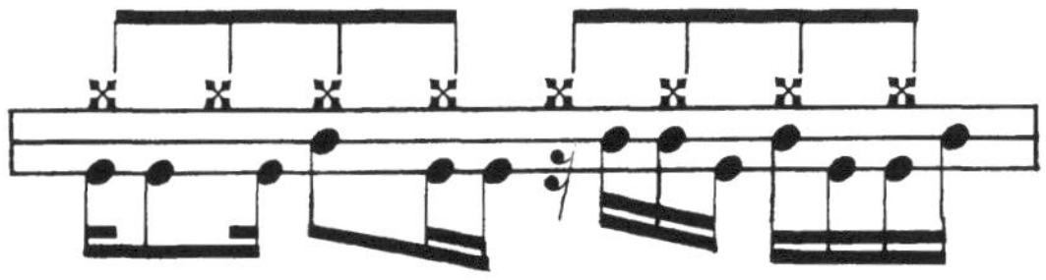

255

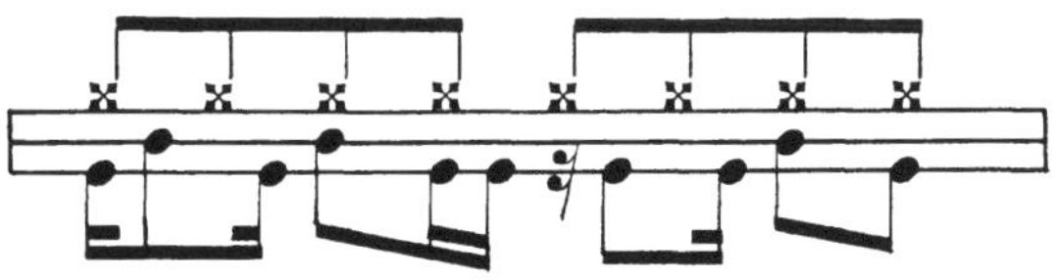

256

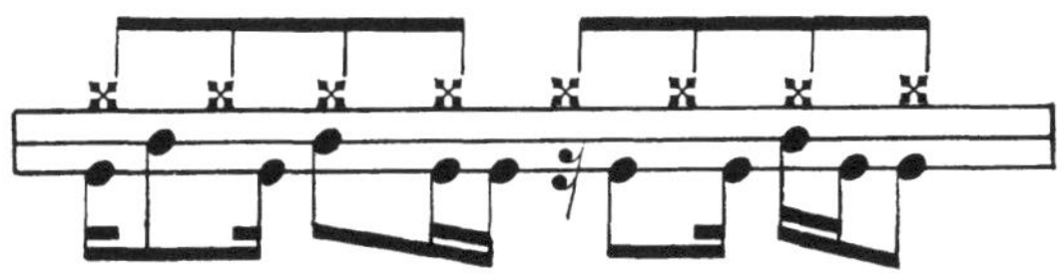

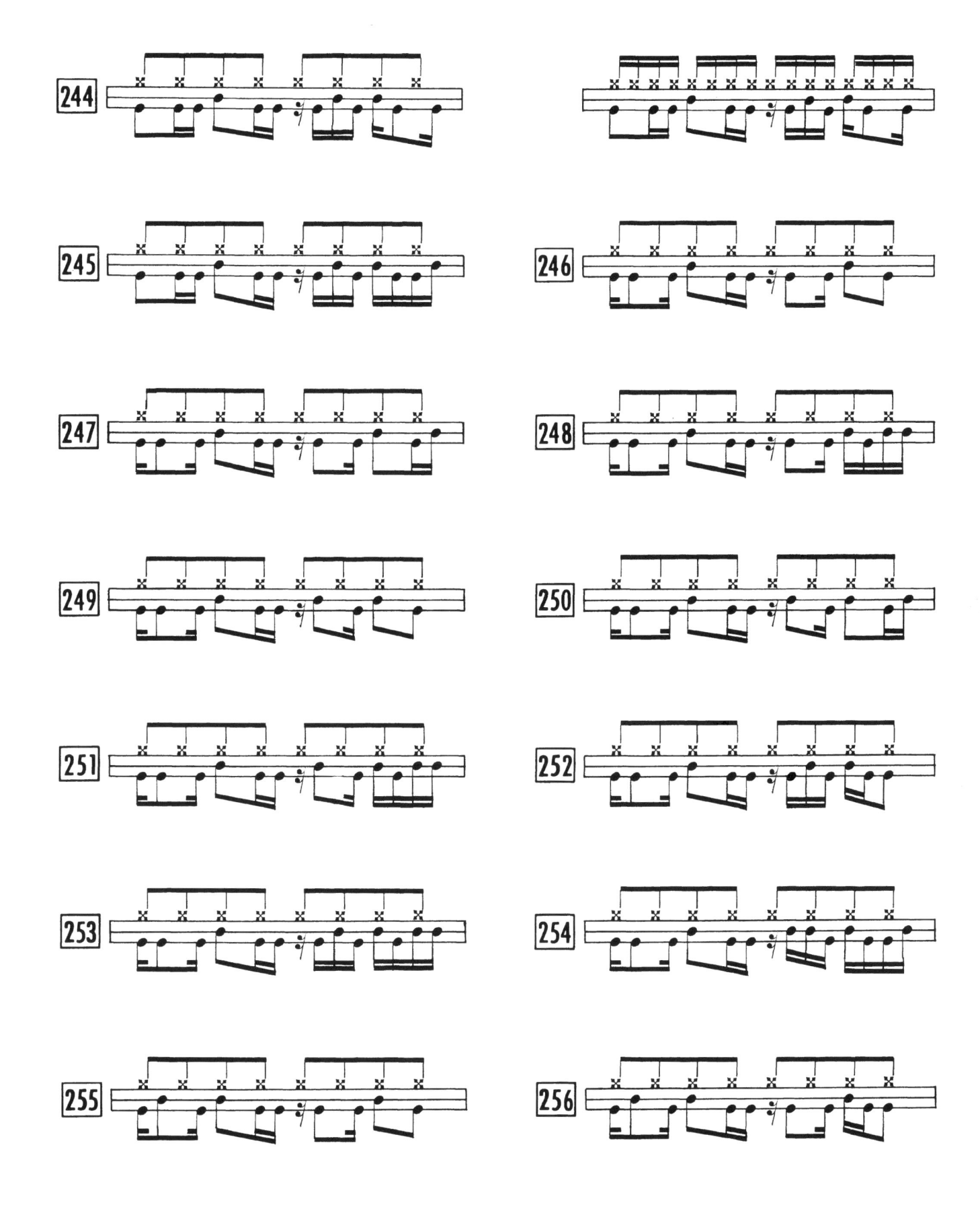

257
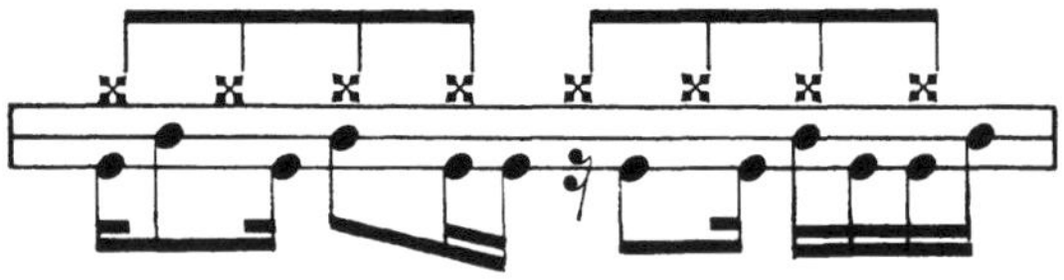

258
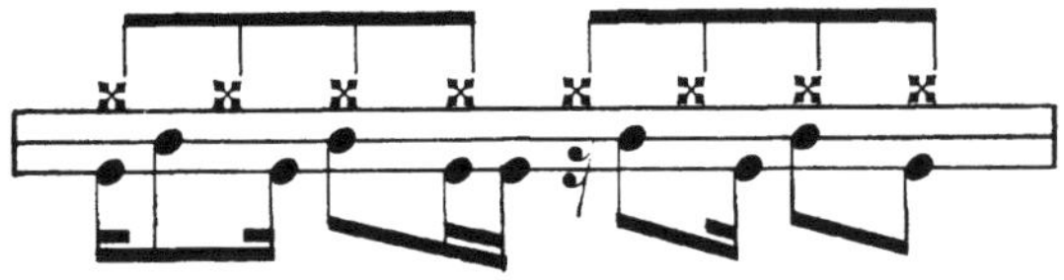

259
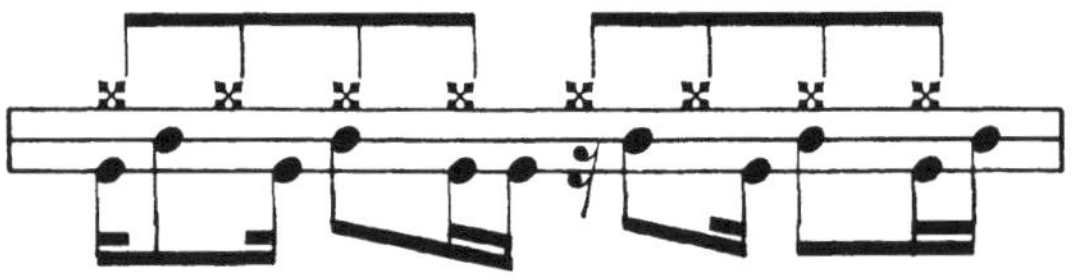

260
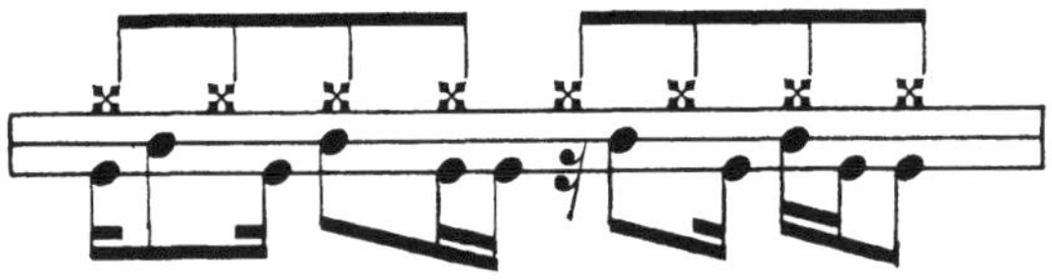

261
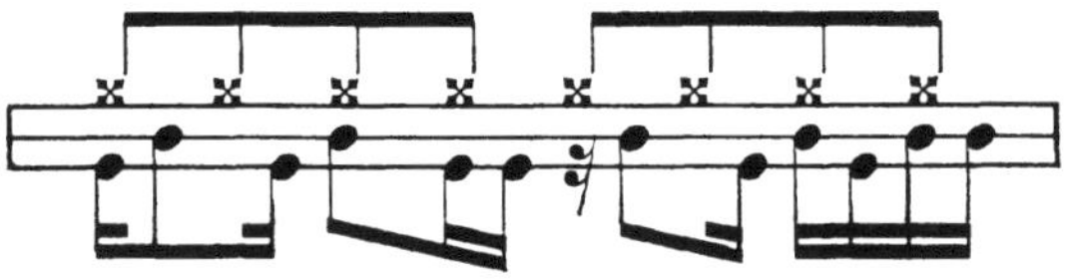

262
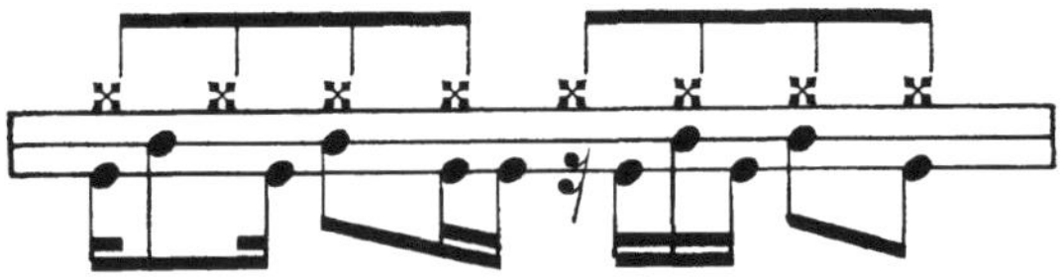

263
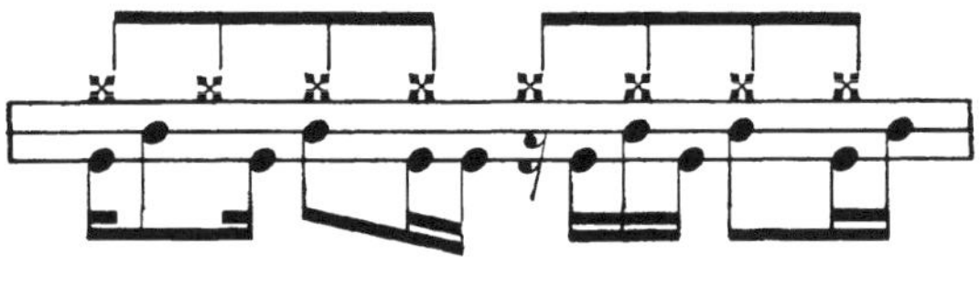

264
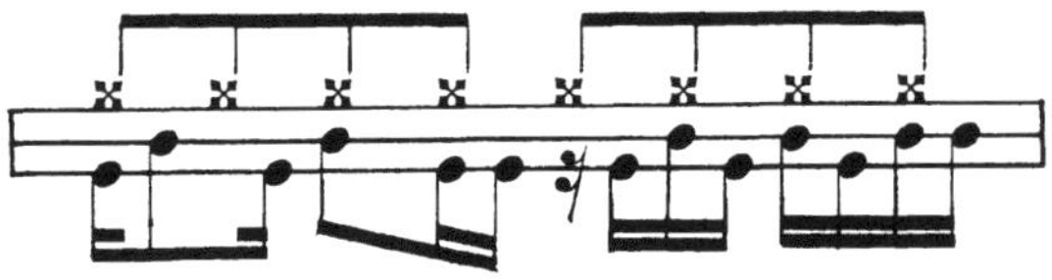

265
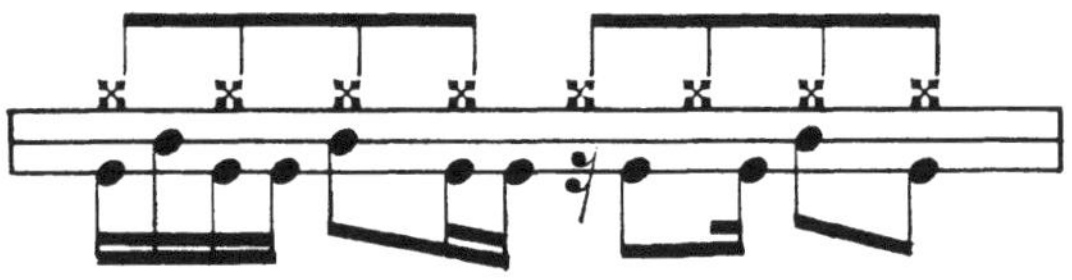

266
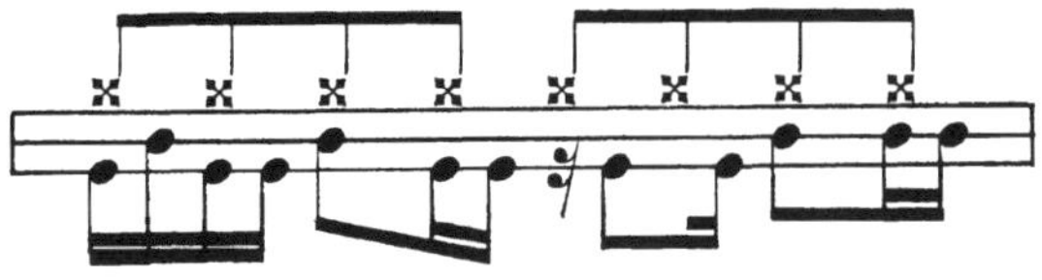

267
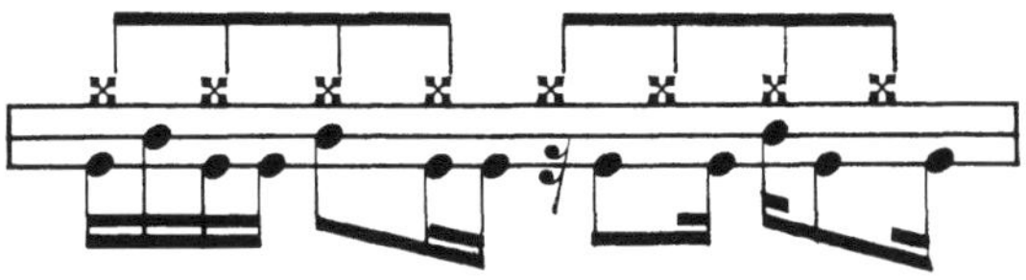

268
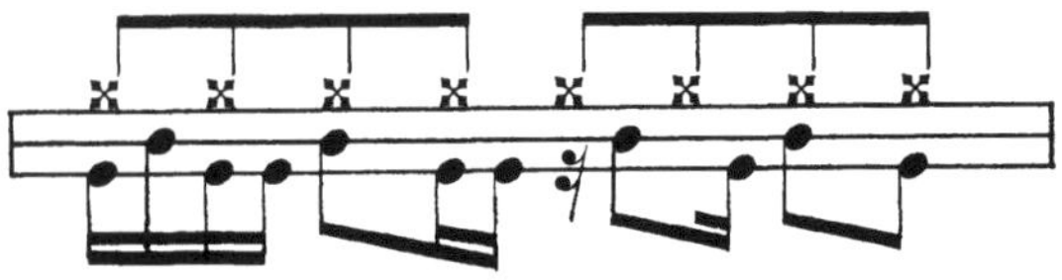

269
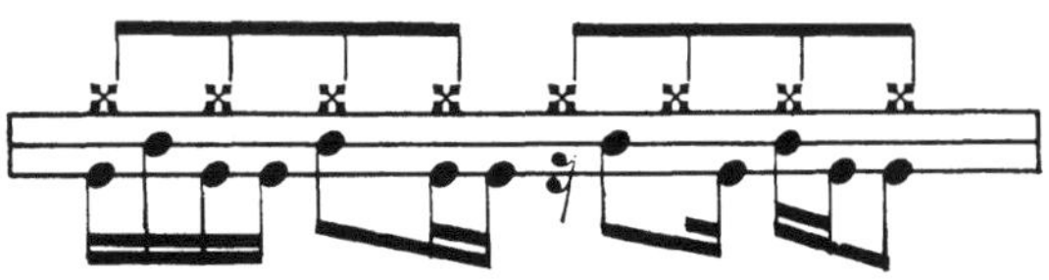

270
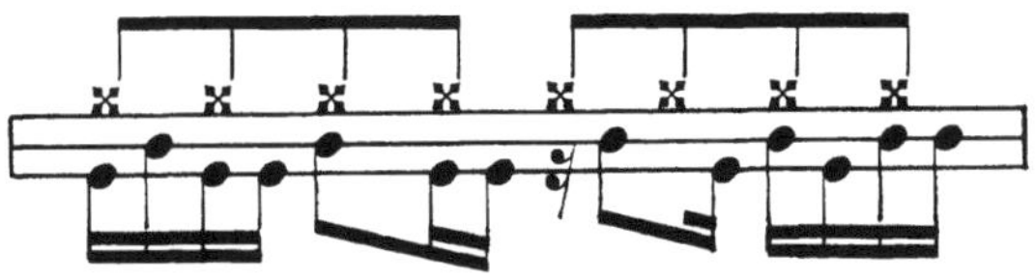

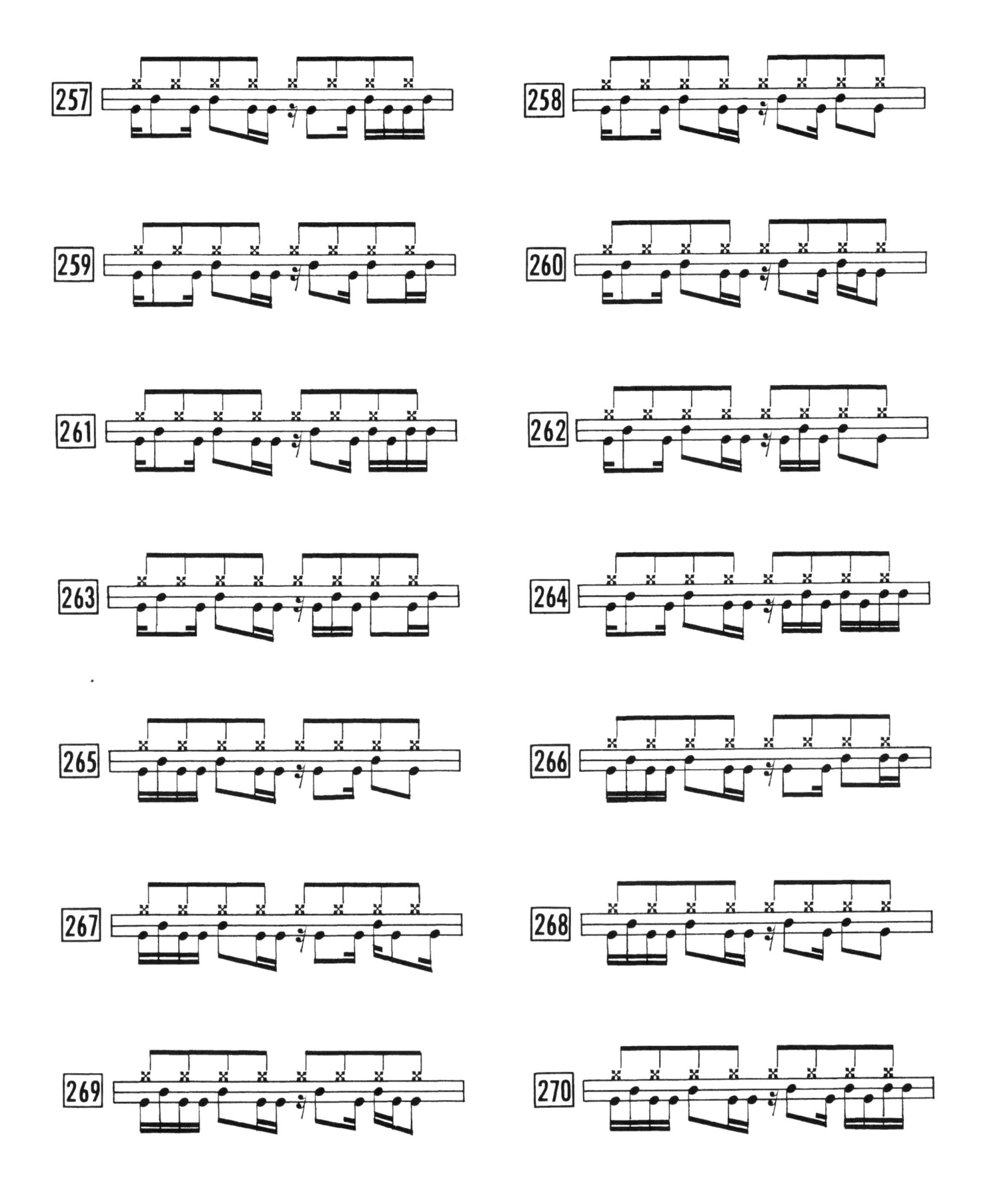

59

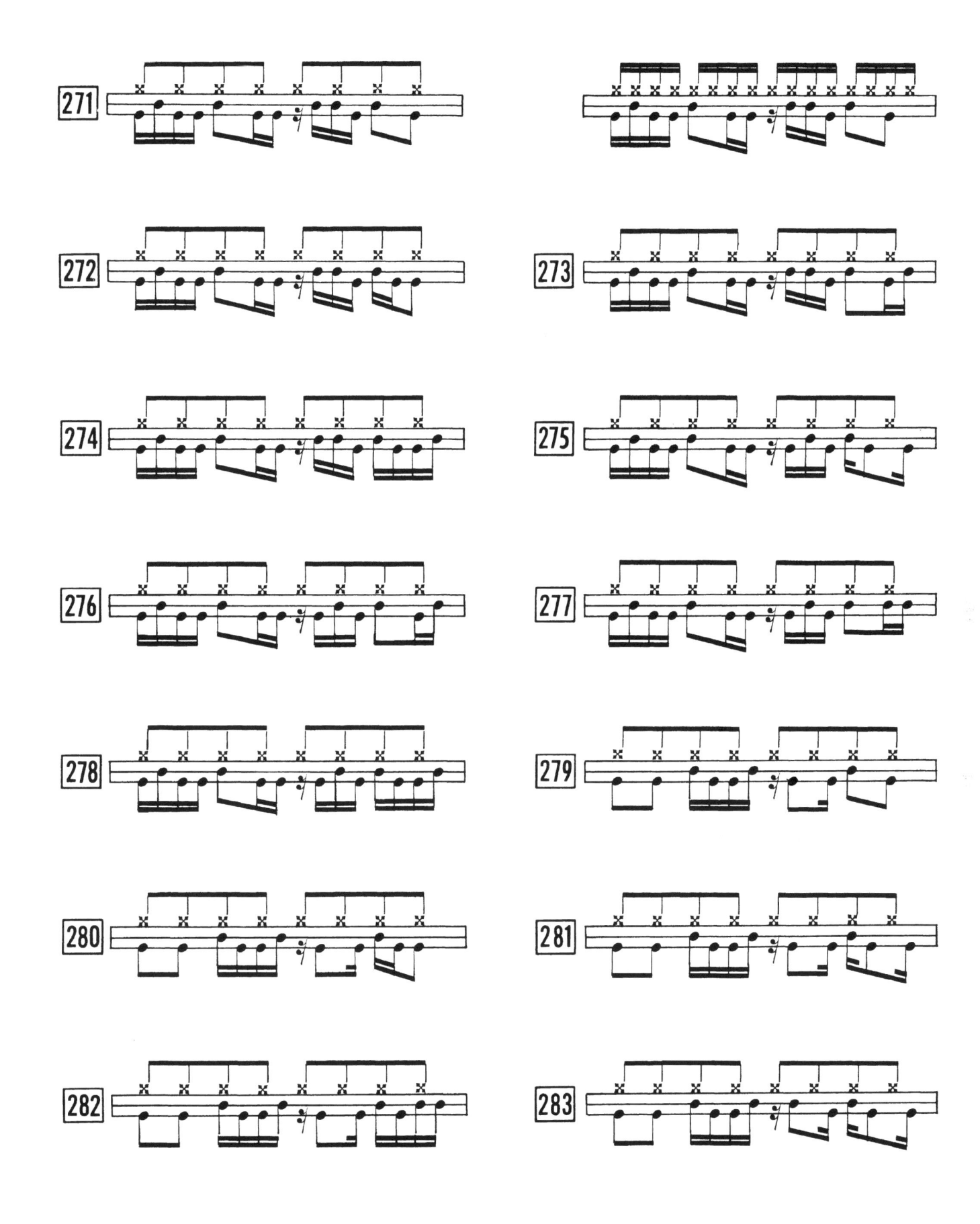

284
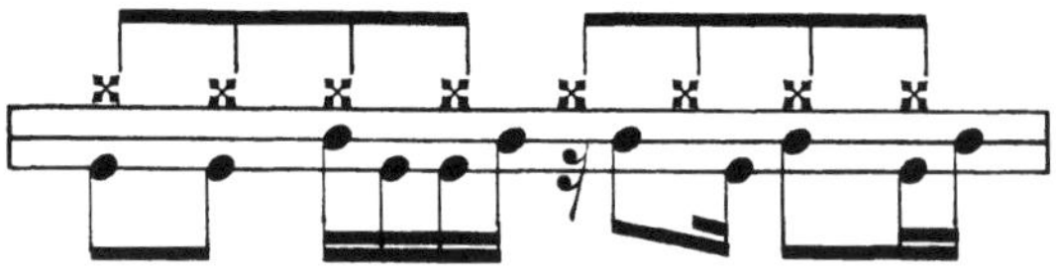

285
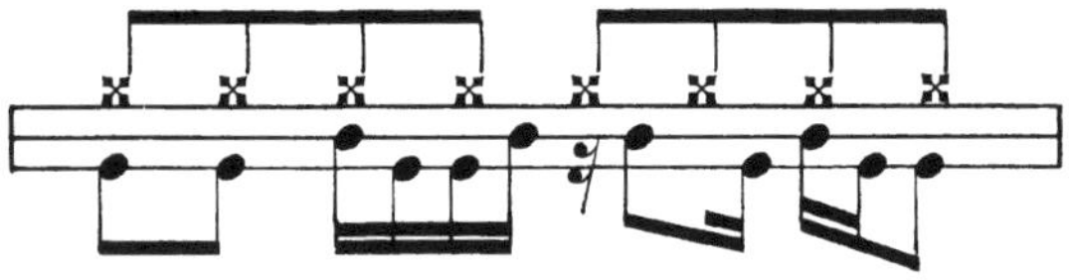

286
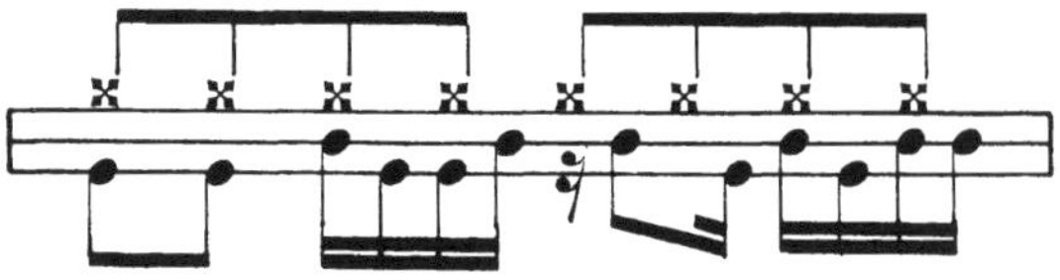

287
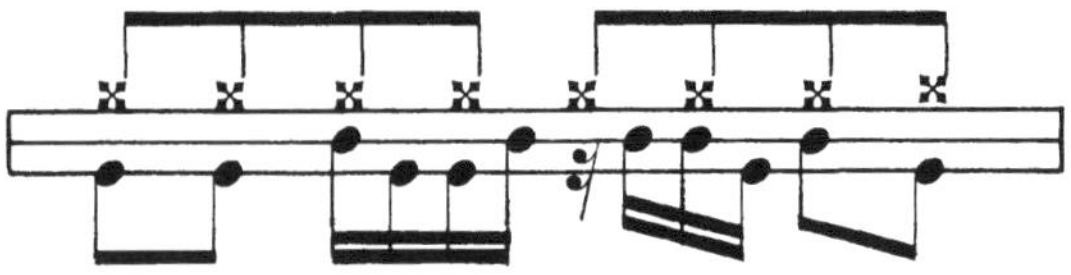

288
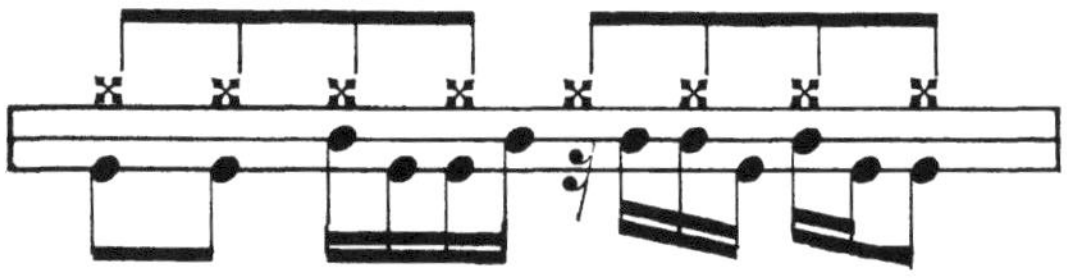

289
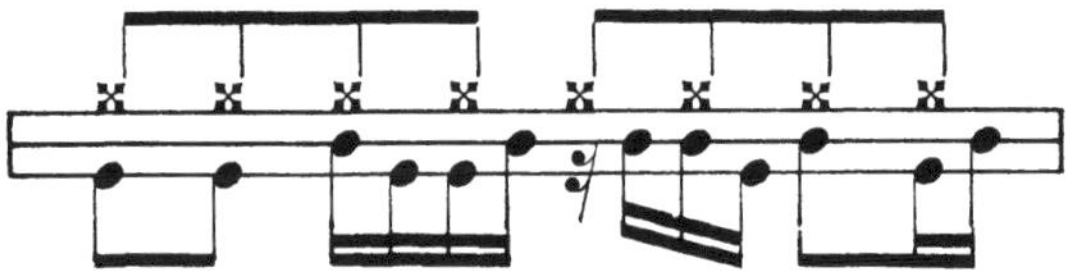

290
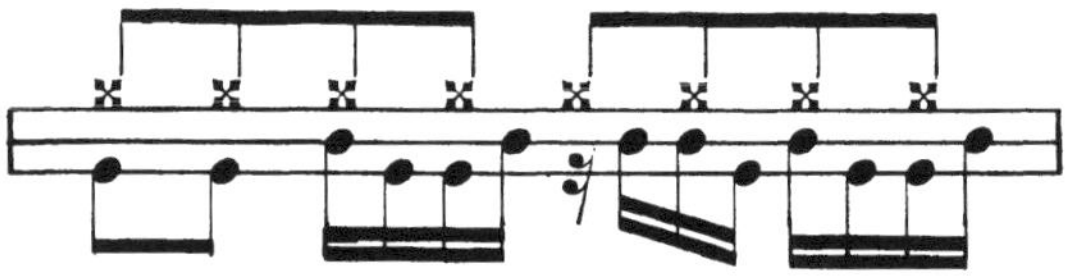

291
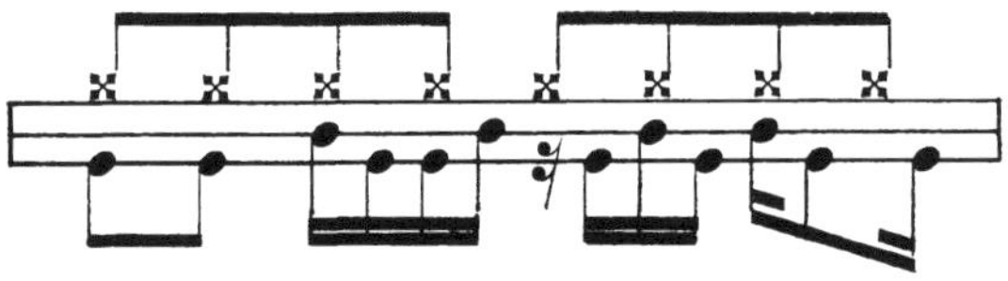

292
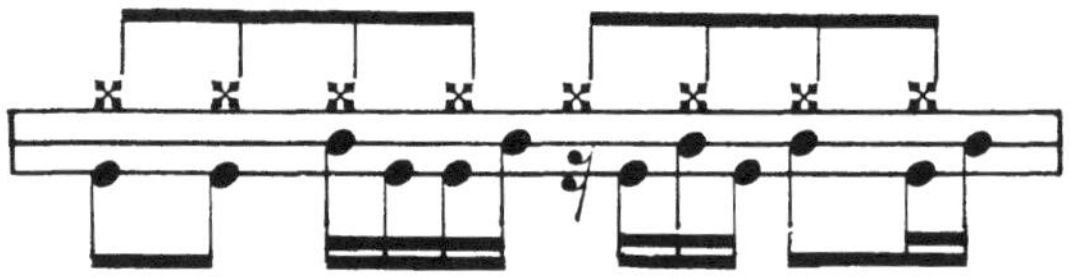

293
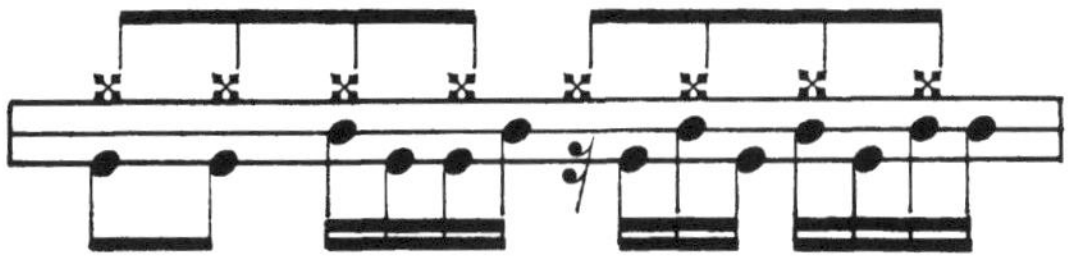

294
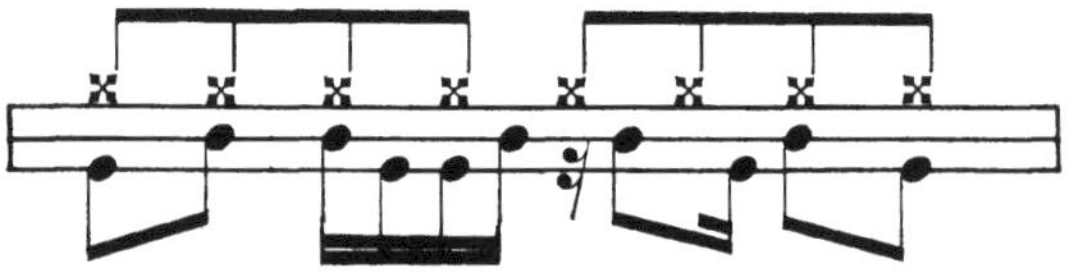

295
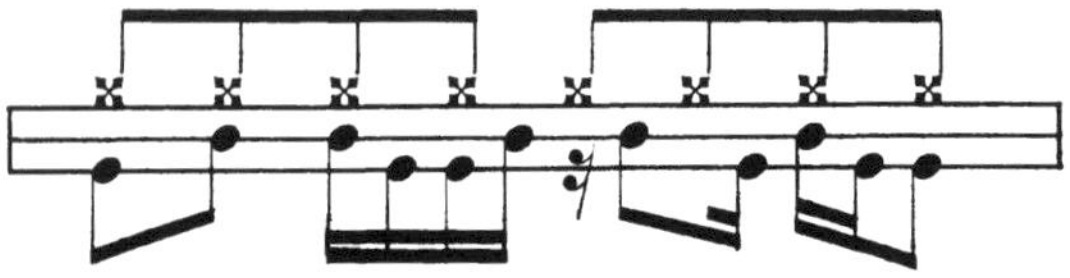

296
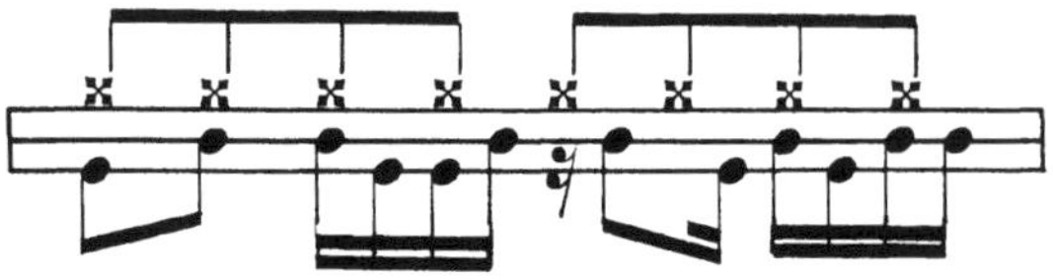

297
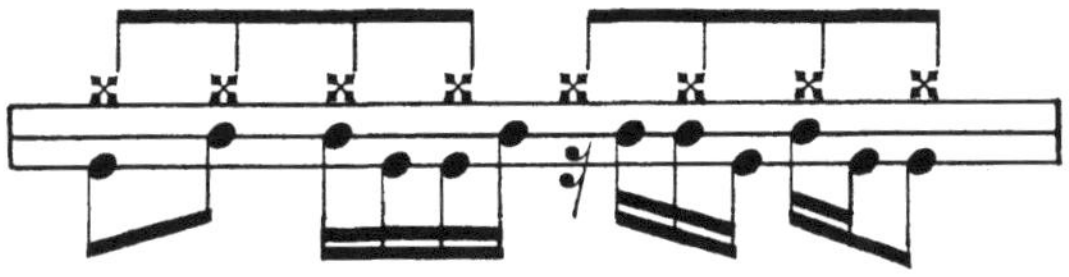

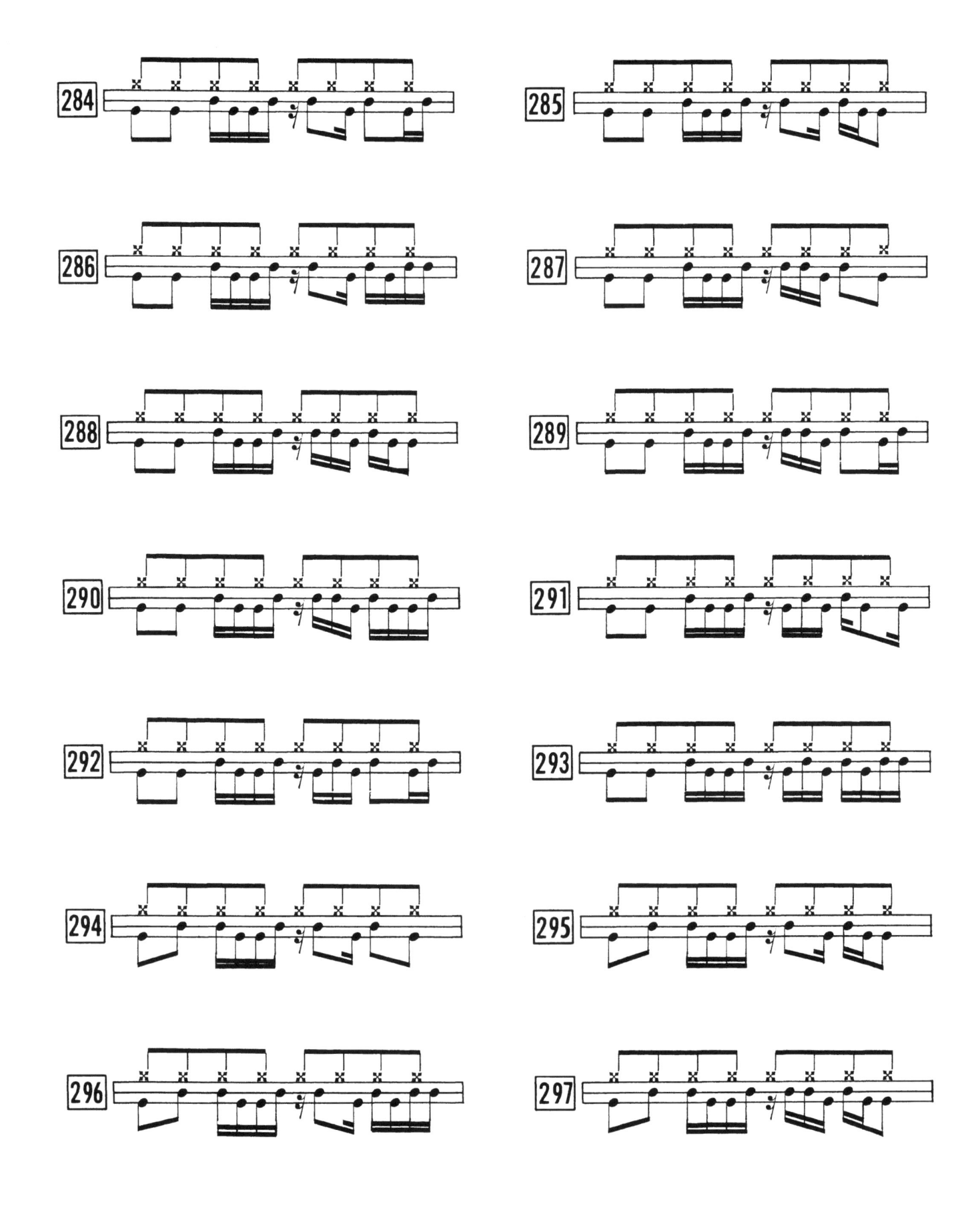

NOTE! USE ♩♩♩♩, ♫♫♫♫, RIDE FOR ALL FIGURES

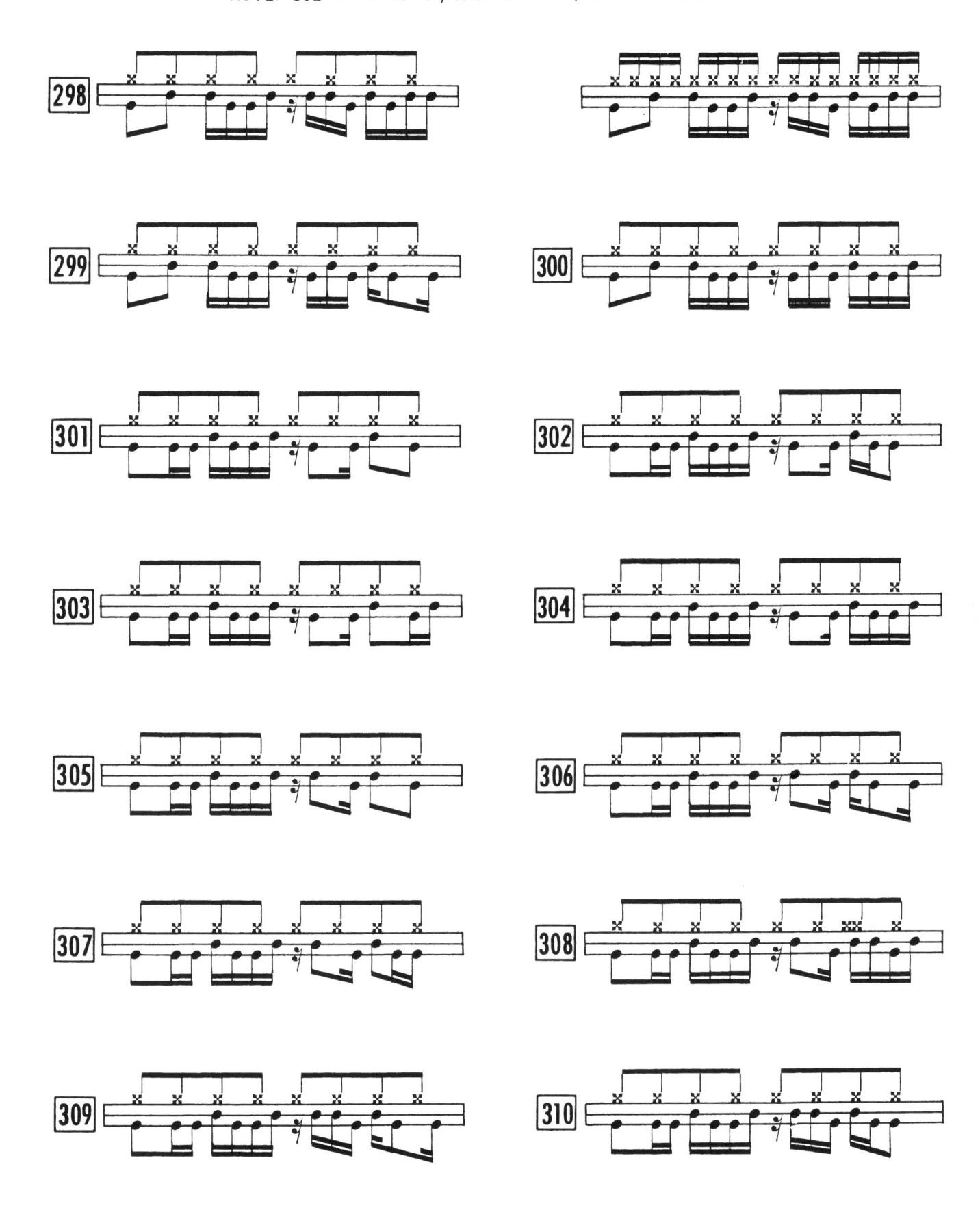

311 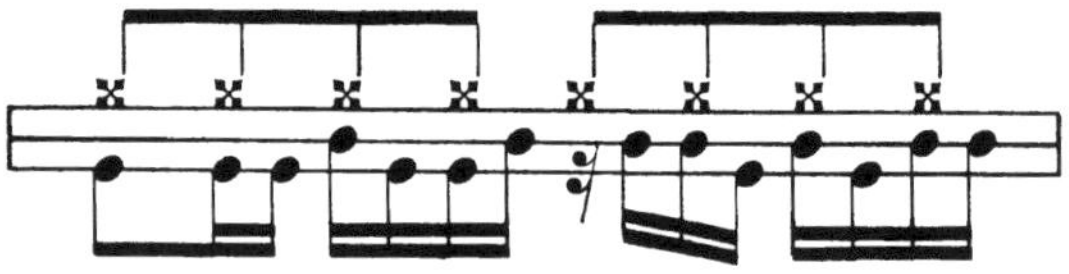

312 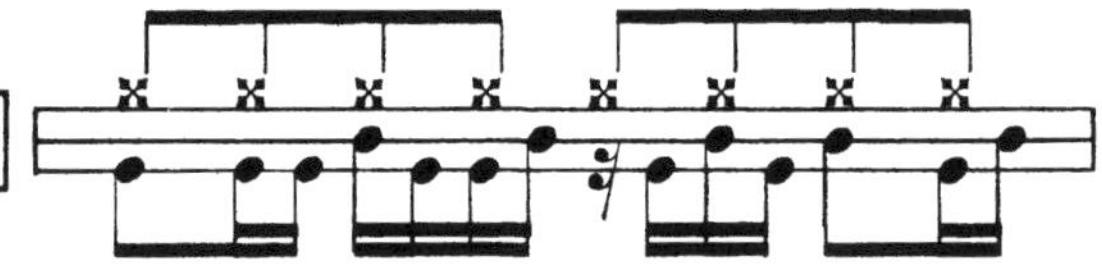

313 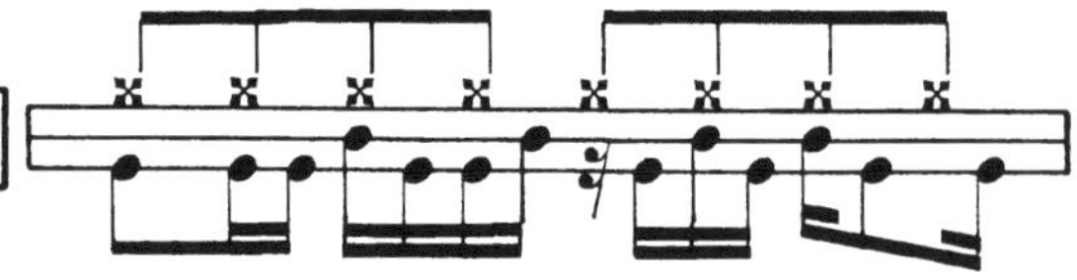

314 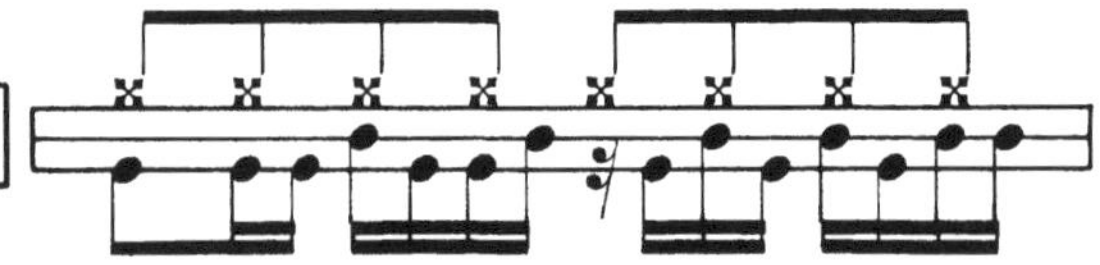

315 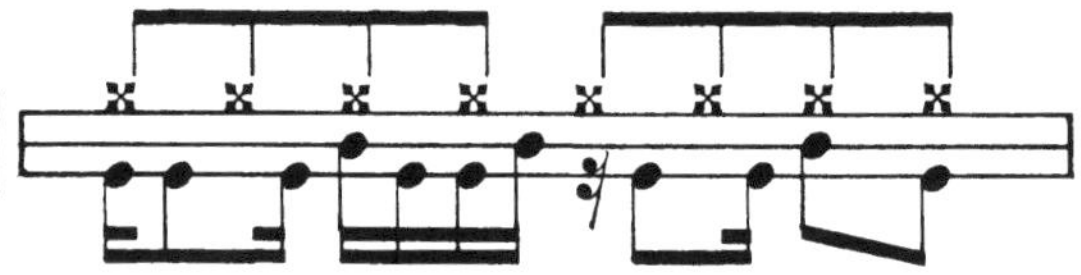

316 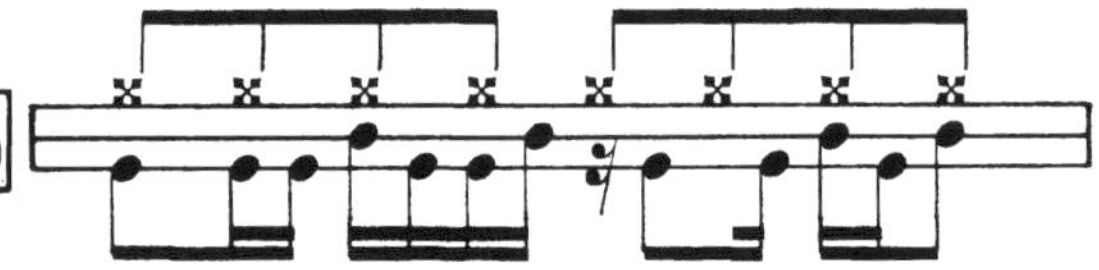

317 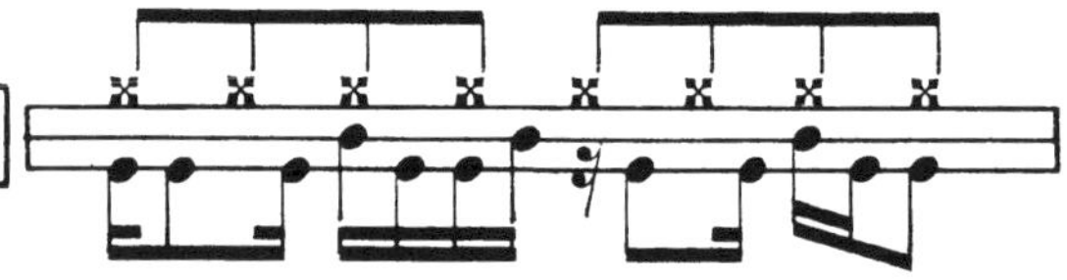

318 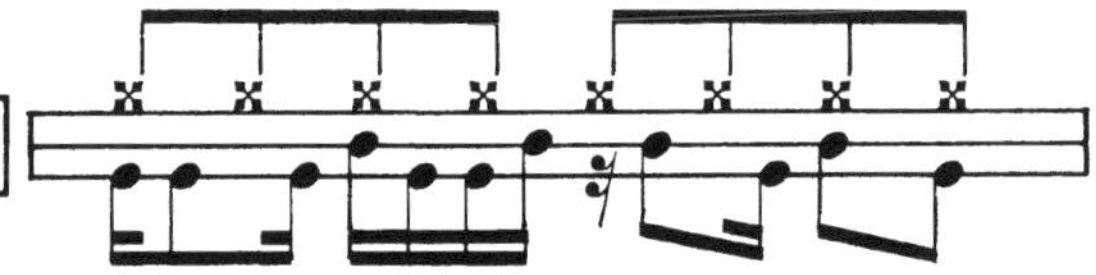

319 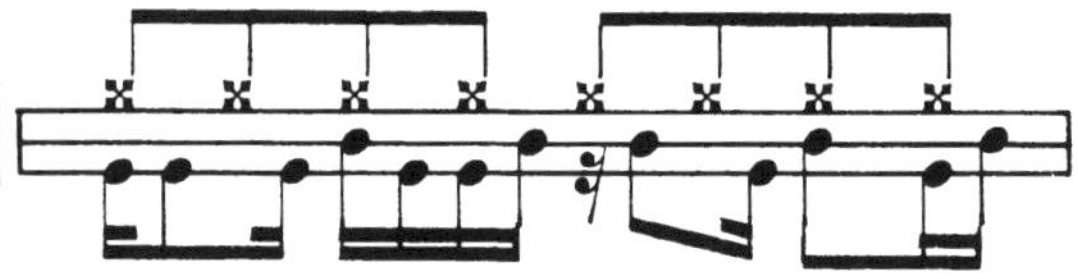

320 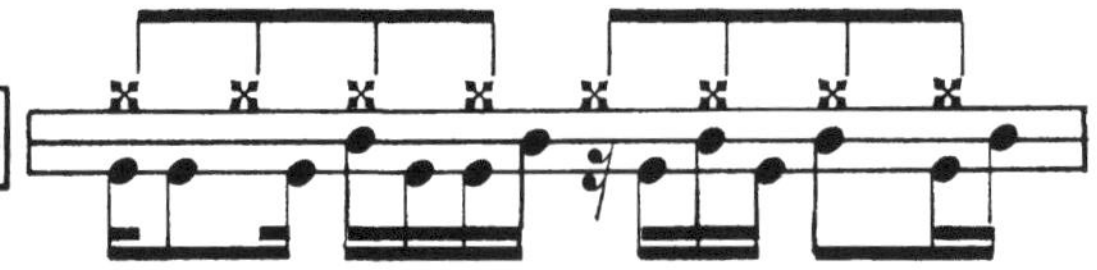

321 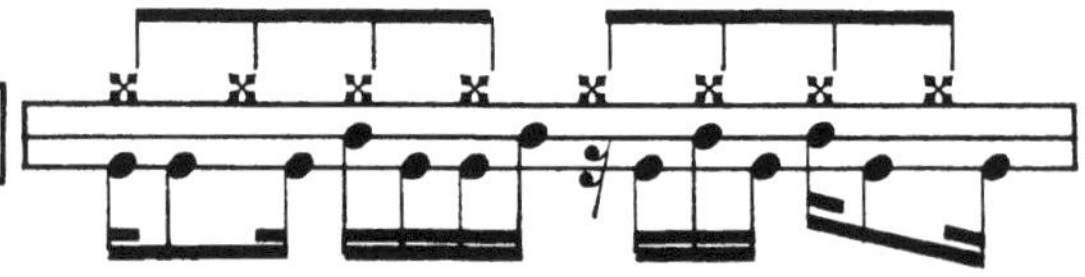

322 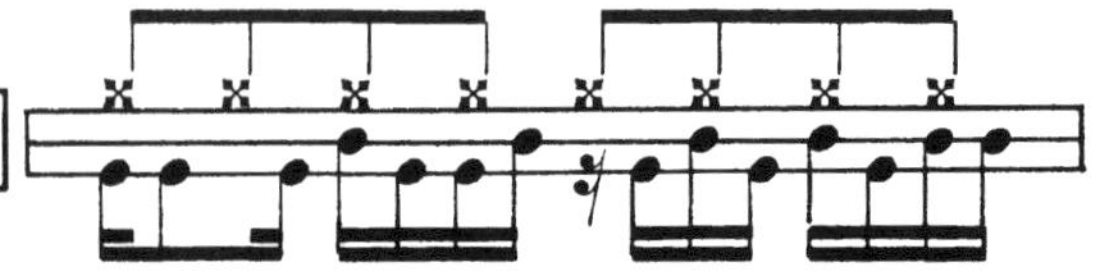

323 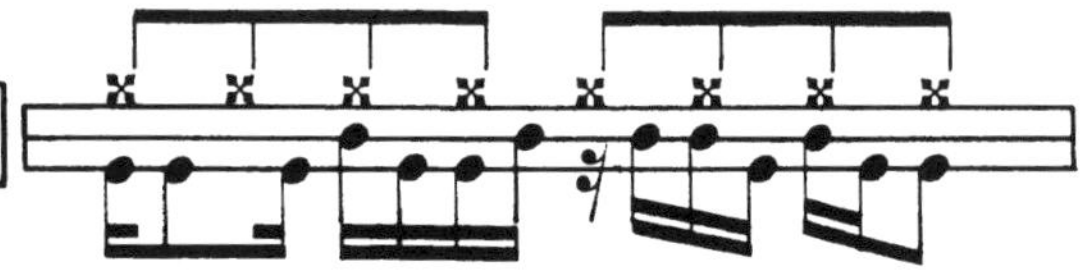

324 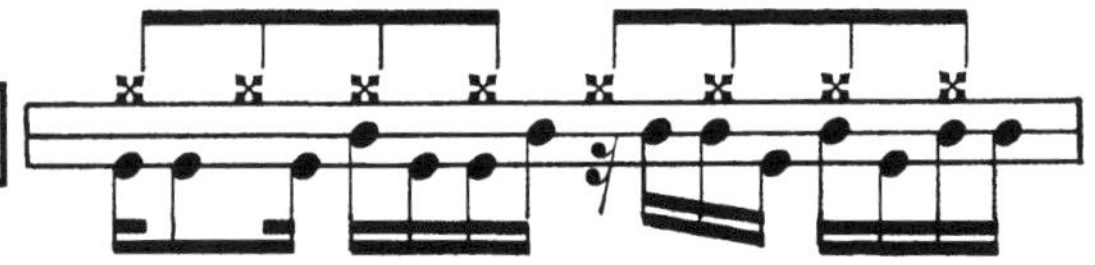

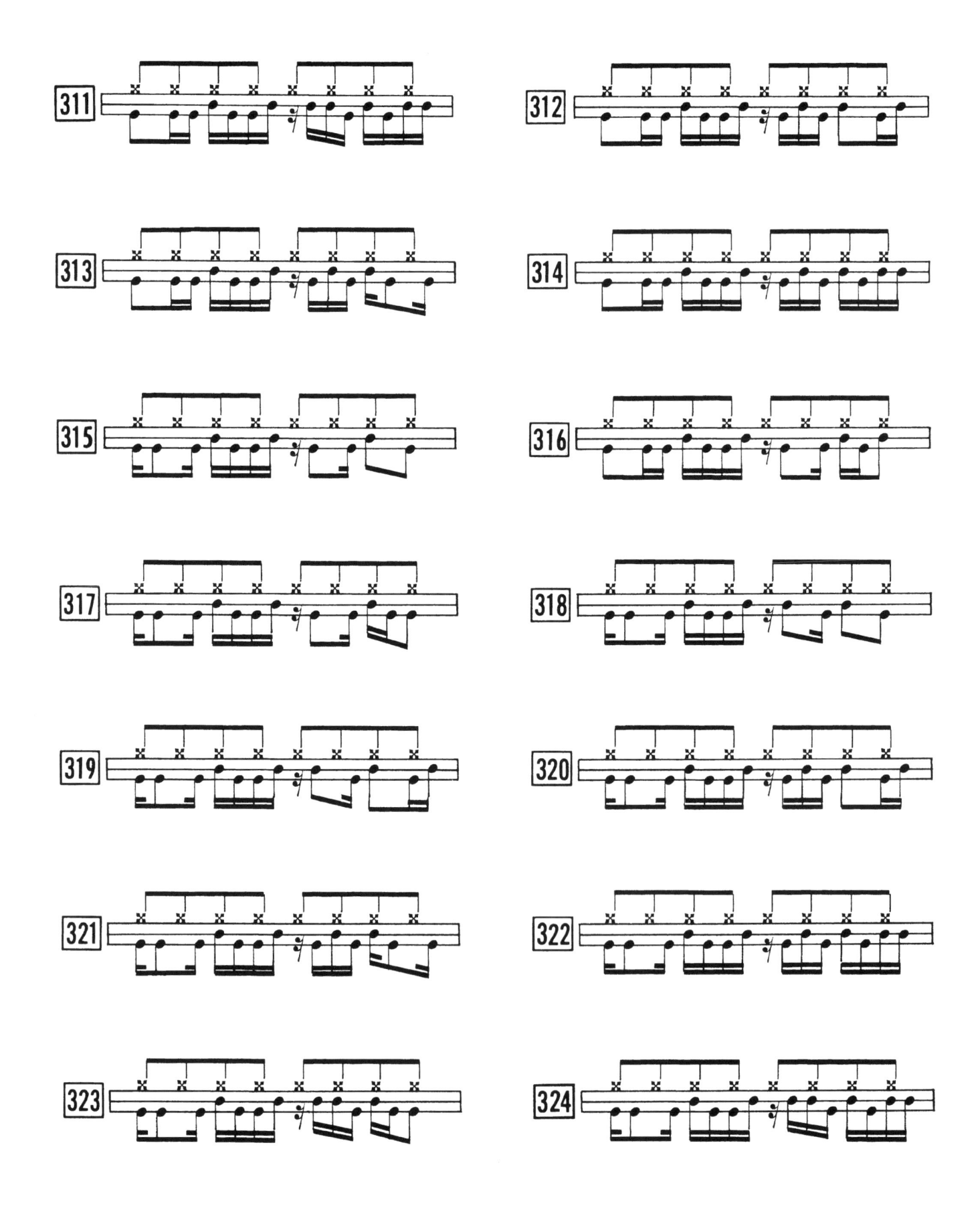

63

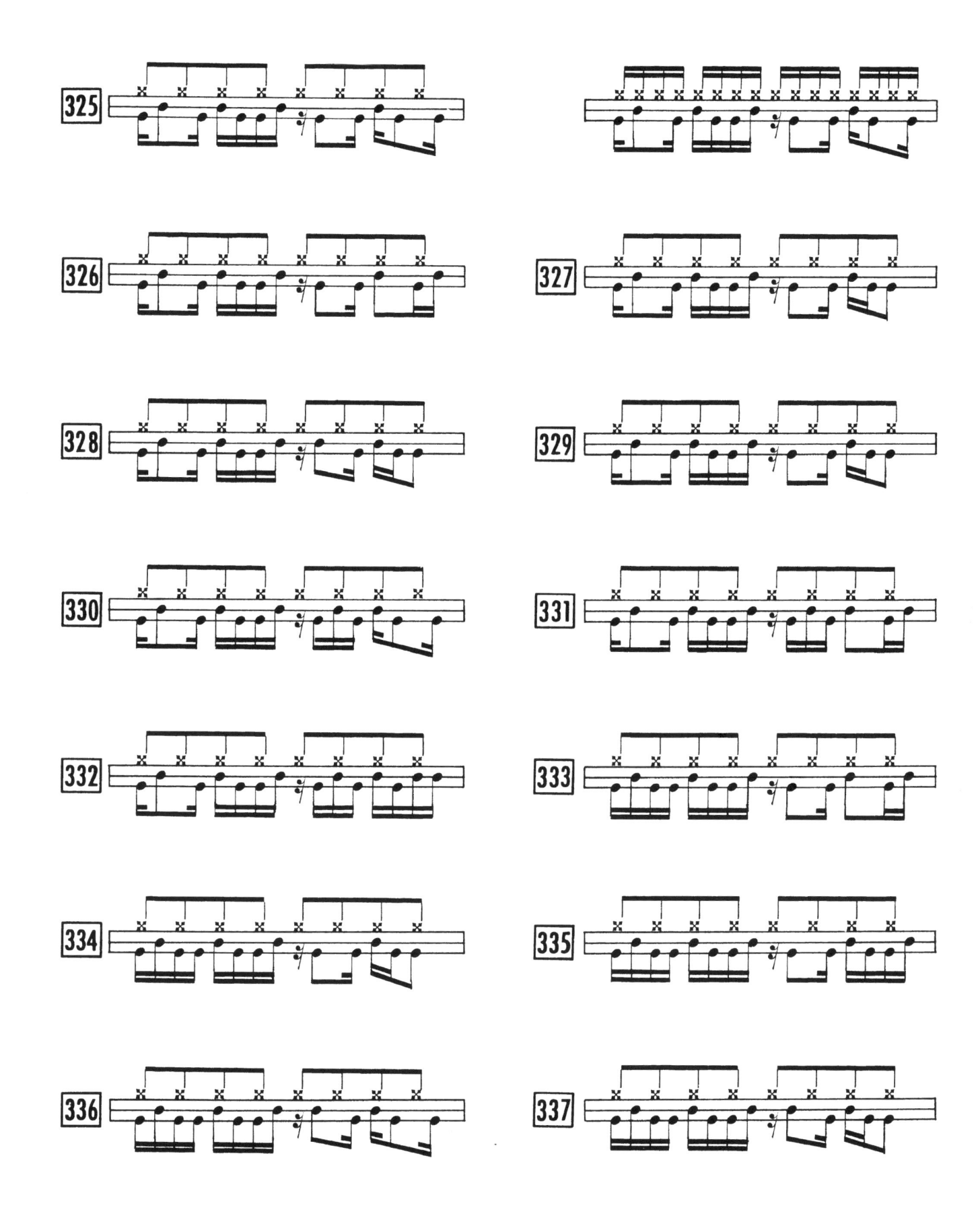

338
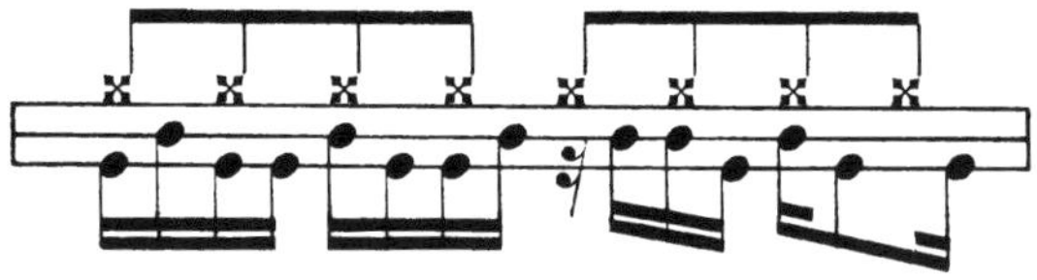

339
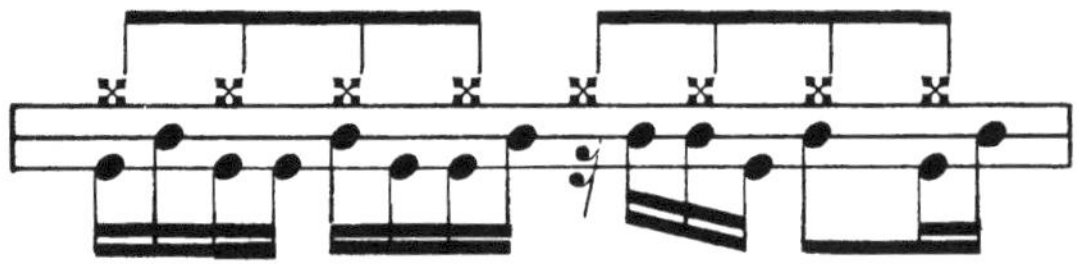

340
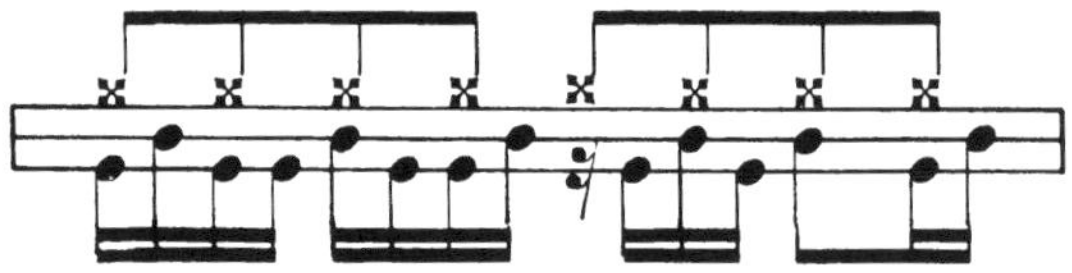

341
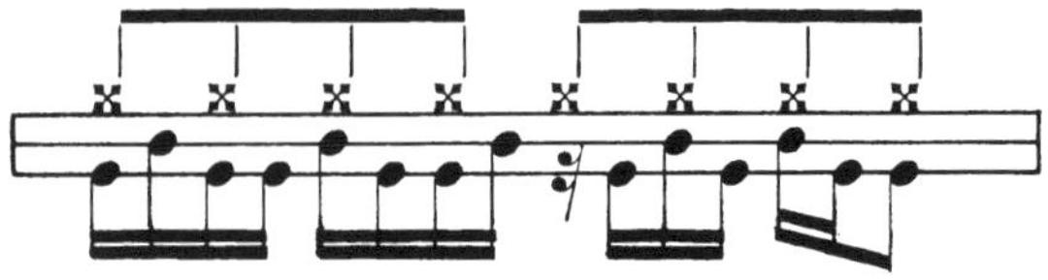

342
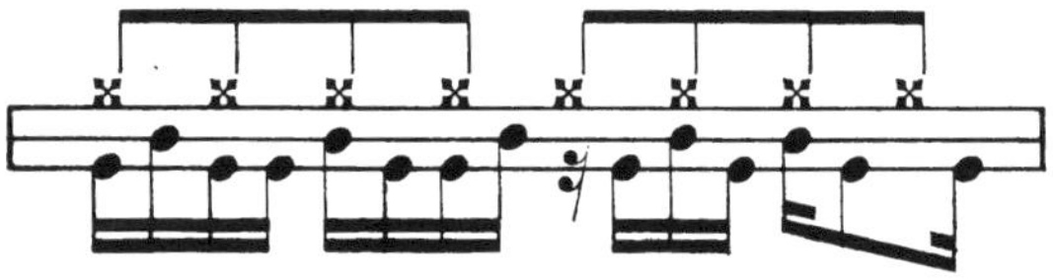

343
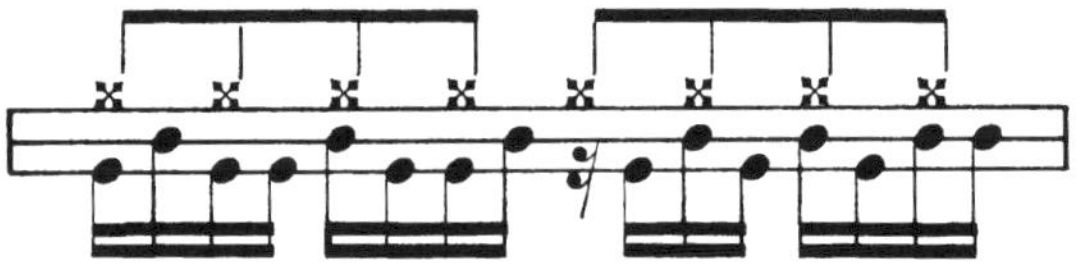

344
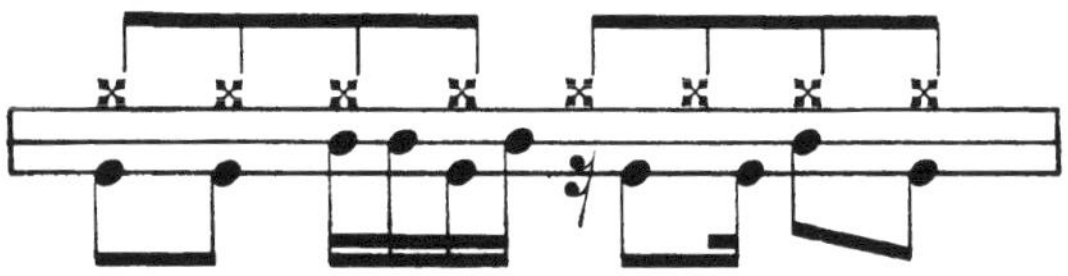

345
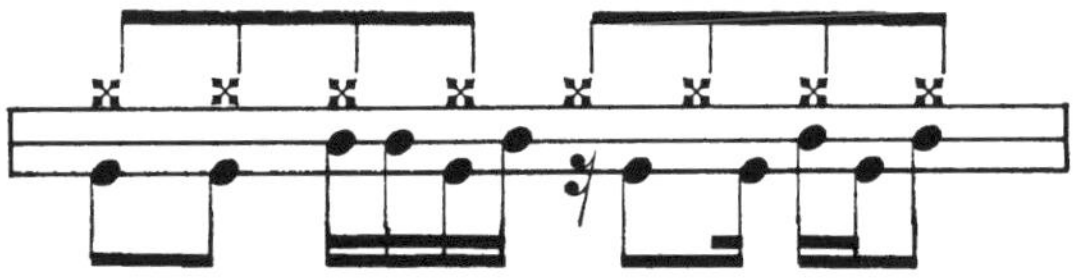

346
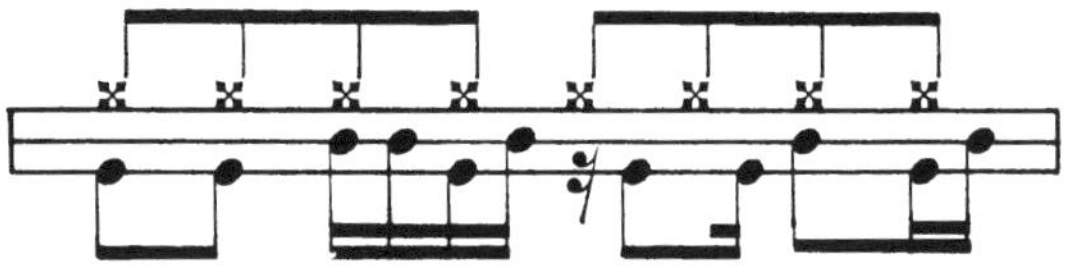

347
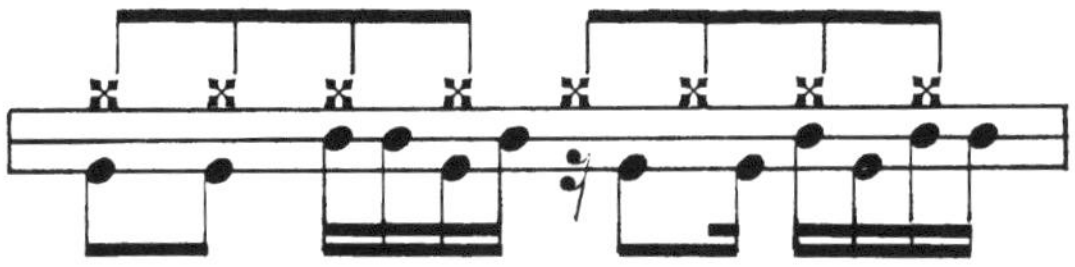

348
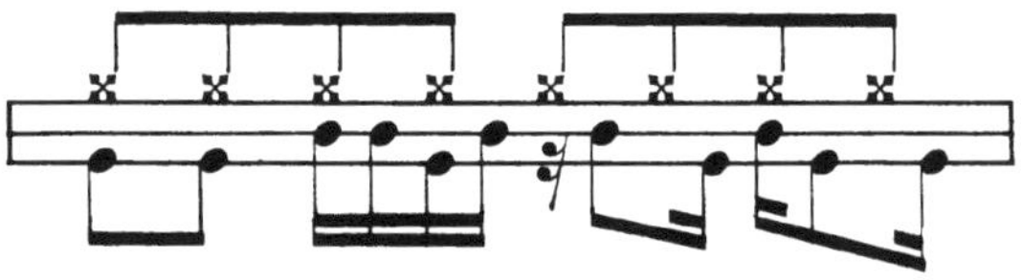

349
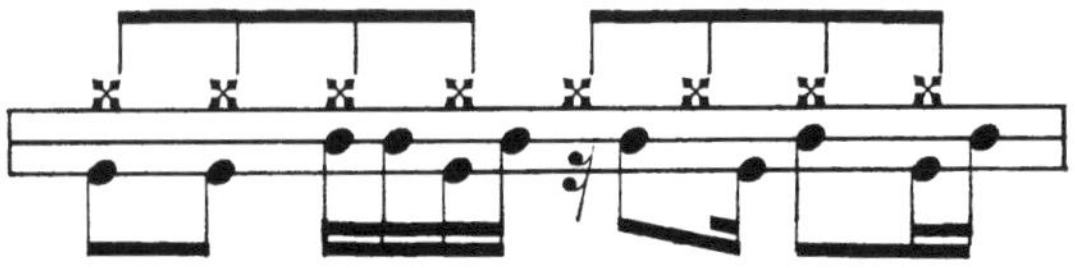

350
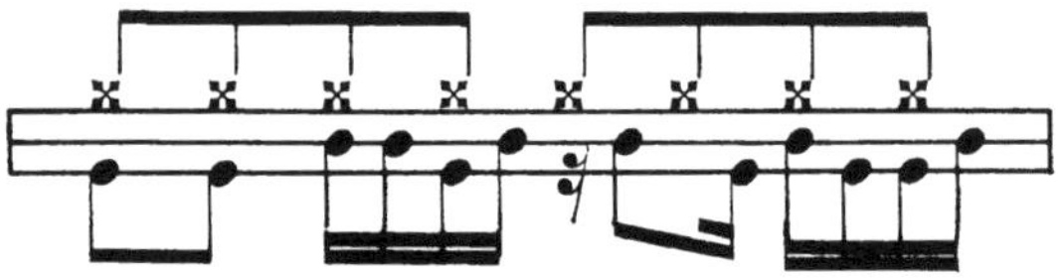

351
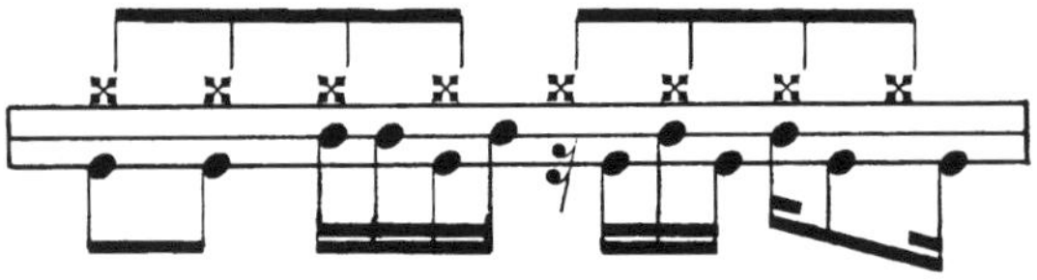

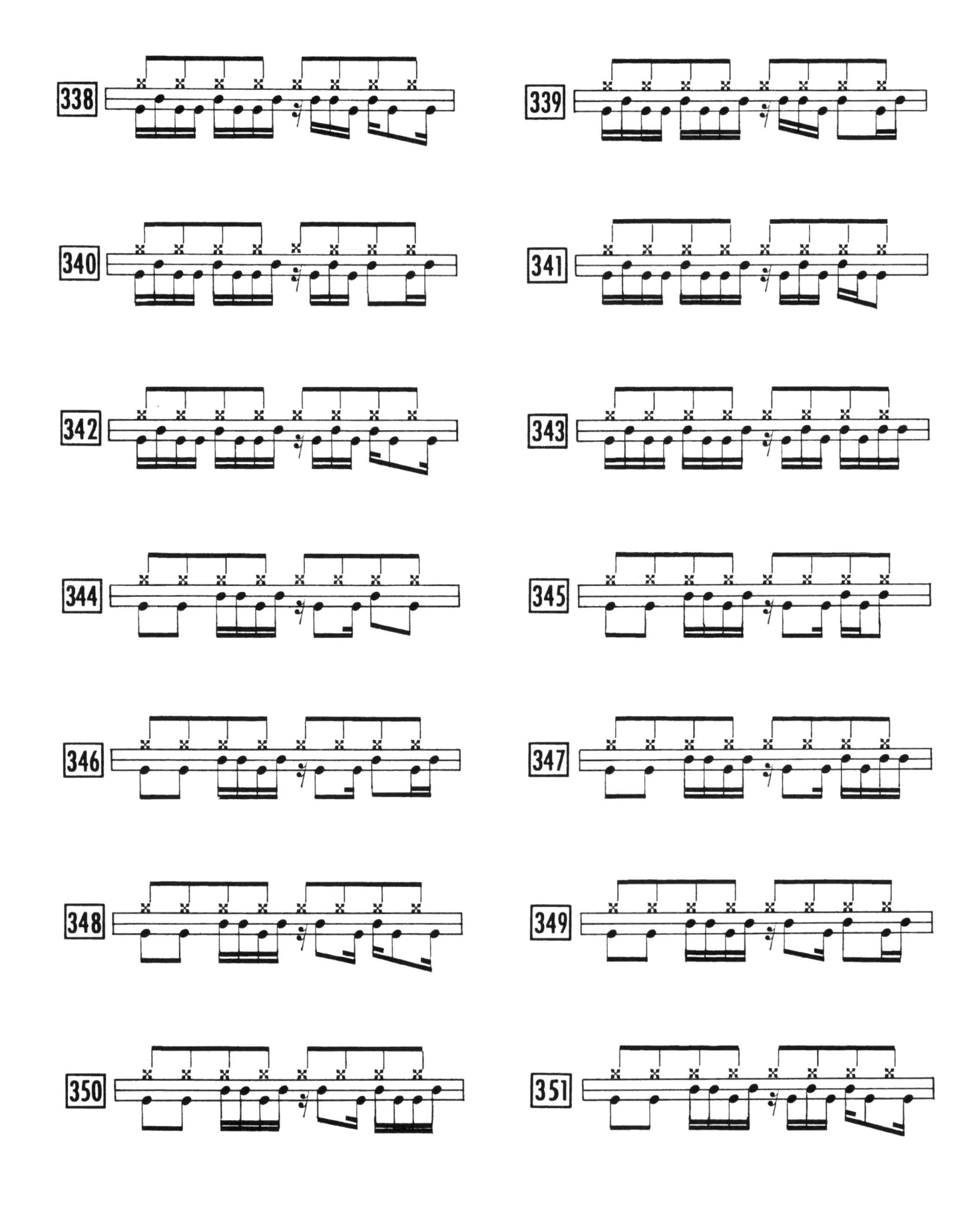

352
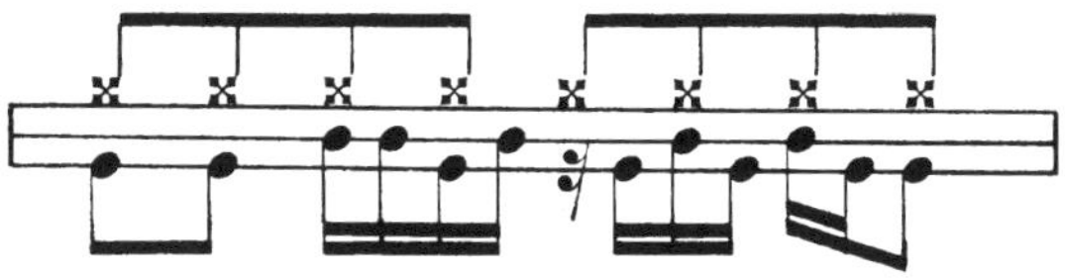

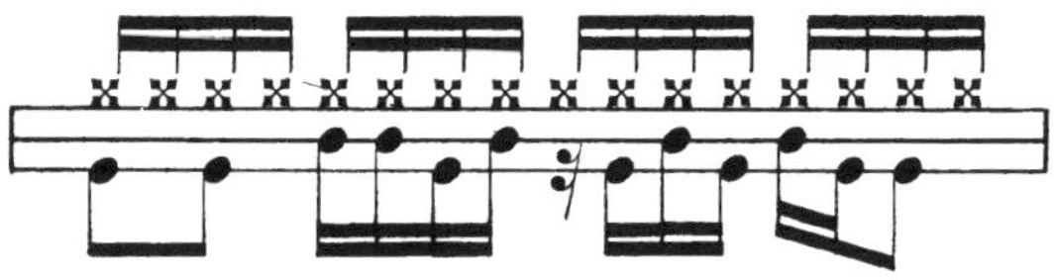

35
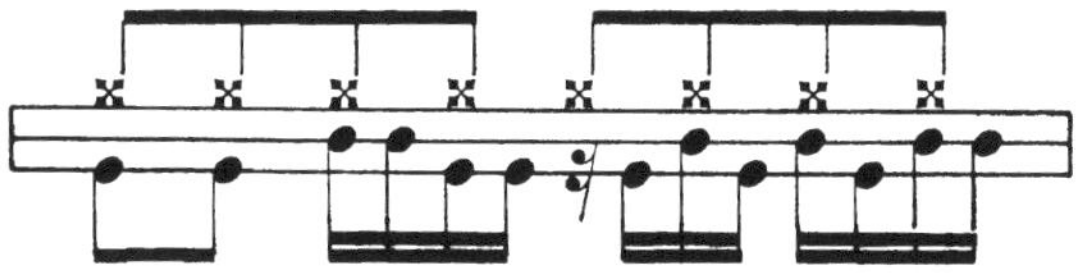

354
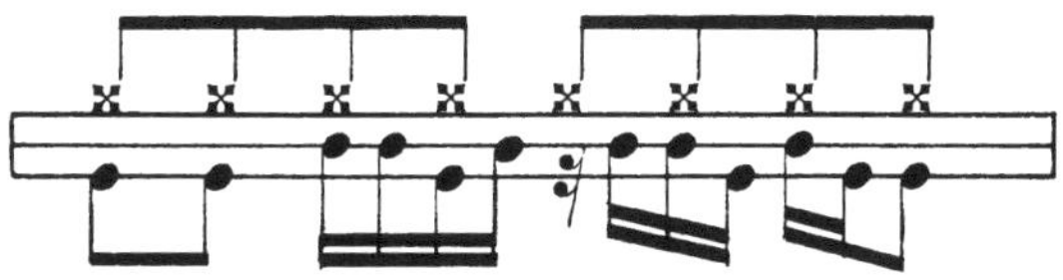

355
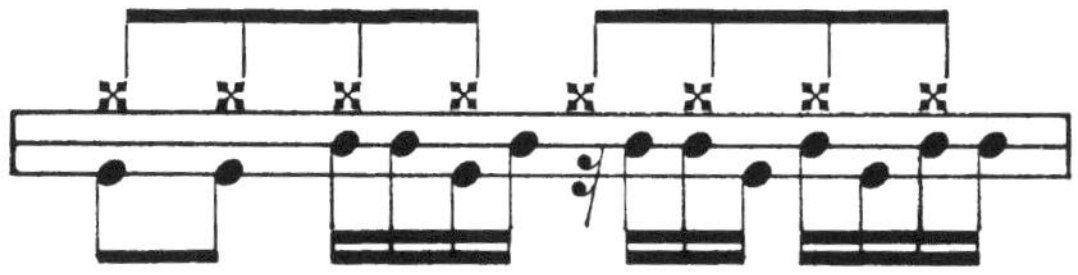

356
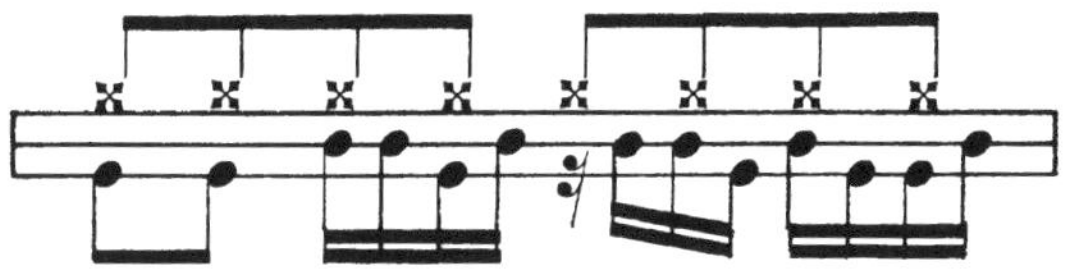

357
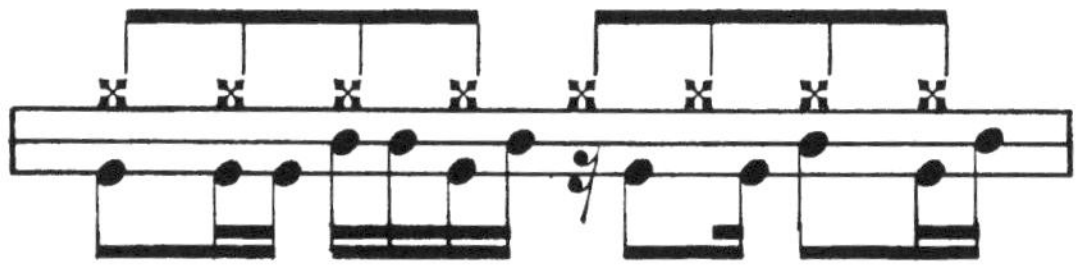

358
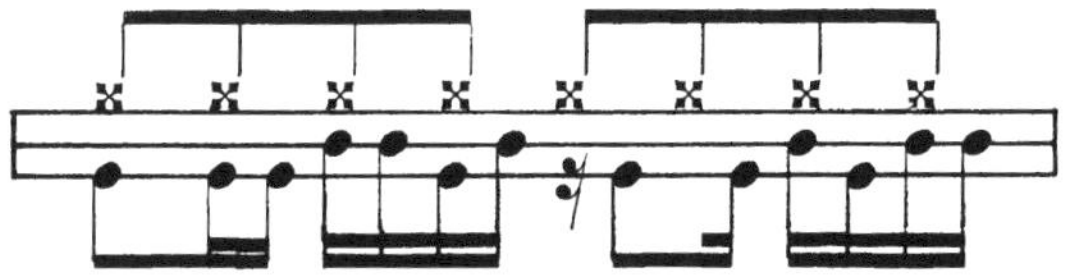

359
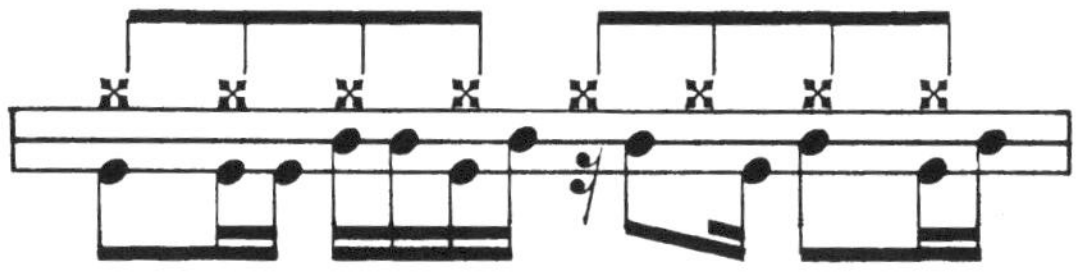

360
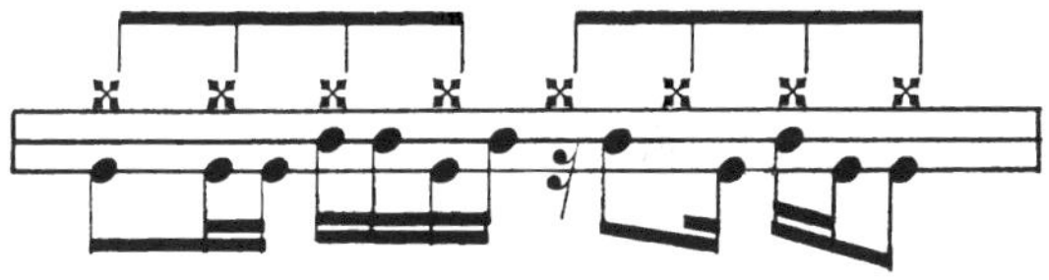

361
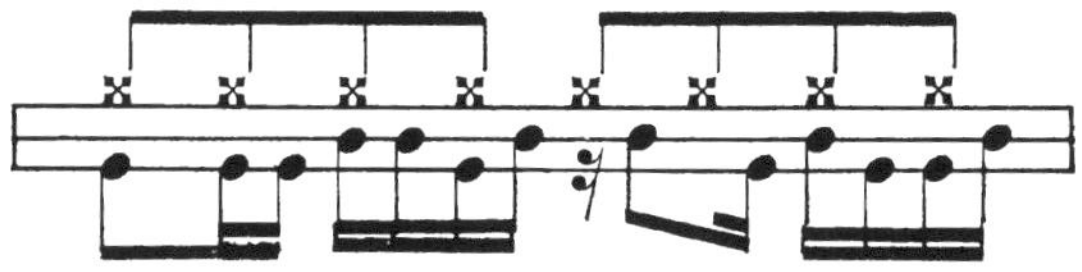

362
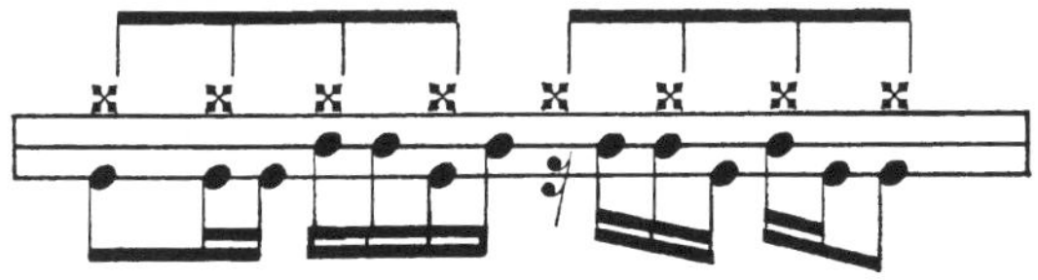

363
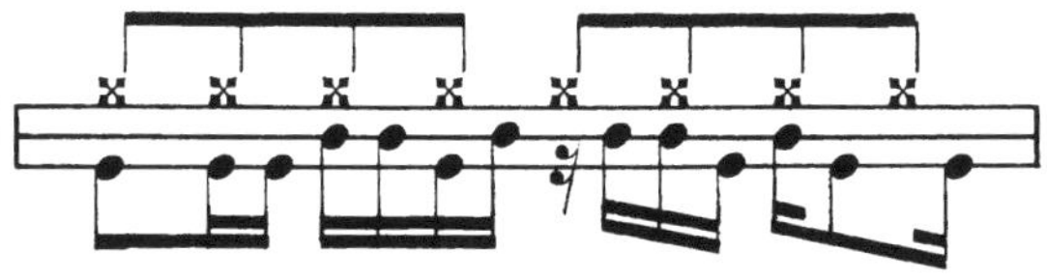

364
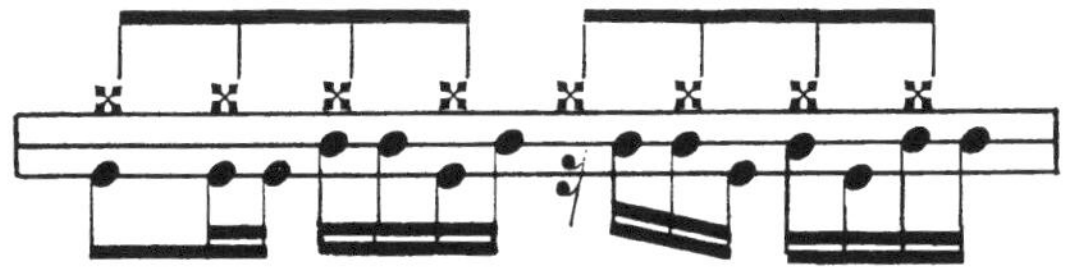

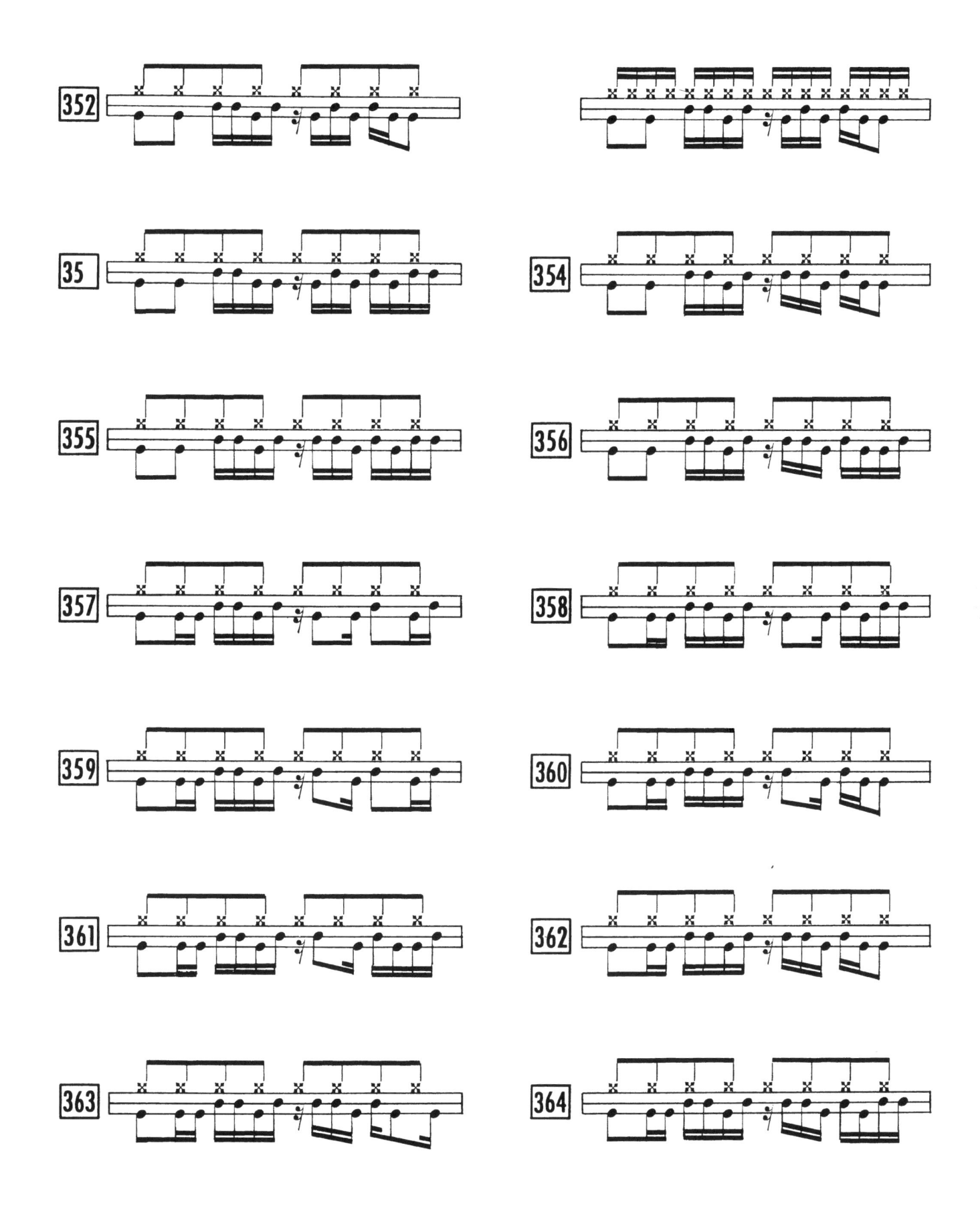

365
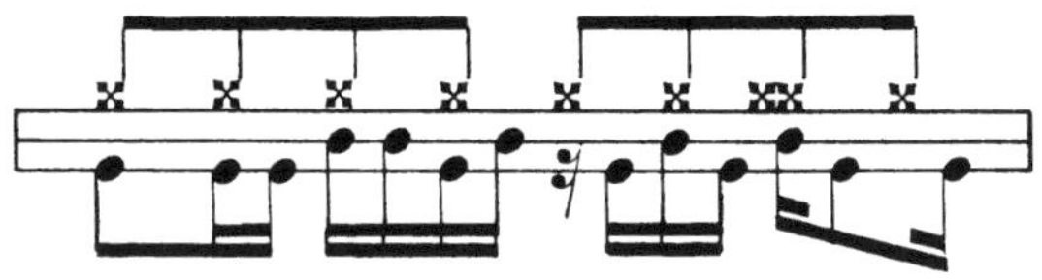
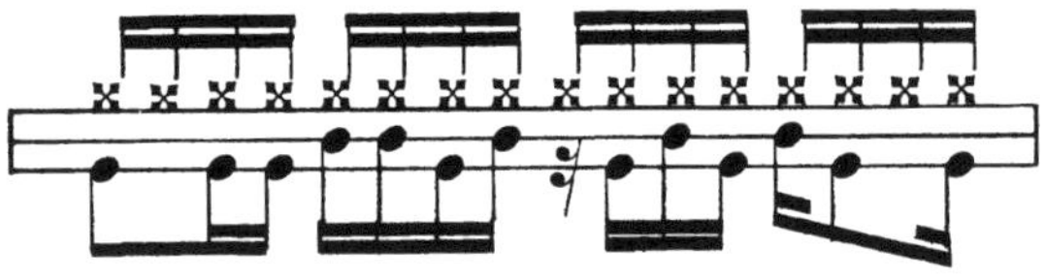

366
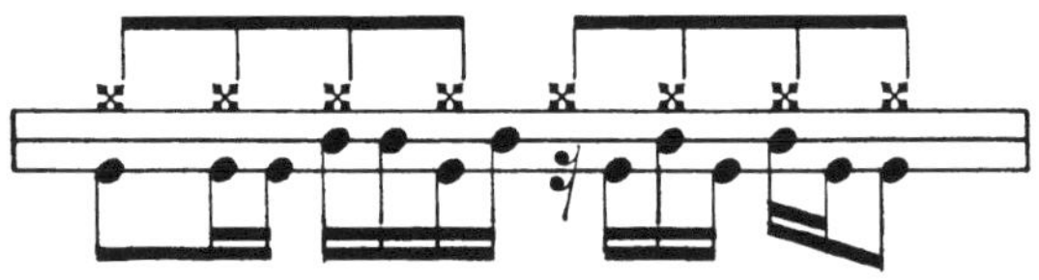

367
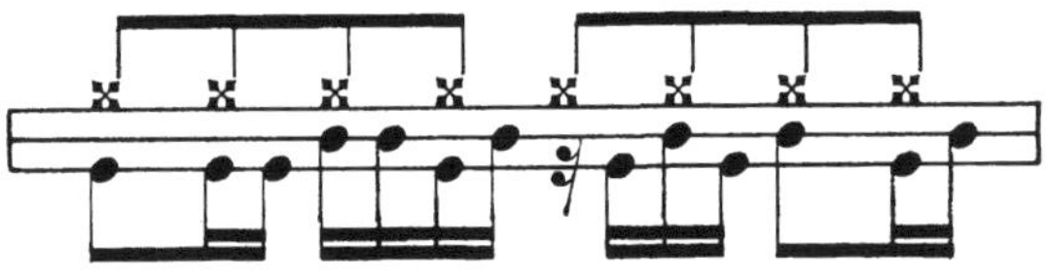

368
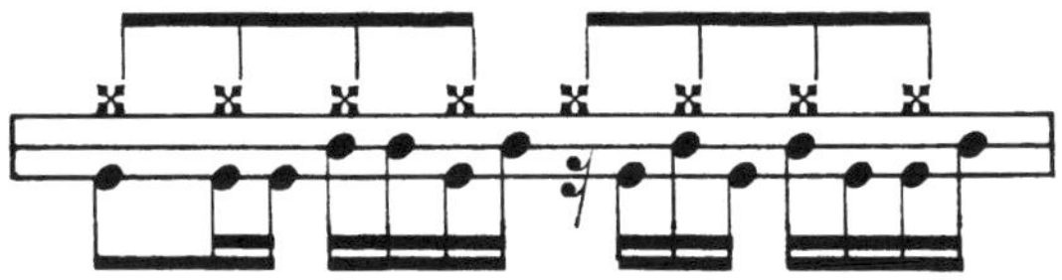

369
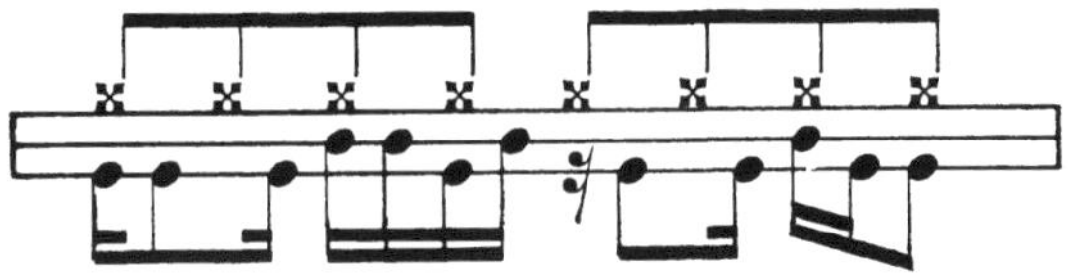

370
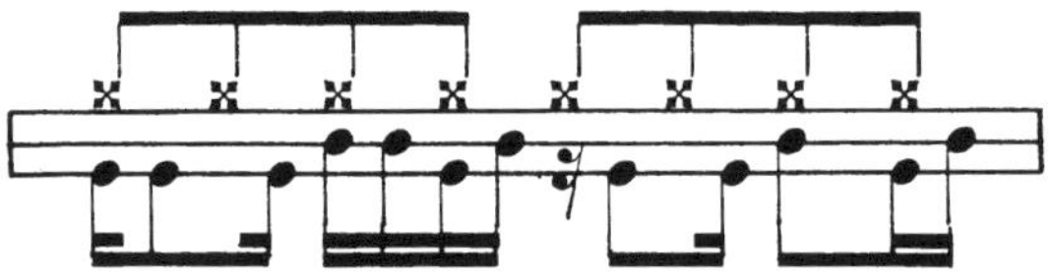

371
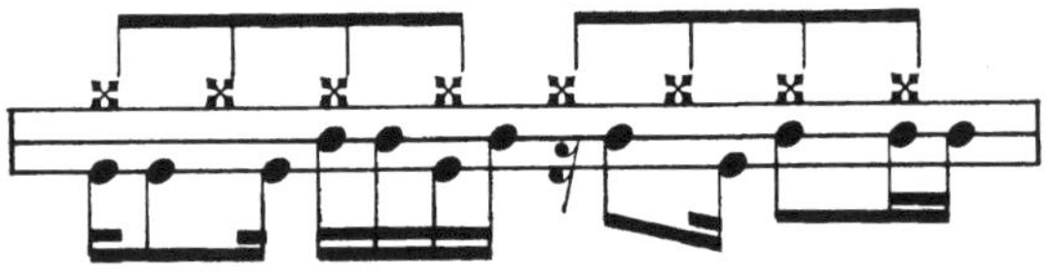

372
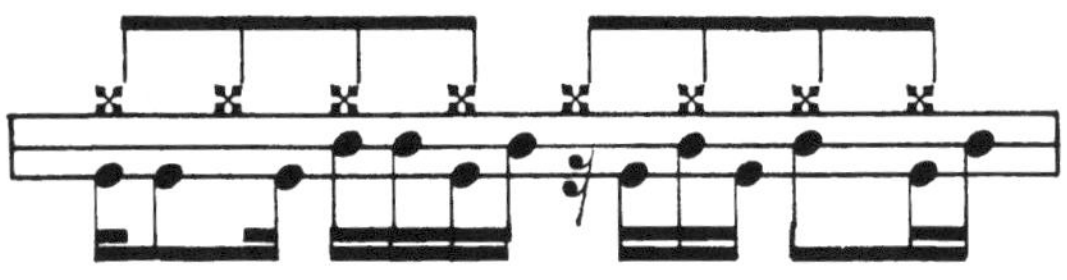

373
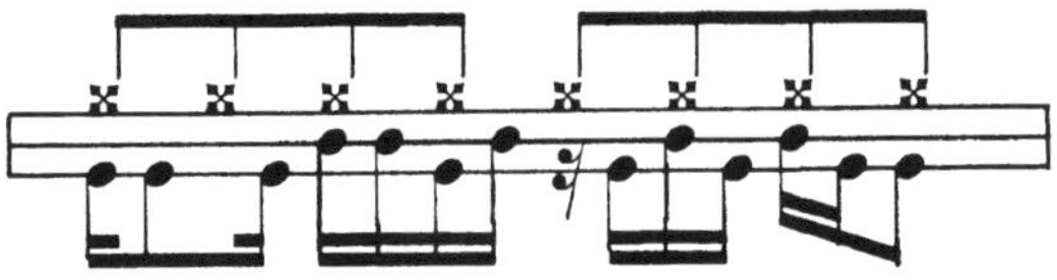

374
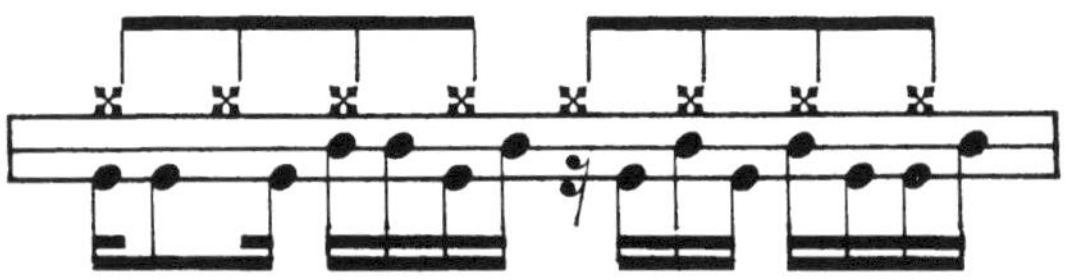

375
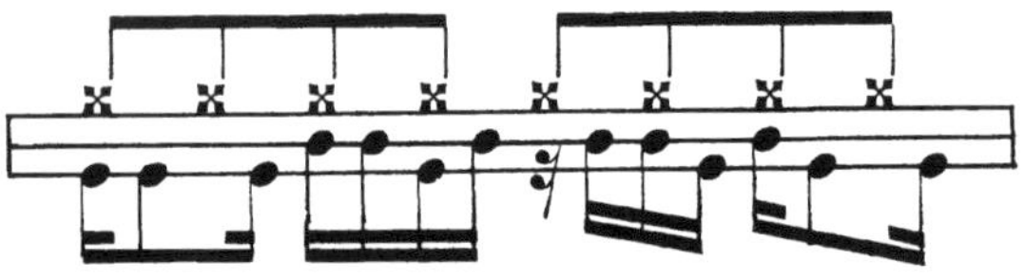

376
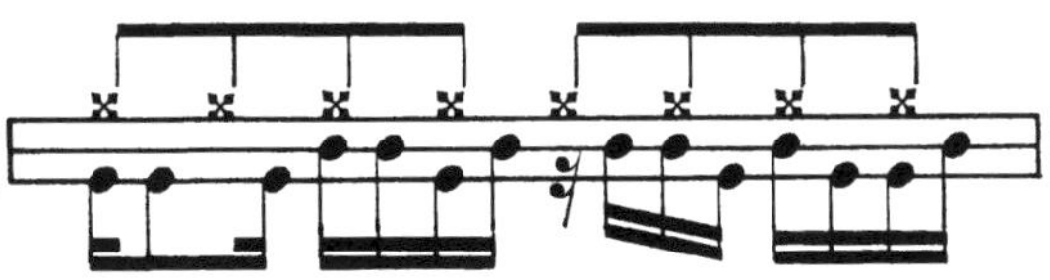

377
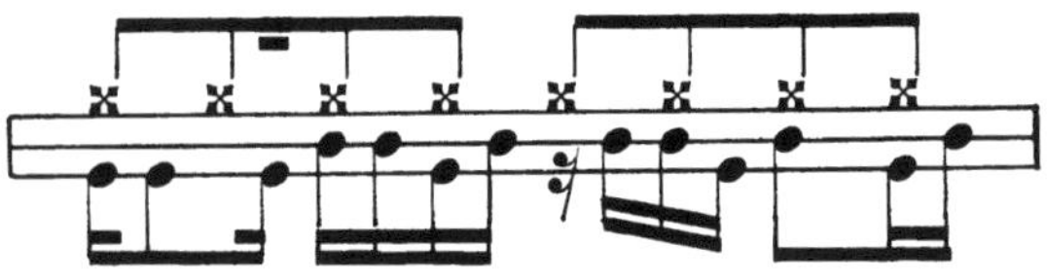

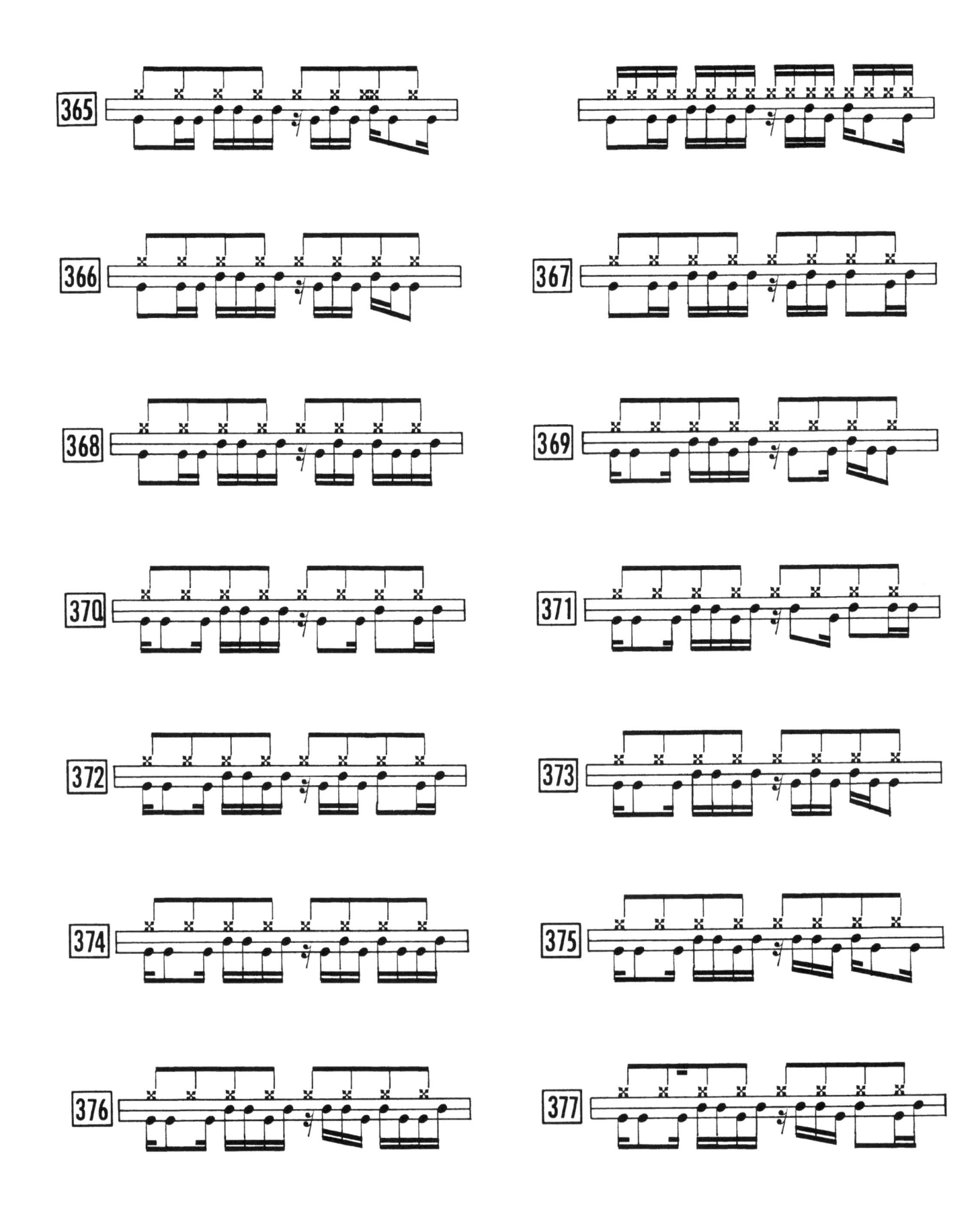

379
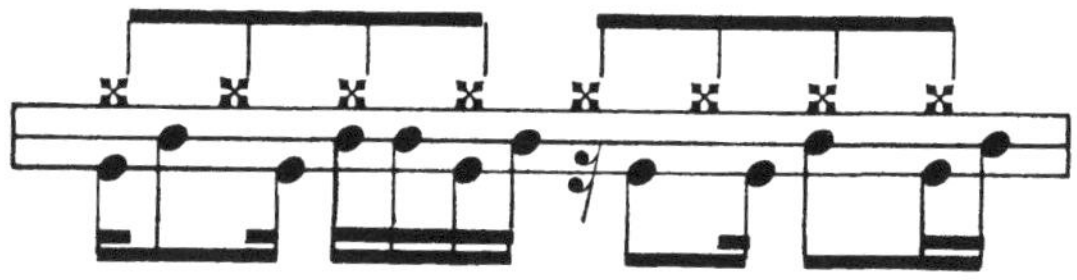

380
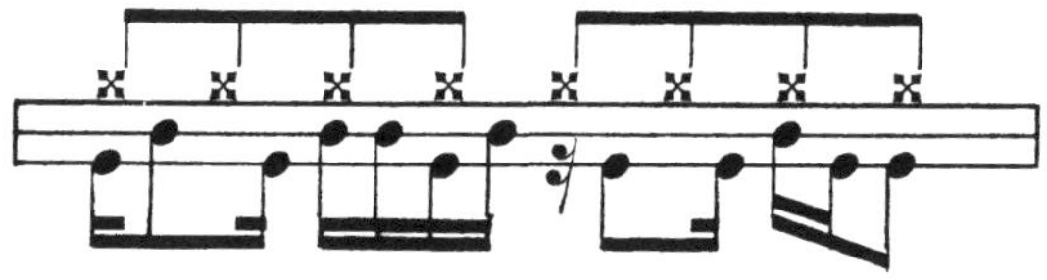

381
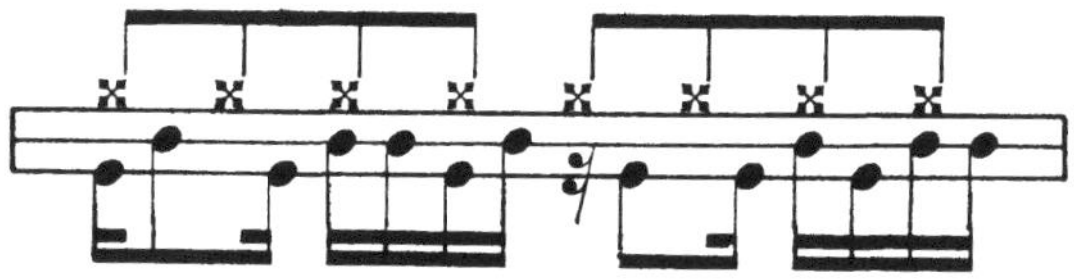

38
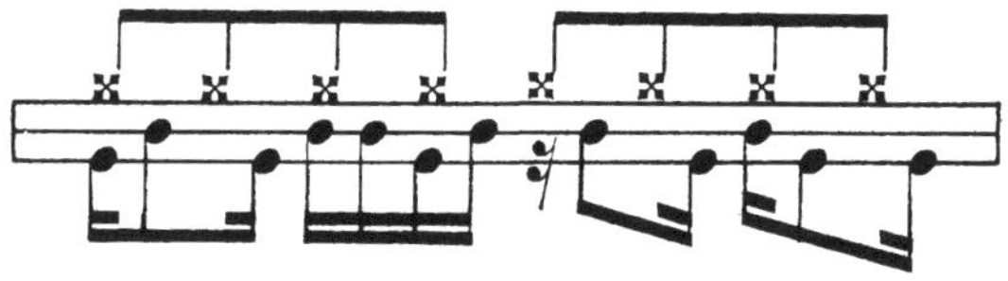

383
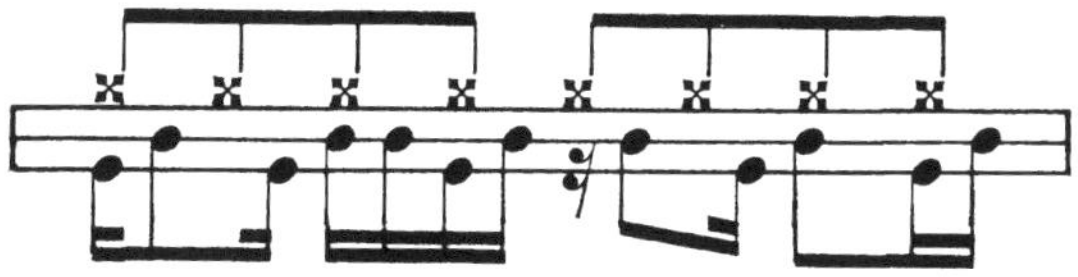

384
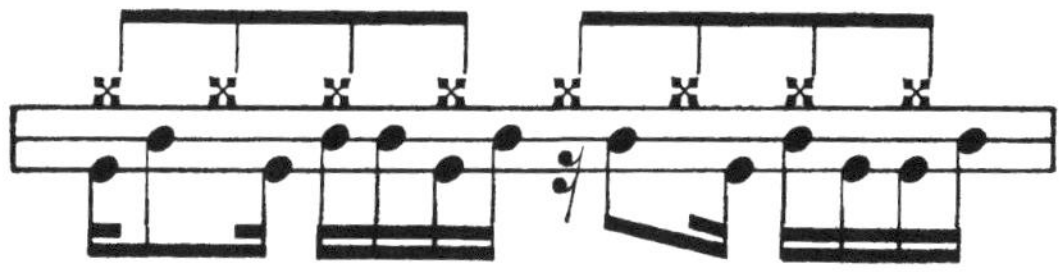

385
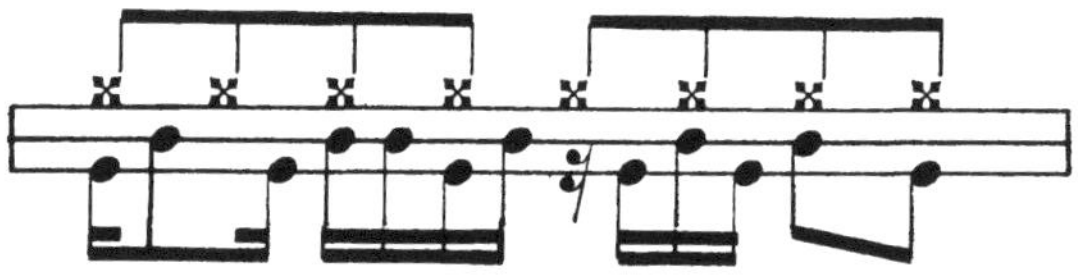

386
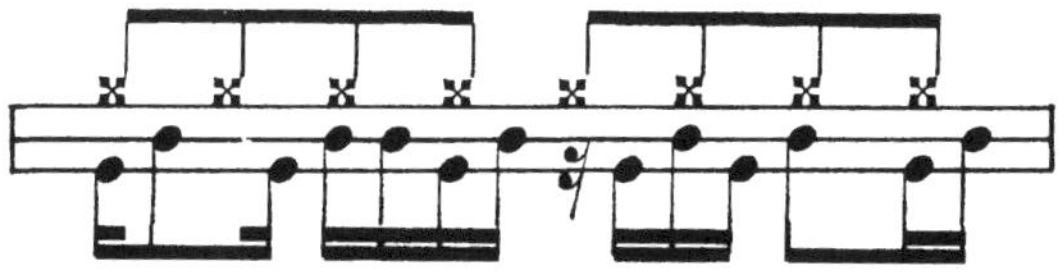

387
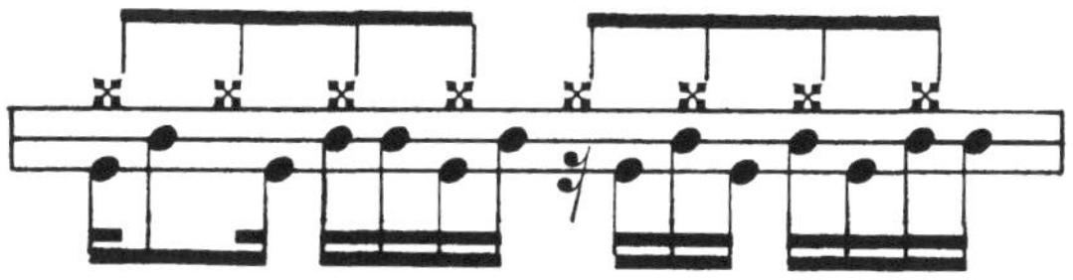

388
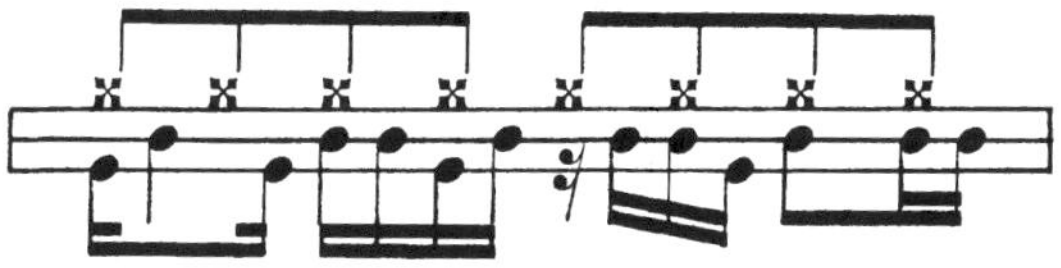

389
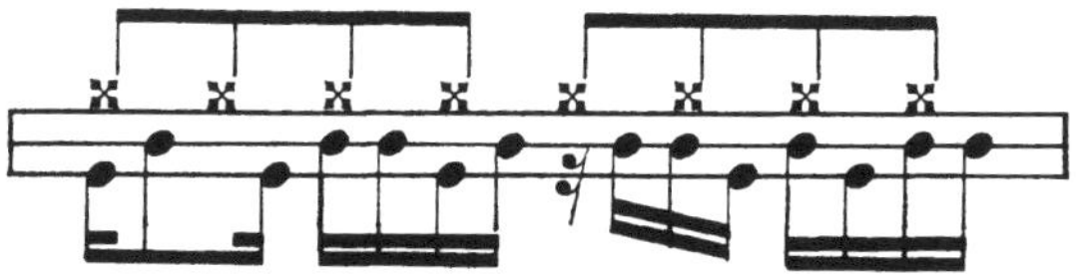

390
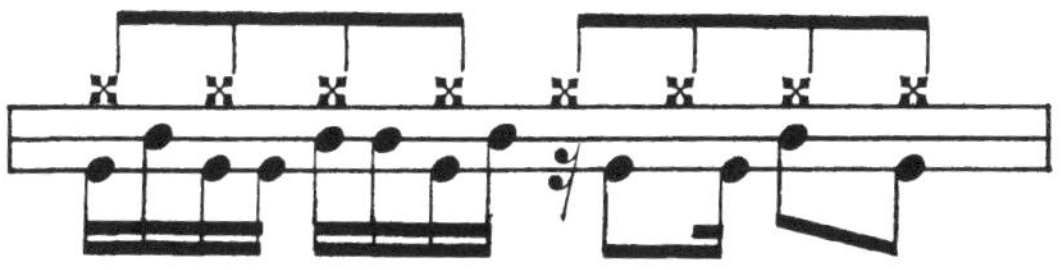

391
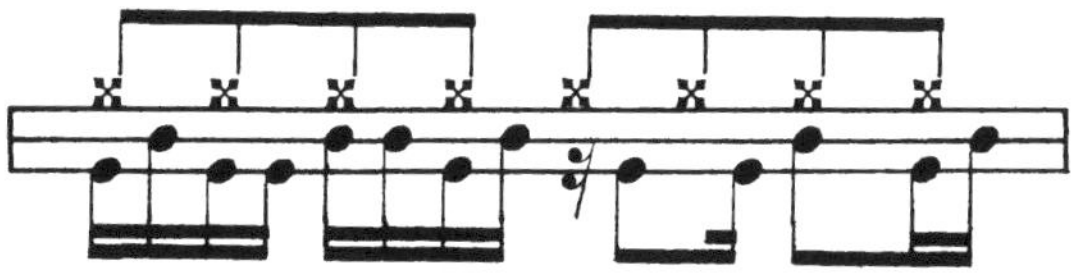

392
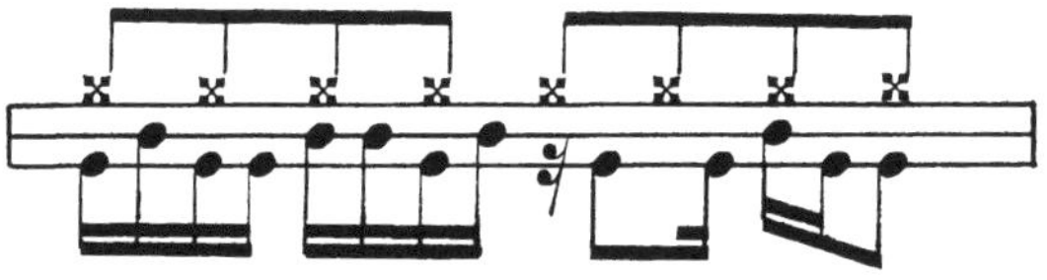

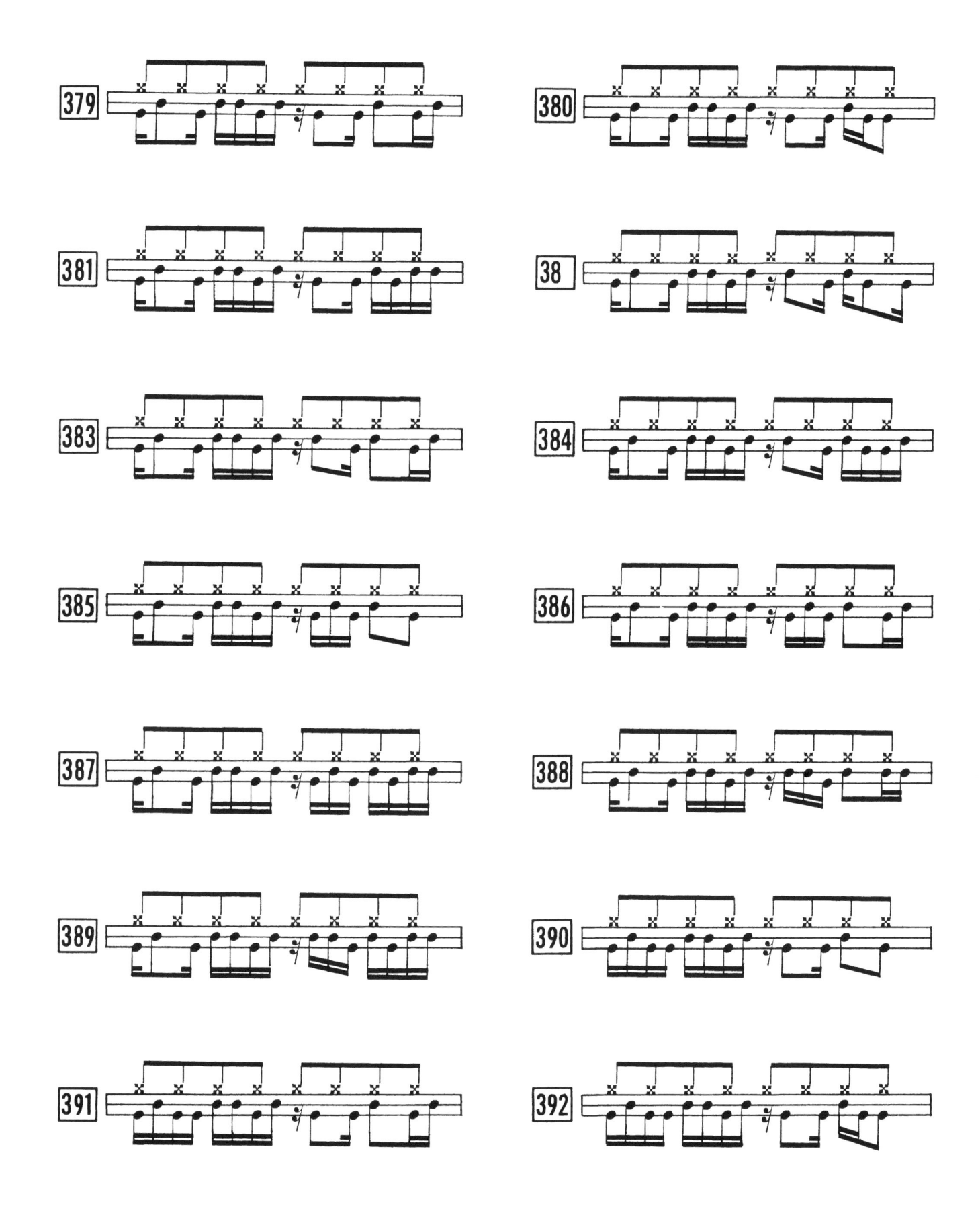

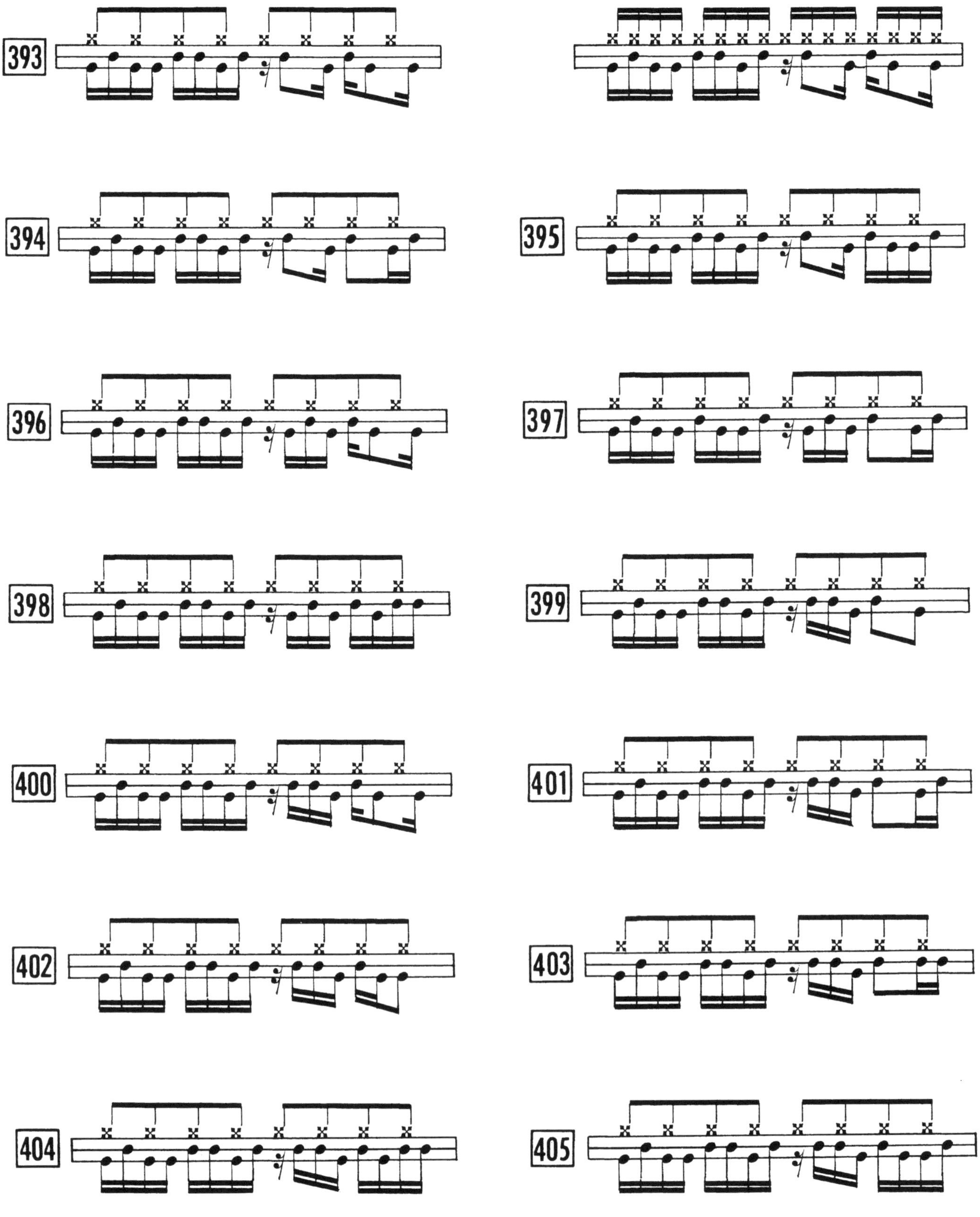
393
394
395
396
397
398
399
400
401
402
403
404
405

CHAPTER II

PART III

RHYTHMIC IMPROVISATION

    The following are a few eight bar solos designed to demonstrate, in practice, the theory of improvising rhythmically. Most of the figures used are the variations shown in parts one and two. They are connected together in solos in an effort to show how a one or two bar figure can be turned into a longer phrase. 4, 8, 12 bars, etc.

    The solos as they are, are playable. However, in an actual musical situation, the solos would probably be played much looser and would not stick quite as close to the basic beat. How close to the basic figure the drummer stays depends largely on the musical situation.

ABOVE ALL ELSE, MUSICIANSHIP AND TASTE MUST BE EMPHASIZED!

TECHNIQUE IS ALWAYS SECONDARY TO MUSICIANSHIP.

Note: Once again it must be emphasized that all the solos must be played with both an eighth note and a sixteenth note ride on he right hand. The sixteenth note ride gives an entirely different feeling and sound than does the eighth note ride. For this reason they both must be used.

- 8 BAR SOLOS - BASIC BEAT:

71

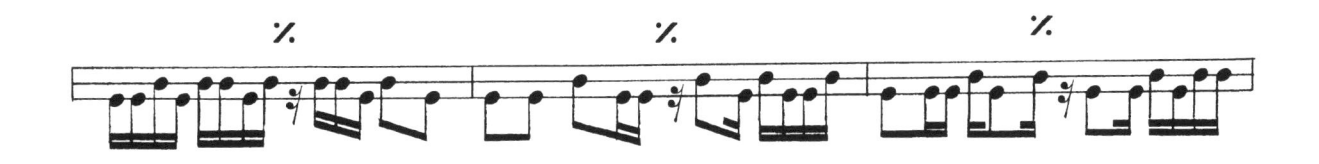

5

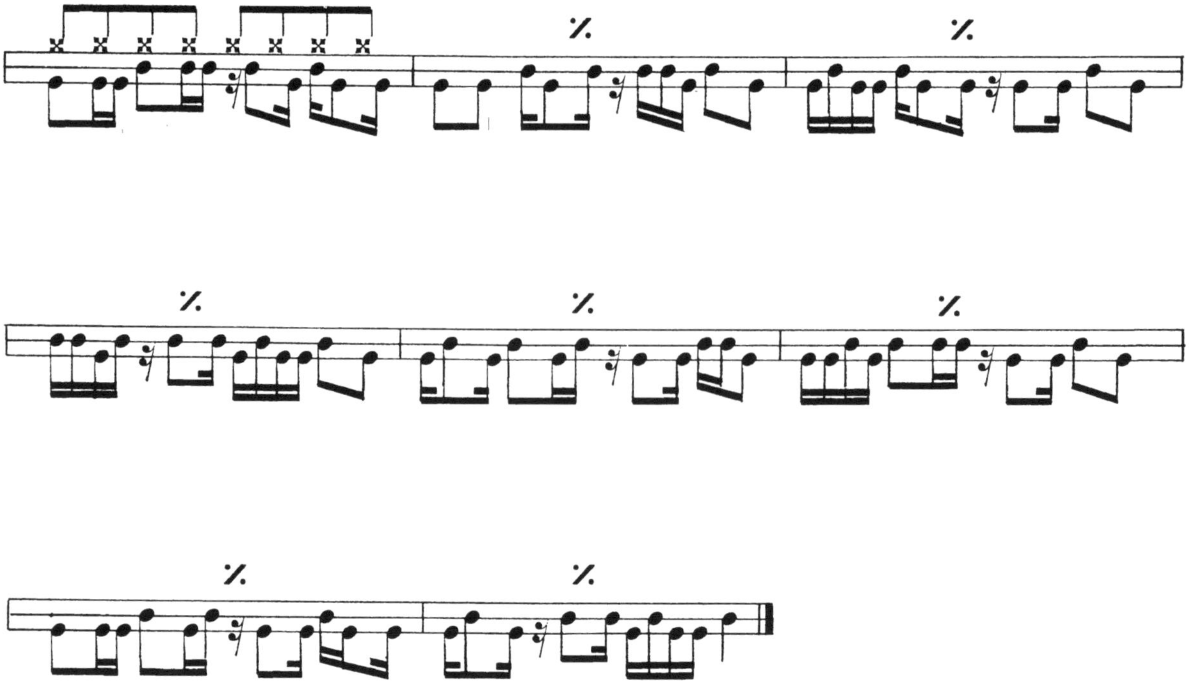

6

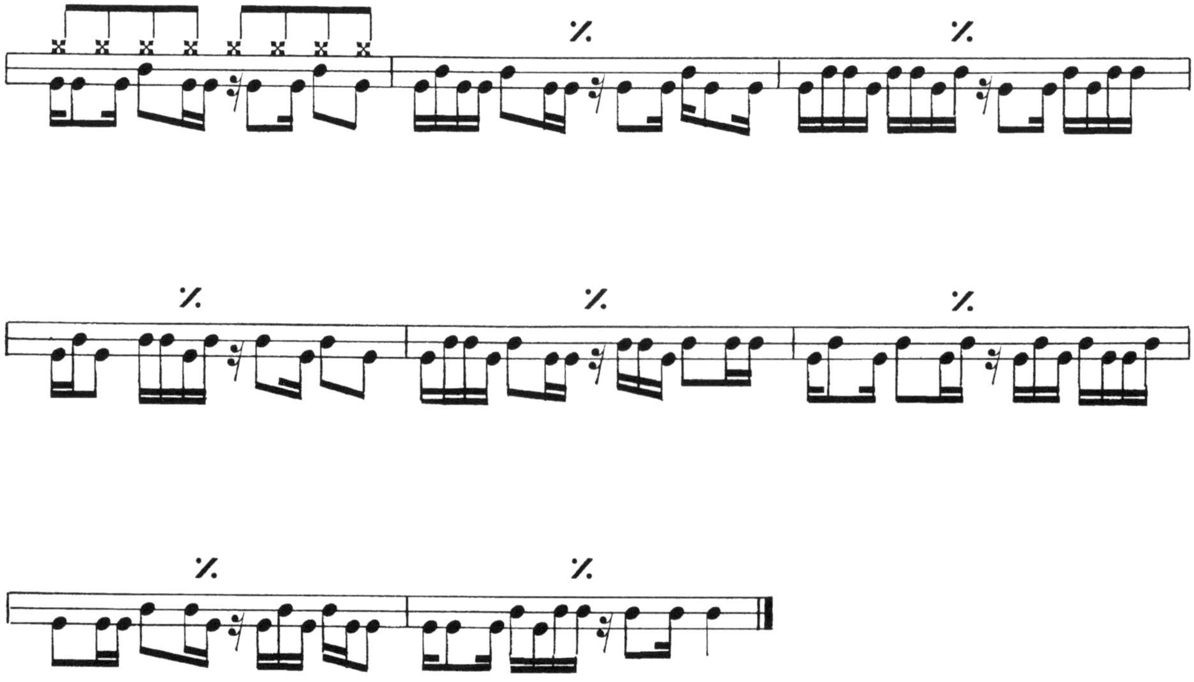

73

CYMBAL VARIATIONS WITH THE RIGHT HAND

The first step to cymbal variations is to change the sound of the ride pattern without actually changing the rhythmic figure. This applies mainly to when the right hand is being played on a closed high hat, a practice that is used quite frequently in rock drumming.

Changing the sound can be accomplished quite simply by opening the high hat cymbals slightly for a short time and then closing them again. When the high hat cymbals are struck in a slightly open position they ring a little, and in contrast to the normal staccato effect of a closed H.Hat, they tend to give a much broader sound, almost changing the duration of the notes.

Note: X denotes a closed H.Hat.   O denotes an open H. Hat.

FOR EXAMPLE:

PLAYED AS: **HEARD AS:**

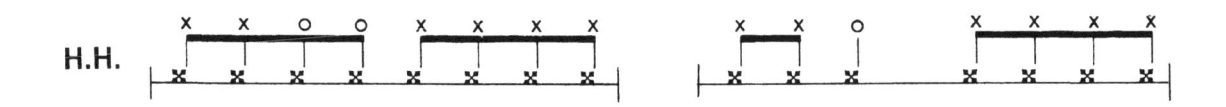

Notice that when the second two eighth notes of the bar (2 &) in the above example, are played with the H.Hat cymbals slightly open it sounds almost as though they were a quarter note held into the third beat of the bar.

Because of the broader sound produced, this practice can be very useful in "re-enforcing" accents played on either the snare or the bass drum. For example, if the H.Hat is opened slightly on the second and/or fourth beats of the bar, along with the usual snare accent a much "heavier", more definite feeling is obtained. It would not be advisable to use this device on every accent (EG: Every 2nd and 4th beat of the bar for the entire tune) however, when used occasionally and with taste it can be quite effective.

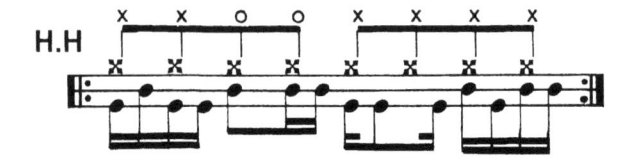

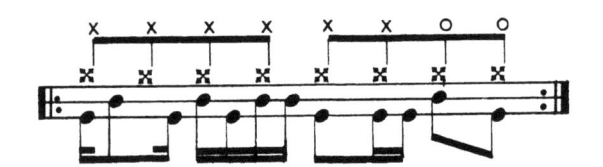

CYMBAL VARIATIONS WITH THE RIGHT HAND (Cont.)

By keeping the H.Hat cymbals open for only one instead of two eighth notes, a shorter, much different effect is achieved. This practice is most effective when played on the off-beat eighth notes (1 & 2 & 3 & 4 &). Definitely not all of these notes, but only when they are in a position so as to make some kind of musical sense.

These shorter little accents have a tendency to lead into something else, thereby making them very handy to use at the end of a phrase. (1 bar, 2 bar, 4, 8, etc.)

FOR EXAMPLE: By placing one of these cymbal figures at the end of a two bar phrase it tends to give the effect of finishing off the one phrase and either leading into a new one or into a repeat of the old one.

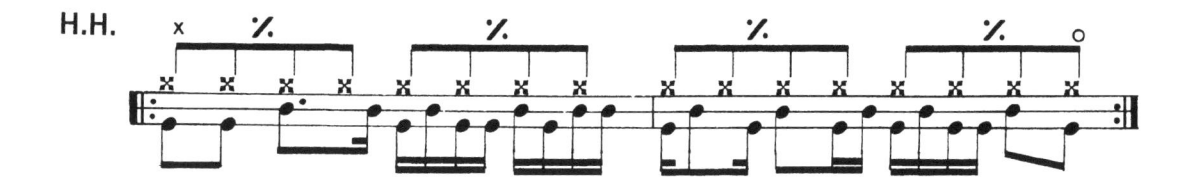

They also come in quite handy in setting up accents, such as the usual ones on the 2nd and 4th beats of the bar. Once again, if used to excess they will lose their effectiveness.

EG:

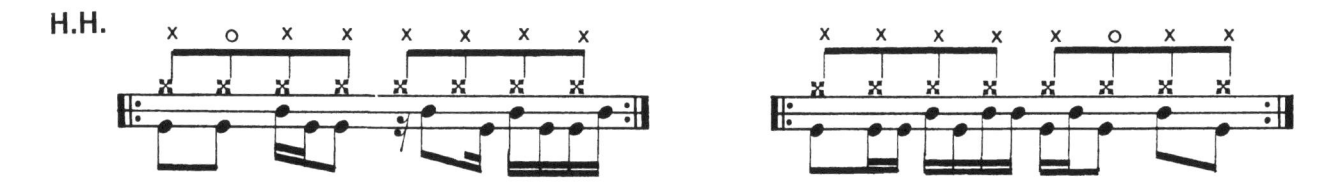

CYMBAL VARIATIONS WITH THE RIGHT HAND (Cont.)

THE FEW HIGH HAT ACCENTS DESCRIBED ON THE PREVIOUS PAGES CAN BE AND SHOULD BE APPLIED TO ALL THE EXERCISES AND FIGURES CONTAINED IN THIS TEXT.

By merely varying the sound of the high hat slightly, the feeling and sound of a figure can be changed substantially. This can add a little variety, and much musical colour and flavouring to your drumming. For the best possible effect, these accents should be applied with taste.

The following are a few figures taken from Chapters One and Two, with the high hat accents added to them.

Note: For the following exercises the cymbal rhythm, unless marked with an **O**, will be played on a closed high hat. Only the notes so marked are to be played on an open H.Hat. If the note immediately following an open note is marked with an **X** it must be played closed.

EG: Both notes played open.   Second note played closed.

CYMBAL VARIATIONS WITH THE RIGHT HAND (Cont.)

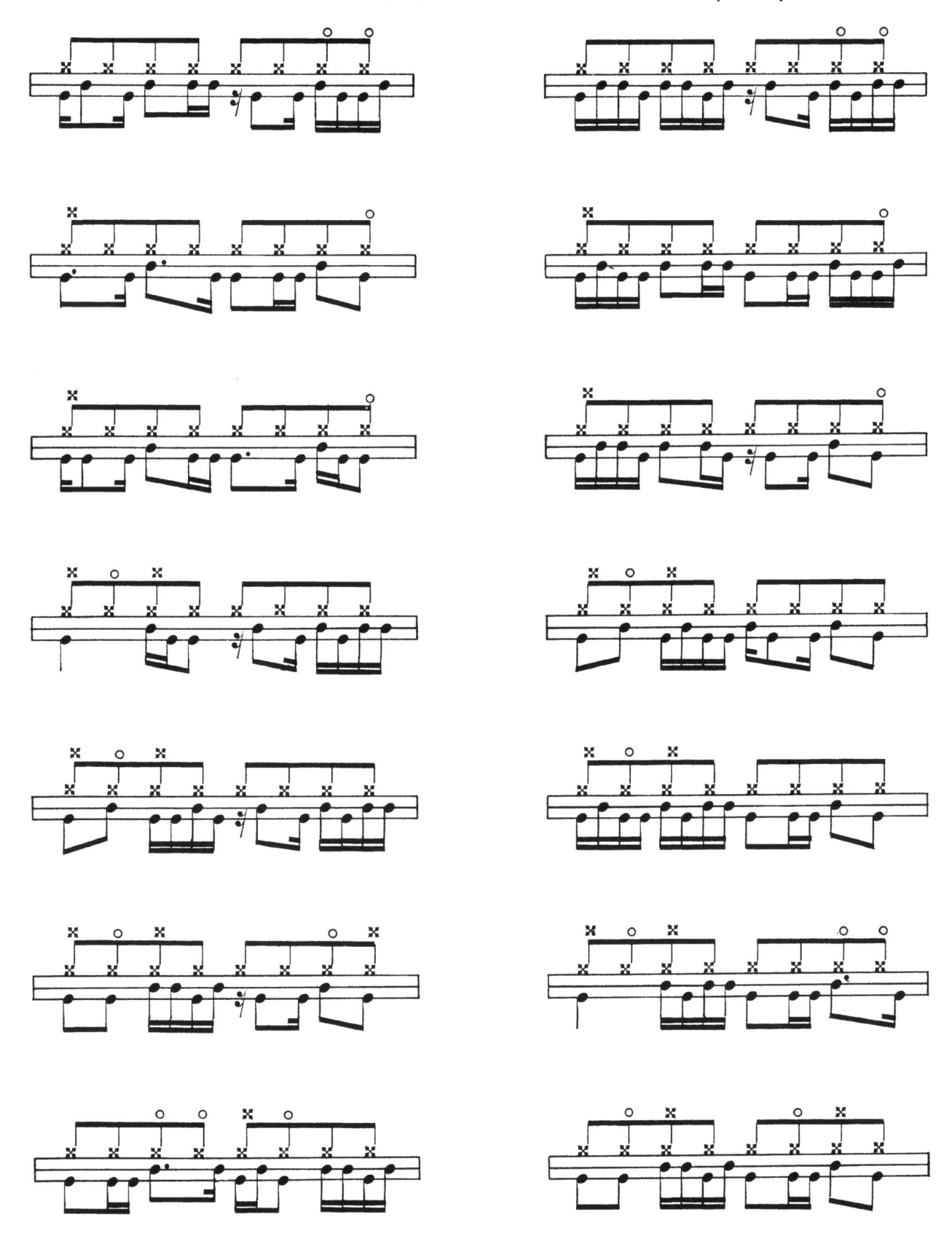

CYMBAL VARIATIONS WITH THE RIGHT HAND (Cont.)

Much care must be taken, when using changing rhythm patterns with the right hand, to ensure that the pulse and feeling of the original rhythm is not disturbed. More so than with any other device in this text, there is a time and place for changing the ride rhythm. Care should be taken to make sure the rhythm doesn't get too busy.

The following are a few examples of some of the figures that can be obtained by changing the rhythmic structure of the right hand. Most of these figures can be played on either the RIDE CYMBAL, THE BELL OF THE RIDE CYMBAL, OR THE CLOSED HIGH HAT. If a figure is more suitable to a closed high hat than the bell of the ride cymbal, etc., it will be indicated beside the figure.

Note: Most of the figures are marked to be played on the H.Hat (o,x.). Play them on the H.Hat, then eliminate the o and x markings and repeat the exercises on the ride cymbal and on the bell.

CYMBAL VARIATIONS WITH THE RIGHT HAND (Cont.)

* These exercises are especially effective when played on the high hat

Mel Bay's Studio/Jazz Drum Cookbook
by John Pickering

Mel Bay Publications, Inc.
Pacific, Mo. 63069

OTHER JAZZ DRUM BOOKS FROM MEL BAY

Made in the USA
Middletown, DE
12 July 2025